E. Ho

CHINESE NATIONALISM

Contemporary China Papers
Australian National University

**Series Editor: Jonathan Unger,
Australian National University**

Titles in this series published by M. E. Sharpe are:

**No. 20: THE PRO-DEMOCRACY PROTESTS IN CHINA
Reports from the Provinces**
Edited by Jonathan Unger

**No. 21: USING THE PAST TO SERVE THE PRESENT
Historiography and Politics in Contemporary China**
Edited by Jonathan Unger

**No. 22: DIRECTORY OF OFFICIALS AND ORGANIZATIONS IN CHINA
A Quarter-Century Guide**
Malcolm Lamb

No. 23: CHINESE NATIONALISM
Edited by Jonathan Unger

Contemporary China Papers
Australian National University

CHINESE
NATIONALISM

JONATHAN UNGER, editor

GEREMIE R.
BARMÉ

ALLEN CHUN

GEORGE T.
CRANE

PRASENJIT
DUARA

JOHN
FITZGERALD

EDWARD
FRIEDMAN

LUCIAN W.
PYE

JAMES
TOWNSEND

JONATHAN
UNGER

WANG
GUNGWU

An East Gate Book

M.E. Sharpe
Armonk, New York
London, England

An East Gate Book

Library of Congress Cataloging-in-Publication Data

Chinese nationalism / edited by Jonathan Unger.
p.   cm. — (Contemporary China papers)
"An East Gate Book"
Includes bibliographical references and index.
ISBN 1-56324-802-6 (hardcover : alk. paper).
ISBN 1-56324-810-7 (pbk : alk. paper).
1. Nationalism and communism—China.
2. Nationalism—China.
3. China—Politics and government—1976–
4. China—Economic policy—1976–
I. Unger, Jonathan. II. Series.
HX550.N3C46   1996
320.5′323′0951—dc20   95-52834
CIP
Printed in the United States of America

The paper used in this publication meets the minimum requirements of
American National Standard for Information Sciences—
Permanence of Paper for Printed Library Materials,
ANSI Z 39.48-1984.

♾

BM (c)   10   9   8   7   6   5   4   3   2   1
BM (p)   10   9   8   7   6   5   4

Contents

Contributors

Geremie R. Barmé is a fellow in Pacific and Asian History at the Australian National University's Institute of Advanced Studies and editor of *East Asian History*. He has published widely in English and Chinese on twentieth-century Chinese culture, history and politics. His latest book is *Shades of Mao: The Posthumous Cult of the Great Leader*.

Allen Chun is a Research Fellow in Anthropology at the Institute of Ethnology of the Academia Sinica in Taipei, Taiwan.

George T. Crane is an Associate Professor at Williams College, where he teaches Chinese politics, East Asian political economy, and Asian studies. His writings include *The Political Economy of China's Special Economic Zones* (1990). He is currently researching economic nationalism in East Asia.

Prasenjit Duara is Professor of History at the University of Chicago. His writings include *Culture, Power and the State: Rural North China, 1900-1942* (1988) and *Rescuing History from the Nation: Questioning Narratives of Modern China* (1995).

John Fitzgerald is Professor of Asian Studies at La Trobe University, Melbourne. He edited *The Nationalists and Chinese Society 1928-1937* (1989) and is the author of *Awakening China: Politics, Culture and Class in the Nationalist Revolution* (1996).

Edward Friedman is Professor of Political Science at the University of Wisconsin, Madison. His most recent books are *Chinese Village, Socialist State* (1991), *The Politics of Democratization: Generalizing East Asian Experiences* (1994) and *National Identity and Democratic Prospects in Socialist China* (1995).

Lucian W. Pye is Ford Professor of Political Science, Emeritus, MIT, and an Associate of the Fairbank Center at Harvard University. He is the author of such books as *The Spirit of Chinese Politics* (1968), *Asian Power and Politics* (1985) and *The Mandarin and the Cadre* (1988).

James Townsend is Professor Emeritus of Political Science and East Asian Studies at the University of Washington, Seattle. His books include *Political Participation in Communist China* and *Politics in China* (3rd edition) (with Brantly Womack).

Jonathan Unger is head of the Australian National University's Contemporary China Centre and co-editor of *The China Journal*. He has published books on Chinese student attitudes, village life, industrial hierarchy, and Chinese political dissidence.

Wang Gungwu is Professor Emeritus of the Australian National University and Chairman of the Institute of East Asian Political Economy, Singapore. He has recently edited a volume of essays, *Global History and Migrations* (1996).

Acknowledgments

A growing interest in Chinese nationalism has emerged as China's economy expands and its role on the world stage concomitantly grows larger. To what extent might nationalist feelings in China be shifting in keeping with China's new place in the world? What has been the content of Chinese nationalism historically, and how might this affect current-day Chinese perceptions and emotions? To what extent has Chinese nationalism been shaped over the decades by the state? How might we best understand nationalistic currents in China in light of the historical experience of nationalism elsewhere in the world?

Given the salience of these questions, in recent years *The China Journal* (formerly *The Australian Journal of Chinese Affairs*) has sought out the most interesting analyses on the nature and ramifications of Chinese nationalism. I am grateful to the nine scholars who have contributed to this effort. Each has conducted extensive research into a different aspect of Chinese nationalism, and each brings their judgments to bear from a different perspective. Most of their papers have been re-edited with their cooperation so as to yet better integrate them into the book's common overarching theme. The chapter by Edward Friedman was written expressly to fill an important remaining gap in the volume's coverage, and special appreciation is owed to Ed.

Gary Anson provided expert assistance in copy-editing and proof-reading the chapters, and Ms. Heli Petryk devised the book's layout and took responsibility for its production. Without their help the volume would never have appeared.

Introduction

Jonathan Unger

Chinese nationalism is emerging as an important issue for reassessment. Under Mao, nationalism was one of the core sources of loyalty to the state, but its salience was shrouded by an overlay of revolutionary ideology. With the demise of Maoist ideology over the past two decades, a vacuum in commitment to public goals has become obvious among the people of China in what Chinese newspapers have called a 'crisis of faith'. In these circumstances, nationalism remains the one bedrock of political belief shared by most Chinese.

Naturally, it is a sentiment that the Party leadership feels it advantageous to play upon. The Party has needed to find a new basis of legitimacy to sustain its rule, and it is staking this on its performance as the architect of economic growth and, just as importantly, as the guardian of national pride. In speeches, top Party leaders have been pushing the need to 'strengthen patriotism' as a leading priority.[1] There is, to be sure, nothing uncommon in this. As the American historian Peter F. Sugar notes, 'there is no corner on the globe where the leaders of the most significant or the most insignificant state do not constantly use all the means of communication (in the widest sense) at their disposal to foster nationalism, the state-supporting loyalty'.[2]

Though the Chinese government today puts itself forward as the guardian of nationalism, thus far it has not actually pursued the nationalist card any more vociferously than many other governments do — or, indeed, further than in the schools and mass media of Mao's day. China's successful opening into the world economy works to play down jingoistic inclinations; China needs to get along internationally in order to get ahead economically. Yet the very success of the current thrust to make China 'rich and strong' (that once-again-fashionable phrase of late 19th-century Chinese nationalist reformers) has

---

[1] Just one example is the speech by Party Secretary Jiang Zemin to the National Propaganda Work Conference (reprinted in full in *Jingji ribao*, 7 March 1994, p.2), where the need to strengthen the spirit of patriotism repeatedly is listed first among priorities.

[2] Peter F. Sugar, 'From Ethnicity to Nationalism and Back Again', in *Nationalism: Essays in Honor of Louis L. Snyder* (Greenwood Press, Westport, 1981), p.69.

begun to feed Chinese pride, and potentially invites thoughts of Great Power muscle flexing. Three decades ago during the Cultural Revolution, Chinese had given vent to xenophobic feelings, even to the point of storming a couple of foreign embassies, but this was of little consequence internationally, in that China at the time was inward looking and temporarily had largely disengaged itself from the world scene. In contrast, China's growing presence in the world economy over the past decade and its ever more prominent role on the world political stage make it of signal importance today whether Chinese nationalism remains relatively benign or becomes jingoistically assertive.

When pondering any country's nationalism, we are dealing, of course, with a powerful and, today, near-universal sentiment. Yet researchers remind us that nationalism is an ideological artefact of relatively recent historical provenance[3] — as is the very notion of a 'nation-state'. Notwithstanding this, when Ernest Gellner wrote that 'It is nationalism which engenders nations, and not the other way round',[4] and when Eric Hobsbawm wrote 'nationalism comes before nations',[5] their quips did not ring entirely true for China. Unlike much of Europe, China was not carved out of a welter of remnant feudal suzerainties and city-states under the impetus of 19th-century nationalist romanticism (it should be recalled that Italy and Germany did not become nation-states until 1870-71). So, too, unlike the great bulk of the present-day nations of the Third World, China was not originally cobbled together by a Western colonial power out of a congeries of disparate peoples.

Yet Gellner and Hobsbawm were at least partly right in that China, although a political and cultural entity stretching back two millenia, comprised a civilization and empire but was not truly a 'nation' whose people were imbued with an abiding sense of 'nationalism' in the full modern sense of those terms. A good deal of research, exemplified by the influential writings of Joseph Levenson, has shown that 'culturalism' — 'Chinese culture as the focus of loyalty'[6] — permeated traditional Chinese thought. The Chinese literati perceived China as the only true civilization, one that embodied a universalist set of values, and all who accepted its teachings and principles, including a conquest dynasty like the Manchu-Qing court, could be incorporated within its culturalist bounds. Nationalist feeling, in contrast,

---

3   Scholars largely agree that nationalism first emerged in parts of Western Europe in the late eighteenth century. See, for example, Anthony D. Smith, *National Identity* (Penguin Books, London, 1991), p.44; Benedict Anderson, *Imagined Communities: Reflections on the Origin and Spread of Nationalism*, revised edition (Verso, London and New York, 1983), p.11; and Anthony Giddens, *The Nation-State and Violence* (Cambridge University Press, Cambridge, 1987), p.119.

4   Ernest Gellner, *Nations and Nationalism* (Cornell University Press, Ithaca, 1983), p.55.

5   E. J. Hobsbawm, *Nations and Nationalism since 1780: Programme, Myth, Reality* (Cambridge University Press, Cambridge, 1990), p.10.

6   Joseph R. Levenson, *Liang Ch'i-ch'ao and the Mind of Modern China* (University of California Press, Berkeley, 1967), p.108.

centres loyalties on the state or an ethnicity or both, and implies nation-states or would-be nation-states that define themselves in contrast to other nation-states.

But the distinction in China was actually not so clear-cut: as James Townsend argues in Chapter One of this volume, a type of ethnic proto-nationalism existed alongside the elite's identification with Chinese culture. So, too, as Townsend also points out, Chinese culturalism did not utterly give way to a modern-day state nationalism. This imparts a special complexity to present-day Chinese notions of nationalism: for anyone who has heard Chinese talk of their patriotism knows that even today it comprises an admixture of political nationalism, ethnic Han identity, and a culturalist pride that is observed in allusions to Chinese civilization as a point of self-identity. All of these sentiments have been influenced and partially shaped and reshaped by the history of this century and by the teachings of successive regimes. This book probes the resultant multi-layered complexity of Chinese perceptions of Chinese nationhood. A premise which is shared by the contributors is that to understand the present and potential ramifications of Chinese nationalism, one must first come to grips with the historically derived *content* of this nationalism.

This effort to decode the content of Chinese nationalism entails considerably more than mere descriptive accounts. Most of the chapters in this volume, as readers will discover, are highly analytical, and some also incorporate a comparative perspective. A consequence is that the book, while of direct interest to students of China, is also likely to be of interest to comparative theorists across a range of fields.

An excellent illustration of this conceptual thrust is Chapter Two, by Prasenjit Duara. Duara notes that his purpose is to suggest new categories for conceptualizing nationalism, inspired in part by post-modernist theories. In a complex discussion whose conclusions complement those of Townsend, Duara suggests that a crucial distinction must be made between the modern nation-state and nationalism: that 'nationalism is never fully subsumed by the nation-state' (p.32) and is best considered in China by way of its complicated relationship to a multiplicity of historical narratives and identities.

The state's effort to transform and monopolize the meaning of the 'nation' and thus the content of the attendant nationalism is the topic of several of the chapters, starting with the historian John Fitzgerald. As Fitzgerald writes in Chapter Three, in China 'each of the major state movements of the past century has advocated a distinctive and mutually exclusive definition of the national self' (p.57). Drawing on recent theoretical writings on post-colonial nationalism and drawing parallels with other nation-building movements such as India's, Fitzgerald focuses on the politically-driven shifts in Chinese nationalist thought: why the late 19th-century Confucian reformers still clung to associating the collective self largely with Chinese civilization; in what respects the turn-of-the-century liberal republicans conceived of the nation as a body of citizens; and how and why

Kuomintang revolutionaries and state-builders defined it as encompassing a Chinese race. He shows the logic by which China's Communists progressively redefined 'nation' and 'nationalism' to take increasing account of class, whereby the ranks of the 'people' who comprise the 'nation' came to exclude persons of suspect class background. Fitzgerald notes, in conclusion, that whereas 'the nations of citizen, race and class may well have been inventions of the state' (p.83), the Chinese people have sustained some alternative notions of how they belong together, and that as China today shifts out of the Party's ideological hegemonic control, 'Patriotic nationalism has taken root outside the state itself' (p.85).

Lucian Pye in Chapter Four explores a form of non-state-driven national identity that, in an earlier period, had provided a potential alternative to both Kuomintang and Communist notions of national identity: the modernizing Chinese culture of the coastal treaty ports. Pye draws a distinction between the Chinese treaty ports, on the one side, and, on the other, the modernizing nationalism that developed elsewhere in the world among the educated elites of colonized peoples. He explains why, whereas 'elsewhere in the post-colonial world nationalism and modernization were reinforcing forces, . . . in China they have been essentially antagonistic forces . . . Whereas elsewhere, the most modernized people were accepted as appropriate spokespersons for the nationalistic ideals of the society, in China they generally were suspected as being less than fully "Chinese"' (p.91). Even the Kuomintang and Communist Parties contained few modernized leaders; and with their roots largely in a parochial interior China, both political leaderships shaped nationalism in a direction that was not to be polluted by modern values. Pye finds China faced today, unhealthily, with an 'inchoate and incoherent form of nationalism' (p.87), and he blames this on that earlier rejection of 'the melding of Chinese nationalism and modernization which was taking place in pre-war coastal China' (p.109).

In Chapter Five, Wang Gungwu, too, sees a thwarted melding of nationalism and modernization, which he situates in the rejection by both political parties of the liberal nationalism of the May Fourth movement of 1919. The Communist triumph of 1949 brought with it a narrow, increasingly exclusive view of nationalism even while Party leaders believed themselves the purveyors of world revolution: in retrospect, they were more Chinese than revolutionary, more inward looking than outward looking.

To be sure, the very notion of a Chinese nationalism, be it in the values developing in treaty-port society, or the patriotism of May Fourth era activists, or Kuomintang nationalism, or Communist Party nationalist teachings, was pertinent only to a portion of the Chinese populace throughout the first decades of this century. Much of the farming population, tied to localistic concerns, as yet had little notion of China as a whole, let alone being attuned to the nationalist sentiments that were developing among the educated classes, in China's urban areas, and among the political parties. One of the signally important aspects of any modern nationalism is its envelopment of ever-widening circles of a populace through the proselytization of modern political movements and governments.[7] China was no exception here. As Wang Gungwu notes, it continues to be a point for debate as to whether the nationalism propagated by Communist Party organizers among the farmers of north China during the guerilla warfare against Japan proved the crucial factor in the subsequent Communist victory against the Kuomintang (as had been argued in a book by Chalmers Johnson).[8] But few would dispute that the war and Communist Party organizational efforts did provide a means to penetrate localism — with, among other things, the teachings of nationalism.

The socialist revolution that followed the establishment of the People's Republic, organized from above in every Chinese town and village, entailed an ever-increasing penetration by the Party-state of local social networks and local lives up through the 1970s. Everyone, urban and rural alike, by necessity became a participant in a work-unit that served as a focus for repeated Party-led proselytization. Modern schooling and literacy programs were also eventually extended into almost every village, and with them state teachings that included heavy doses of nationalism. Mass organizations, mass education, and a mass media for the first time reached into all Chinese communities; for the first time, the institutions and mechanisms of a centralized modern state were fully at work.

Nationalism not only was effectively inculcated; its content was very much manipulated to serve the government. The new sacred symbols of nationhood that were taught all served as symbols both for the nation and the Party-state: the red flag, the National Day on which the establishment of the People's Republic was declared, Tiananmen Square in Beijing, and Chairman Mao, who was portrayed as the sacrosanct father-figure of both nation and Party.[9] The socialist cause, the Party leadership, and Chinese nationhood merged in school-books into a unified identity.

At the same time, across the Taiwan Strait, the Kuomintang was stamping its own imprint on the meaning of nationalism, but in contradistinction to the cultural iconoclasm and radicalism of the mainland government. In a study directly relevant to the broader questions of modern-day Chinese nationalism, Allen Chun deploys in Chapter Six a conceptual framework drawn from post-

---

[7]   As Ernst Gellner observes in *Nations and Nationalism*, 'nationalism is, essentially, the general imposition of a high culture on society, where previously low cultures had taken up the lives of the majority, and in some cases the totality, of the population' (p.57). In this sense, nationalism is an important part of the modern incarnation of what the anthropologist Robert Redfield has called a society's elite Great Tradition as against the Little Traditions of encysted local agricultural communities.

[8]   Chalmers Johnson, *Peasant Nationalism and Communist Power* (Stanford University Press, Stanford; Oxford University Press, London, 1962).

[9]   Jonathan Unger, *Education Under Mao* (Columbia University Press, New York, 1982), pp.82-5.

modernist thought to analyse how the content and images of nationalism were reshaped and propagated by the government exiled in Taiwan so as to meet the Kuomintang's claims to be the true guardian of Chinese nationalism. The Taipei regime did so by attaching nationalism to the 'preservation' of traditional Chinese culture — the glory of Chinese civilization. In so doing, the Kuomintang government inculcated its own reconstructed notions of traditional Chinese values through the machinery of the school, mass media and military, selecting aspects of tradition that promoted discipline and control. As in the PRC, in short, the nationalist ideology was very much shaped and driven by the state and its needs.

Today, in Taiwan and the Chinese mainland alike, the state is losing its recent hegemonic capacity to define the content of nationalism, as political controls in both the PRC and Taiwan loosen and social forces reassert themselves. As James Townsend observes, in the PRC today 'the official gloss portraying a united people striving together for China's modernization does not jibe with the realities of Chinese behaviour' (p.22). Increasingly, thus, the content of Chinese nationalism has been up for grabs. As noted throughout the book, a reservoir of sentiments exists available to be tapped, ranging from Han-wide ethnic nationalism, a retooled and redrawn state-driven political nationalism, through a culturalistic interpretation of nationhood. Surveying this landscape, Prasenjit Duara is drawn to conclude that 'At no other time is this multiplicity of political identities, with its ambivalences and conflicts, clearer than in our own confused time . . .' (p.55).

In counterpoint to the isolationist sentiments of Mao's day, when many Chinese believed China to be self-reliantly forging ahead to national glory, under Deng many Chinese have had to come to terms with a world economy in which China is merely the largest under-developed country, far outstripped by its economically sophisticated East Asian neighbours. In this circumstance, feelings of national pride and national identity are being rebuilt in diverse ways. The plasticity of this post-Mao national identity is demonstrated clearly by George T. Crane in Chapter Seven in his discussion of the symbolic significance of the special economic zones that have sprung up and flourished along China's coast. Crane shows how the zones and the economic practices that they represent were initially portrayed as exceptions to Chineseness, as an 'otherness'. He shows, too, how over time, to strategic parts of the leadership and populace, the zones have come to represent national aspirations and a shift in the paradigm as to what constitutes China's national identity. The conceptual framework that Crane employs regarding 'national economic identity' renders this chapter very much relevant to analytically minded readers who may have little direct interest in the zones *per se*.

As the recurrent shifting debates over the zones suggest, different schools of thought regarding Chinese nationalism and national identity, which appeal to different constituencies and sectors of the country, have emerged over the past decade. But for the most part, as Crane and Townsend suggest, the popular mood has not militated for any intense nationalism; instead, for most

Chinese the 1980s and 1990s have comprised a time of openness to ideas and influences from outside.

In Chapter Eight, Edward Friedman emphasizes this liberal thrust of new ideas about nationalism that have taken hold outside the government among large sectors of the urban population. Friedman notes, among other things, the redefinition of Chinese identity by way of a 'southern narrative', in which people from Guangdong, Fujian, Shanghai, and other regions of the coastal south have turned against the historical myth of a single northern, Yellow River origin of Chineseness and instead accentuate a diversity of origins and traditions. Disdaining a rooted inward-looking national image built upon the northern interior, the southern narrative posits a new national identity of mercantile openness, international interaction, decentralization, and southern cultural pre-eminence.

Geremie Barmé, in contrast, points in Chapter Nine to an undercurrent of more militantly nationalist thought — in some cases, ultra-nationalist — that is emerging among portions of the intelligentsia and that has been favourably received in mass culture as the sub-theme of a number of popular books and television series. Barmé notes that 'since 1989 there have been numerous indications of a growing disenchantment with the West and its allies' (p.187), and he finds in the nationalistic narratives an implicit 'desire for revenge for all the real and perceived slights of the past century' (p.184). He sees this manifested both in writings that betray a nationalistic braggadocio and in writings of self-hatred that bitterly deprecate Chinese capacities and accomplishments.

Friedman and Barmé are laying out two scenarios that seem diametrically at odds with each other. Nonetheless, several contrary trends in thinking do seem to be simultaneously in progress today in China. In part, this is because various constituencies among the populace are responding differently to the vast changes that China is undergoing. In part, too, it is because a confusion of beliefs and emotions exists within the minds of a great many individuals, who at one and the same time feel both open to the possibilities provided by peaceful outward-looking development and yet harbour doubts and fears about China's place in the world — and thus are not immune to the blandishments of jealously nationalistic sentiment and self-loathing breastbeating.

Chinese nationalism today seems like Joseph's biblical coat of many colours. It does not consist of a single cloth, a single easily comprehended sentiment. Rather, it comprises an inter-stitching of state-inculcated patriotic political appeals, Han ethnic identification, and culturalist pride; a confusion of aspirations for national greatness alongside growing sub-national assertions of regional identity; open-minded optimism and anti-foreign resentment. So long as the economy continues to do well, so long as the future seems bright for China in the world economy, openness may well prevail, with perversely nationalistic sentiments emotionally satisfying within popular entertainment but muted in real-life appeal. If, contrarily, the current economic expansion sours, if Chinese aspirations come to nought, a repertoire of highly nationalist emotional sentiment is available for more serious consideration.

We cannot predict with any certainty what form of nationalism might prevail, any more than we can make accurate long-term forecasts about the Chinese economy or domestic political scene. But with knowledge about the historical content of Chinese thought, with evidence concerning the multi-faceted current mood, and with the conceptual insights provided by the contributors to this volume, we are in a position to come to grips intellectually with the complex weave of Chinese nationalist sentiment, today and in future.

ONE

Chinese Nationalism

James Townsend*

Nationalism was the 'moving force' of the Chinese revolution, wrote Mary Wright, capturing in a phrase a conviction widely shared among students of modern China.[1] In this perspective, a 'rising tide' of nationalism is a constant factor, perhaps the only one, in China's long revolutionary era. As the metaphor suggests, the waters of nationalism steadily engulf all that stand in their path — imperial, Republican, and Communist institutions, elite and popular classes, coastal and interior regions, reformist and conservative factions, Chinese at home and abroad. Other movements and ideologies wax and wane, but nationalism permeates them all.

The paradigm that governs this perspective is what I call the 'culturalism-to-nationalism thesis'. It is a loose paradigm at best and has no single source or definitive formulation, but its underlying assumptions pervade the academic literature on modern China. The core proposition is that a set of ideas labelled 'culturalism' dominated traditional China, was incompatible with modern nationalism and yielded only under the assault of imperialism and Western ideas to a new nationalist way of thinking. The history of modern China, then, is one in which nationalism replaces culturalism as the dominant Chinese view of their identity and place in the world. Because this was a transformation of collective cultural and political identity, it was a long and traumatic process that left its mark, and continues to do so, on all periods and divisions within the modern era.

*   An earlier version of this essay was written for a conference honouring the teaching and research of Robert A. Scalapino, held in Berkeley, California, in March 1990. It is based on research supported by grants from the Joint Committee on Chinese Studies of the Social Science Research Council and the American Council of Learned Societies, the Jackson School of International Studies at the University of Washington, and the Research School of Pacific and Asian Studies at the Australian National University.

1   Mary Clabaugh Wright, 'Introduction: The Rising Tide of Change', in Wright (ed.), *China in Revolution: The First Phase, 1900-1913* (Yale University Press, New Haven, 1968), p.3, passim.

This culturalism-to-nationalism thesis is a useful and provocative generalization about the rise of nationalism in modern China. The reality and importance of this phenomenon is not in dispute: all observers see a century or more of vigorous Chinese nationalist rhetoric and activity, a 'rise of nationalism' that distinguishes modern China from its imperial past. However, I believe that Chinese nationalism remains poorly understood and inadequately studied. The thesis has made an important contribution, but it is conceptually imprecise and empirically oversimplified in its vision of the historical change in question. The purpose of this essay is to summarize the thesis and its implications, to offer a critique of its conceptual and empirical limitations, and to suggest an alternative approach — which might be called 'bringing the nation back in' — to supplement the thesis and help strengthen the study of Chinese nationalism.

The Culturalism-to-Nationalism Thesis

Over twenty years, ago, in a concise survey of the scholarly literature on Chinese nationalism, James Harrison observed that 'the traditional Chinese self-image has generally been defined as "culturalism", based on a common historical heritage and acceptance of shared beliefs, not as nationalism, based on the modern concept of the nation-state'.[2] He emphasized that this self-image, developed over more than two millenia following the Qin-Han imperial unification that began in 221 BC, did not preclude some political or nationalistic loyalties. The long span of imperial history offered some evidence of patriotism, of a sense of racial distinctness and xenophobia, and of commitments to imperial institutions and ruling dynasties. Nonetheless, the primary Chinese identity was cultural, with no perception of a Chinese state or nation apart from the cultural heritage. Supreme loyalty attached to the culture itself, not to the state, and there could be no justification for abandoning or even changing the cultural tradition in order to strengthen the state.[3]

Harrison noted two prime elements in the construction of culturalism. One was the notion that China was the only true civilization, its cultural superiority unchallenged. Non-Chinese peoples might be military threats, but they could never be true rivals because of their backwardness and because they could never rule China except in a Chinese way. There was no concept of or need for nationalism in this world devoid of cultural or interstate competition. The other element was the political prescription that rulers must be educated in and govern according to Confucian principles, which were of universal value. Because the standard rested on education, legitimate rule was not limited to ethnic Chinese; aliens who accepted and exemplified Confucian

---

2   James Harrison, *Modern Chinese Nationalism* (Hunter College of the City of New York, Research Institute on Modern Asia, New York, n.d. 1969?), p.2.

3   Ibid., pp.3-14.

norms might also rule. The political elite's loyalty was to principles that defined a manner of rule, not to a particular regime or nation.[4]

Culturalism's refusal to acknowledge a world of formally equal states and its insistence that legitimate rule rested on adherence to Confucian norms dampened the nationalistic impulses that occasionally surfaced in the course of fluctuating imperial fortunes and houses. Its essential integrity as a worldview, supported by the size, wealth and power of the empire, gave it great lasting power, enabling it to bridge periods of disunity and infuse new governments, whether Chinese or alien, with values supportive of the tradition. Culturalism — so the thesis goes — thus explains not only the empire's capacity to survive for so long but also why it fell when a truly competitive alien culture penetrated China. Foreign imperialism did not have to conquer the empire to destroy it. It had only to demonstrate that its formidable military power carried an explicit challenge to the Chinese view of the world by agents who assumed their own cultural superiority. With culturally-based confidence and identity in doubt from setbacks administered by these avowed challengers, and lacking a nationalist base to fall back on, imperial China disintegrated. The logical outcome of the crisis was rejection of culturalism and development of a nationalism that would provide a new basis for China's defence and regeneration.

Harrison provides a useful overview of the culturalism-to-nationalism thesis, but it was Joseph Levenson who produced its most subtle, provocative, and influential elaboration, presenting the core concepts as poles around which the swirling currents of modern Chinese thought might be organized. In his first book, Levenson traced the intellectual evolution of Liang Qichao (1873-1929) in his search for a formula to halt the disintegration of both culture and empire that characterized the final decades of the Qing dynasty (1644-1911).[5] Passages in this book describe how Liang 'fought his way through from culturalism-to-nationalism'.[6] Elsewhere, Levenson portrayed 'culturalism and nationalism as competitors for loyalty' among turn-of-the-century intellectuals, seeing the era as one in which 'nationalism invades the Chinese scene as culturalism helplessly gives way'.[7]

Many others have found culturalism a useful term to distinguish a mainstream Confucian image of China as a culturally-defined community from competing images of an ethnically-defined ('racism') or politically-

---

4   Ibid., pp.4-5.

5   Joseph R. Levenson, *Liang Ch'i-ch'ao and the Mind of Modern China*, 2nd revised ed. (University of California Press, Berkeley, 1959).

6   Ibid., esp. pp.108-22; quotation from p.108.

7   Joseph R. Levenson, *Confucian China and Its Modern Fate: A Trilogy* (University of California Press, Berkeley, 1968), vol.1, pp.98-104

defined community ('modern nationalism').[8] Sometimes a slightly variant term is used, as in Ishwer Ojha's analysis of the evolution of Chinese foreign policy from 'culturism' to nationalism, the former term representing a 'non-territorial concept', a loyalty to and preoccupation with culture that differs fundamentally from nationalism, which 'treats culture only as a means' to aid the nation.[9] Joseph Whitney has analysed China's shift 'from cultural entity to political entity' as the Confucian idea of the state was replaced by an imported nationalism.[10] Not surprisingly given the ubiquity of this theme, several students of comparative nationalism have accepted the thesis as an authoritative interpretation. It appears in Hugh Seton-Watson's history of nations and nationalist movements, where Chinese nationalism is a purely modern product of European ideas and incursions;[11] and in Selig Harrison's reference to China's historical sense of identity as a self-centred 'culturalism' that was replaced by nationalism in the twentieth century.[12]

The most explicit formulations of the thesis concentrate on the late Qing and early Republican periods, especially the years between 1895 (when defeat by Japan catalysed Chinese nationalism) and 1919 (when the May Fourth Movement marked culturalism's eclipse) — as this was the era of competition between culturalism and nationalism and the replacement of the former by the latter. However, the full range of the thesis includes studies of earlier imperial history that emphasize the weakness or absence of nationalism in China's political tradition as well as studies of the modern period charting the tributaries that feed the swelling nationalist tide. There is no shortage of evidence to support this nationalist triumphalism. Nineteenth-century xenophobia and turn-of-the-century anti-Manchuism blend into the more fully developed ideas and movements of the May Fourth era, with their dedication to anti-imperialism and national salvation and regeneration. From this point on, observers have invoked nationalism in at least partial explanation of a remarkable range of phenomena: aversion to foreign ideas and promotion of foreign ideas; repudiation of traditional culture and celebration of national

---

8   See, for example, John Fincher, 'China as a Race, Culture, and Nation: Notes on Fang Hsiao-ju's Discussion of Dynastic Legitimacy', in David C. Buxbaum and Frederick W. Mote (eds), *Transition and Permanence: Chinese History and Culture: A Festschrift in Honor of Dr. Hsiao Kung-ch'uan* (Cathay Press, Hong Kong, 1972), pp.59-69; and Laurence A. Schneider, *Ku Chieh-kang and China's New History: Nationalism and the Quest for Alternative Traditions* (University of California Press, Berkeley, 1971), p.270.

9   Ishwer C. Ojha, *Chinese Foreign Policy in an Age of Transition: The Diplomacy of Cultural Despair,* 2nd ed. (Beacon Press, Boston, 1971), pp.ix-xiv, 1-50.

10   Joseph B. R. Whitney, *China: Area, Administration and Nation-Building* (University of Chicago Department of Geography Research, Chicago, 1969), pp.26-9, 160-2.

11   Hugh Seton-Watson, *Nations and States: An Enquiry into the Origins of Nations and the Politics of Nationalism* (Westview Press, Boulder, 1977), pp.9, 274-87, 423.

12   Selig S. Harrison, *The Widening Gulf: Asian Nationalism and American Policy* (The Free Press, New York, 1978), pp.69-86; reference to culturalism on p.70.

traditions; Nationalist victory in 1927 and Communist victory in 1949; Sino-Soviet alliance in 1950 and the conflict a decade later; Cultural Revolution Maoism and post-Mao modernization. The implication is that nationalism permeates Chinese affairs, manifesting itself even among ideas and movements differing widely in other respects.

At some point in its intellectual history, the thesis parted company with its favourite metaphor. This is a tide that never ebbs. Once triumphant in Chinese political identity, as dominant now as culturalism was in the past, nationalism places its stamp on each new departure in Chinese politics. The recent post-Mao period links nationalism to the outward orientation of the 1980s and 1990s, producing what some observers have called an 'assertive' or 'confident' phase of Chinese nationalism.[13] Once mainly internal in orientation, nationalism now has profound implications for unresolved territorial claims and how a modernized China might use its power.

The rise of Chinese nationalism is obviously of global importance but it is neither novel nor surprising in the light of comparative history. A primary assumption about the modern era is that it is an age of nationalism, linked to the institutions and doctrines of the modern nation-state that came into being with the European age of revolution and Napoleonic Wars. These doctrines and institutions eventually spread throughout the world, so that today virtually all the world's states and peoples have made the transition from an absence of nationalism, or at most possession of some form of 'pre-modern nationalism', to an embrace of modern nationalism. If this is all the thesis tells us — that China, too, has moved from a pre-nationalist world — it is scarcely news. There is more to the thesis than that, I think. First, it tries to explain why the Chinese empire was so much more durable than other pre-modern systems, finding the answer in China's kind of cultural identity. Second, it argues that China's entry into a world of sovereign nation-states was unusually prolonged and traumatic because it forced the Chinese to reject their age-old cultural identity and to adopt a new politicized one. Third, it suggests that this long, wrenching 'identity crisis' makes contemporary Chinese nationalism unusually intense, becoming in the resolution of the crisis something like the religion of modern China. I will argue that each of these three propositions remains more problematic than the thesis allows, but they clearly raise important issues.

Some might argue that the culturalism-to-nationalism thesis is a straw man, an outdated interpretation reflecting the uncritical application to China of modernization theory, or other allegedly ethnocentric biases of Western scholarship, whereas more recent scholarship has challenged and modified

---

13   Allen Whiting, 'Assertive Nationalism in Chinese Foreign Policy', *Asian Survey* vol.23, no.8 (August 1983), pp.913-33; and Michel Oksenberg, 'China's Confident Nationalism', *Foreign Affairs,* vol.65, no.3 (1986-87), pp.501-23.

many of its propositions.[14] However, the thesis about nationalism seems much more durable than the broader modernization paradigm to which it is obviously related. It remains influential in the work of China scholars[15] and is widely accepted outside the China field as an authoritative interpretation. Although recent scholarship offers many new insights into issues relating to Chinese nationalism, I know of no published work that directly engages the thesis' portrayal of Chinese nationalism. The critique that follows identifies some conceptual problems with the key terms of nationalism and culturalism, then notes some empirical problems, and closes with a brief evaluation of the thesis.

A Critique of the Thesis

Conceptual Problems

Benjamin Akzin called the literature on nationalism a 'terminological jungle',[16] and more than one explorer has been lost in it. The most important point to note here is that the word covers a wide range of social phenomena, so there is no way to assess the thesis without specifying some of these. I must also clarify how I will use the equally troublesome word 'nation'.

Among all the definitional controversies about nationalism, says Anthony Smith, none has been so prolonged and confusing as that between 'statists' and 'ethnicists'. The former define the nation as a 'territorial-political unit', with nationalism involving an aspiration for self-government; the latter see the nation as a 'large, politicized ethnic group defined by common culture and alleged descent', with nationalism turning into a cultural movement.[17] This confusion permits the meaning of nation to range from an ethnic group that does not constitute a state, to a state that contains more than one ethnic group. My discussion adopts the 'ethnicist' view that a nation is a particular kind of ethnic group. The ethnic group itself is 'defined by common culture and alleged descent', or more precisely as a group of people who differentiate themselves from others on the basis of a set of perceived cultural differences.[18]

---

[14]   A thorough discussion of this issue, with citation and analysis of scores of scholarly works that challenge older paradigms with which the thesis is clearly associated, is found in Paul A. Cohen, *Discovering History in China: American Historical Writing on the Recent Chinese Past* (Columbia University Press, New York, 1984).

[15]   For example, a recent synthesis of Chinese history challenges many older interpretations but emphasizes the 'lack of unequivocal nationalist feelings among the Chinese' and the classical focus on 'culturalism rather than nationalism'. Ray Huang, *China: A Macrohistory* (M. E. Sharpe, Armonk, 1988), p.114, and pp.29, 187 and 191.

[16]   Benjamin Akzin, *State and Nation* (Hutchinson, London, 1964), pp.7-10.

[17]   Anthony D. Smith, *Theories of Nationalism* (Harper and Row, New York, 1971), p.176.

[18]   This formulation draws on Fredrik Barth, 'Introduction', in Barth (ed.), *Ethnic Groups and Boundaries: The Social Organization of Cultural Differences* (Little, Brown,

Although there is also dispute on what sets a nation apart from the general category of ethnic group, there is some consensus on the idea that the nation is a 'large, politicized ethnic group', or an ethnic group that seeks or has acquired some degree of political recognition or autonomy.[19] In other words, for our purposes, a nation is a cultural community that is or seeks to become a political community as well.

This concept of nation clarifies the core idea of nationalism. Ernest Gellner says it is 'the striving to make culture and polity congruent'.[20] Nationalism proposes that nations should become states (or at least politically autonomous) and states should become nations (or at least relatively unified and distinct from others in culture). Smith's earlier distinction now supports two families of nationalism: ethnic nationalism, in which an existing ethnic group strives to attain, enhance, or protect its nationhood, perhaps by becoming an independent state; and state nationalism, in which an existing state strives to become a unified nation (the idea of nation-building) or claims that its goals embody those of a nation and are essential to its nationhood. Nationalism may serve either a state or a nation, or a mix of these communities. But *how* does nationalism serve them? Again, scholars disagree, offering three versions of what nationalism is.

One view sees nationalism as a doctrine or set of ideas. For Hans Kohn, it is a 'political creed' that 'centres the supreme loyalty of the overwhelming majority of the people upon the nation-state, either existing or desired', and that regards the nation-state as both an ideal and indispensable organization.[21] The doctrine may be specified more precisely, and ethnocentrically, as 'a doctrine invented in Europe at the beginning of the nineteenth century [which] holds that humanity is naturally divided into nations . . . and that the only legitimate type of government is national self-government'.[22] For others, nationalism is political action or movement. It is 'the assertion of the will to constitute an autonomous political community by a self-conscious group'[23] or

---

Boston, 1969), pp.9-38; Paul R. Brass, 'Ethnicity and Nationality Formation', *Ethnicity,* vol.3, no.3 (September 1976), pp.225-41; and George DeVos and Lola Romanucci-Ross (eds), *Ethnic Identity: Cultural Continuities and Change* (Mayfield, Palo Alto, 1975), pp.5-41.

[19] The idea that a nation is distinguished from other ethnic groups by a higher degree of politicization is found in Akzin, *State and Nation*; Brass, 'Ethnicity and Nationality Formation'; and Smith, *Theories of Nationalism*. See also the seminal work of Karl Deutsch, *Nationalism and Social Communication,* 2nd ed. (MIT Press, Cambridge, 1966), esp. pp.96-105.

[20] Ernest Gellner, *Nations and Nationalism* (Cornell University Press, Ithaca, 1983), p.43.

[21] Hans Kohn, 'Nationalism', *International Encyclopedia of the Social Sciences* (1968), vol.11, p.63.

[22] Elie Kedourie, *Nationalism* (Hutchinson, London, 1960), p.9.

[23] Charles W. Anderson, Fred R. von der Mehden and Crawford Young, *Issues of Political Development* (Prentice-Hall, Englewood Cliffs, 1967), p.17.

'an ideological movement, for the attainment and maintenance of self-government and independence on behalf of a group, some of whose members conceive it to constitute an actual or potential "nation" like others'.[24] Finally, some define nationalism as sentiment, consciousness, or state of mind, emphasizing individuals' awareness of and loyalty to the nation and its traditions.[25]

To summarize, my critique of the thesis departs from the idea that a nation is a large politicized ethnic group; that nationalism consists of doctrines, movements or sentiments supporting a nation; and that state and ethnic nationalism are two different, although possibly overlapping, varieties of nationalism. Some authorities insist that nationalism has existed only in modern times, generally since about 1800, whereas others allow for some pre-modern forms. Smith accepts the pre-modern possibility in what he calls 'ethnocentric nationalism', and Akzin cites China as an ancient nation that entered modern history with nationality and nationalism both present.[26] I accept the possibility of a pre-modern nationalism that lacks the core propositions of modern nationalism: that nations should be states, holding formally equal status in a world order properly composed of such states, whose members are citizens with equal rights and obligations. The thesis emphasizes none of these distinctions, although by nationalism it clearly means modern nationalism.

Culturalism raises problems of a different sort because it is a word that does not appear in standard dictionaries and seems little used outside the China field. China scholars are at liberty, therefore, to use it as they please. The main usage has been the 'culturalism as identity' idea outlined in earlier passages. It has always been a difficult term to handle, however, and Joseph Levenson himself recognized two difficulties in his concept of culturalism.

The first was that culturalism as identity was difficult to distinguish from what I will call 'culturalism as movement'. The distinction arises from what culturalism means in two different political contexts. In one context, loyalty to the culture and belief in its superiority is so profound that bearers of the culture recognize no competition. This is culturalism as identity, an unquestioned worldview that cannot conceivably be lost or proven wrong. The other context involves awareness of competition, hence the prospect of choice among alternatives and the need for some defence and legitimation of the culture, even by those — indeed precisely by those — who believe most intensely in its superiority. This is 'culturalism as movement', in which

---

24   Smith, *Theories of Nationalism*, p.171.

25   See Akzin, *State and Nation*, pp.41, 46, 77-9; Royal Institute of International Affairs, *Nationalism* (Kelley, New York, 1966), p.xviii; Boyd C. Shafer, *Nationalism: Myth and Reality* (Harvest, New York, 1955), p.10; and Louis Snyder, *Global Mini-Nationalisms: Autonomy or Independence* (Greenwood, Westport, 1982), p.xv.

26   See the discussion in Smith, *Theories of Nationalism*, ch.7, and Akzin, *State and Nation*, pp.181-2.

conscious argument and action become necessary to defend a culture under threat. Levenson emphasized that 'true culturalism' had no conception of rivalry whereas Liang Qichao knew China and its culture had rivals; therefore, Liang's was not 'true' but rather 'decaying culturalism', a 'cultural loyalty which he feels he must justify' and which Levenson sometimes labelled 'culturalistic'.[27] Others, too, have noted how easily culturalism supported or merged with a 'cultural nationalism' that vigorously defended Chinese culture against foreign competitors.[28] If culturalism as identity slides easily into culturalism as movement, despite the fact that the latter reverses a key condition of the former, it is not surprising to see the word stretched in other ways as well. In one version it becomes a label for the imperial political and social system as a whole.[29] In another it refers to the approach of scholars (like Levenson) who emphasize this cultural problem, not to the Chinese view of their culture.[30]

Levenson's second cautionary note on the use of culturalism came as an afterthought in reflections on the dichotomies he analysed in his four books on Confucian China and its modern fate. The passage is worth quoting at length:

> Accordingly, when I conjure up dichotomies — objective/subjective, intellectual/emotional, history/value, traditional/modern, culturalism/ nationalism, Confucianist/legalist, and the like — these are offered, not as stark confrontations really 'there' in history, but as heuristic devices for explaining (not conforming to) the life situation. Only categories clash, categories of explanation . . . Antitheses are abstractions, proposed only to let us see how, and why, their starkness in definition is mitigated in history.[31]

In effect, Levenson is telling us not to take the thesis too literally because he poses the contrast between culturalism and nationalism as a 'heuristic device', not as a confrontation really 'there' in history. The thesis is a metaphor for China's modern transformation, not a precise description of historical processes. It suggests a set of categories to study, with every expectation that the student will find the 'starkness' of these categories 'mitigated in history'. The problem is that some may adopt the concept but not

27   Levenson, *Liang Ch'i-ch'ao*, pp.2, 110-19.

28   Ojha, *Chinese Foreign Policy*, pp.x-xi, 26-50; John King Fairbank, *The United States and China,* Fourth ed. (Harvard University Press, Cambridge, 1979), p.99.

29   Leon E. Stover, *The Cultural Ecology of Chinese Civilization* (Mentor, New York, 1974).

30   Arif Dirlik, Culture, Society and Revolution: A Critical Discussion of American Studies of Modern Chinese Thought, Working Papers in Asian/Pacific Studies, Duke University, Asian/Pacific Studies Institute, Durham (1985), esp. pp.7-8, 40, 52.

31   Levenson, *Confucian China,* p.xi.

Levenson's caution about the method. Great misunderstanding can result if metaphors are taken literally.[32]

The vulnerability of the thesis to conceptual confusion is compounded by certain assumptions and normative judgments that bedevil the study of nationalism in general. Assumptions about nationalism's supremacy, universality, and irresistibility appear in definitions that stipulate it centres 'supreme loyalty' on the nation-state, or that proclaim its capacity to override all other political loyalties and objectives. They appear as well in the tidal metaphor so favoured by analysts of the rise of modern nationalism and nation-states. These assumptions often prove true but they are not laws of history. Contrary to much that is said about nationalism by its analysts or adherents, nations fluctuate in boundaries, in beliefs about what is essential to their existence, in intensity of commitment from members, and in how members' loyalties are shared with other communities. Nationalist movements and doctrines rise and fall, expand and contract, and change their statements about what the nation is or is going to be. Most states today include more than one nation or potential nations, with complex overlapping or competing national claims on their citizens. The survival or revival of 'ethnic nationalisms' within states once supposed to be assimilating them is well documented.[33] There is more than one kind of nation, and the nation is but one kind of political community. The study of a particular nation and its nationalism requires appreciation of its changing relationships with other nations and political communities.

Normative judgments about nationalism are also common. To the ardent nationalist it is a good thing, but many contemporary analysts, sobered by two centuries of imperialism, revolution and war, take a negative view. Isaiah Berlin saw nationalism as a 'bent twig', a pathological reaction to science and rationalism, an 'inflamed condition of national consciousness' usually caused by 'some form of collective humiliation'.[34] John Dunn called it 'the very tissue of modern political sentiment', yet condemned its 'moral shabbiness' as 'the starkest political shame of the twentieth century'.[35] Karl Deutsch synthesizes much of this doubt and condemnation in his idea that nationalism produces for a nation and its leaders 'a gain in power and a loss in

---

[32] For a parallel argument that misuse of a 'metaphor of growth' has distorted Western theories of development, see Robert A. Nisbet, *Social Change and History: Aspects of the Western Theory of Development* (Oxford University Press, London, 1969).

[33] See, in particular, Walker Connor, 'Nation-Building or Nation-Destroying?', *World Politics,* vol.24, no.3 (April 1972), pp.319-55; and Anthony D. Smith, *The Ethnic Revival in the Modern World* (Cambridge University Press, Cambridge, 1981).

[34] Isaiah Berlin, 'The Bent Twig: A Note on Nationalism', *Foreign Affairs,* vol.51, no.1 (1972), pp.11-30.

[35] John Dunn, *Western Political Theory in the Face of the Future* (Cambridge University Press, Cambridge, 1979), pp.55-7.

judgment'.[36] Because it is thought to unite and strengthen a nation internally but to enhance its fear and misunderstanding of external forces, nationalism may be thought a good thing for a country fighting for unity or independence, a bad thing for one strong enough to impose its will on others. Not surprisingly, many prefer to describe the sentiments of their own citizens as 'patriotic', whereas others are 'nationalistic' (currently a preferred Chinese perspective). How do these normative notions come into play in the culturalism-to-nationalism thesis? There is a tendency, I think, to see the absence of nationalism in imperial China as a fatal weakness; once the tide is running, failure to join it becomes a moral flaw akin to treason. Yet in the era of the PRC, nationalism begins to assume an irrational and dangerous quality that distorts China's true interests and threatens other states.

This discussion yields three conclusions. First, both nationalism and culturalism carry multiple meanings and refer to complex phenomena, so the thesis is bound to be confusing unless one specifies how its terms are used. It is especially important to consider the nation as a kind of political community, to examine its relationships with other communities, and to distinguish among varieties of nations and nationalisms. Second, the thesis errs in opposing culturalism to nationalism and ethnicity, in arguing that culturalism blocked nationalism and had to dissipate for the latter to rise. Culturalism was actually an assertion of Chinese ethnicity, as it emphasized the cultural distinctions separating Chinese from others and the importance of maintaining those distinctions. Because one of the key distinctions in question was the imperial system, culturalism also asserted the existence of a nation — an ethnic group with its own political order. Culturalism was quite different from modern nationalism, but it was not inherently incompatible with ethnicity and nationalism. Third, the thesis is sometimes used metaphorically, and like all references to nationalism may carry questionable assumptions and normative connotations. Such usages may be illuminating and appropriate at times, but we must handle them with caution.

Empirical Questions

The next step is to apply the ideas introduced thus far in a discussion of the thesis' empirical validity. The thesis covers far too much ground to examine carefully in a chapter, and the range of knowledge required to do so is, in any case, beyond my capacity. What I will do is pose a few questions and hypotheses inspired by fragmentary evidence to suggest where the thesis' strengths and weaknesses might lie. The discussion follows a periodization suggested by the thesis: culturalist dominance (Imperial China), transition to nationalism (c.1860-1919), and nationalist dominance (post-1919). It employs the concepts already introduced of nation, state and ethnic nationalism, and

---

[36]   Karl W. Deutsch, *Nationalism and Its Alternatives* (Knopf, New York, 1969), pp.32-3.

nationalism as doctrine, movement and sentiment. Such a discussion cannot proceed, however, without resolving the problem of what culturalism means.

The idea of culturalism as 'identity' — the most common formulation — works as a 'heuristic device' for Levenson but is difficult to apply in more rigorous fashion. It seems obvious that Chinese 'identity' did not literally transform itself from 'cultural' to 'national' in the past one or two centuries. There is no single identity of either sort for all Chinese in either period, and the two identities in question actually go together in complex ways. It is better to think of culturalism as a belief, doctrine or set of ideas that can be specified with a bit more precision, and then to ask how strong it was among different groups at different times.

Accordingly, for purposes of this discussion, I take culturalism to be the belief that China was a cultural community whose boundaries were determined by the knowledge and practice of principles expressed through China's elite cultural tradition; that this community was unique and unrivalled because it was the world's only true civilization; that it was properly governed by an emperor who held absolute authority over his subjects, consisting of all those participating in the civilization; and that the political authority of the emperor and his officials rested in principle on superior cultural attainments, especially learning and a capacity to govern by moral example. This set of beliefs had several important implications for the community it defined. Most importantly, it specified a particular set of cultural markers, drawn mainly from the Confucian philosophical and moral tradition, that would be distinguished from, and exist independently of, more general cultural characteristics demarcating ethnic groups. Chinese, Mongols, Manchus, Arabs, Turks and the like could all join the community by accepting the principles, and be excluded from it if they did not. It was intellectual commitment to the principles that counted, not the specific culture into which one was born, because the principles could be learned or renounced. The community's precise membership and boundaries could fluctuate so long as the belief was maintained in significant regions. Rulers, too, could gain or lose legitimacy, which was based on superior command or demonstration of the principles, and not on ethnic background.

There is no doubt that this set of beliefs was extremely important to the maintenance of empire. It established grounds for accepting the downfall of Chinese dynasties and the installation of alien ones. It justified imperial rule over non-Chinese peoples and recruitment of some of them into the imperial bureaucracy. It rationalized fluidity of the empire's territorial boundaries and population. It influenced the language of imperial discourse and the quality of imperial relationships with other communities. But what was culturalism's actual extent and influence? My first hypothesis is that the thesis overstates culturalism's strength, which was limited in two important ways.

The first limitation was largely one of class. Culturalism derived from an elite tradition passed on through scholarly study and official practice, making it unlikely that many ordinary subjects understood or accepted the core beliefs.

This is not to suggest a sharp separation of elite and folk cultures but rather a complex mixture of class and ethnic distinctions. Each of the many ethnic groups that comprised the empire had its own cultural markers, readily recognized by itself and the others with which it had contact. The Chinese were by far the most numerous of these groups, and for imperial history as a whole they were the most powerful in every respect — although one or another of the non-Chinese groups held military superiority at times. The Chinese were also a nation (so, too, were some of the others) because the imperial political system was primarily theirs in population, territory, officialdom and culture. Culturalism was strongest among a community of elites that occupied the upper levels of these diverse peoples, which were distinguished by language, religion, food, dress, rituals and the like, and its influence extended into the general population. But although it was a major cultural identification for those at the top, for the majority it would have been of less importance than their primary ethnic identification. It seems likely that most Chinese thought of their cultural and political community — their nation — as a Chinese one, and that culturalism, to the extent that they understood it, reinforced their sense that the empire was also properly Chinese.

The second limitation is that there were alternatives to culturalism, as statecraft and ethnicity both competed or intermingled with it; 'pure' culturalism was modified by considerations of state power as well as by Chinese ethnic assertiveness. The imperial state had to be concerned about territory and its defence, sometimes interacting with others on an equal footing that violated culturalist assumptions.[37] Internally, its law distinguished between subjects and aliens, asserting sovereignty over resident aliens despite the culturalist logic that foreigners ('barbarians') would not be subjects of the empire.[38] Aliens were recruited into the bureaucracy, sometimes in significant numbers, taking Chinese names and demonstrating the idea that the empire was a community based on culturalist belief and practice. But the Mongol and Manchu dynasties established legal distinctions among Chinese and non-Chinese subjects, some non-Chinese continued to be marked as foreigners long after they were almost wholly assimilated, and some aliens served with honour as imperial officials even as their households were still registered locally as foreigners.[39] Scholars like Wang Fuzhi (1619-92) gave doctrinal

---

37   Morris Rossabi (ed.), *China Among Equals: The Middle Kingdom and its Neighbors, 10th-14th Centuries* (University of California Press, Berkeley, 1983).

38   R. Randle Edwards, 'Ch'ing Legal Jurisdiction over Foreigners', in Jerome Alan Cohen, R. Randle Edwards and Fu-mei Chang Chen (eds), *Essays on China's Legal Tradition* (Princeton University Press, Princeton, 1980), pp.222-69; and Vi Kyuin Wellington Koo, 'The Status of Aliens in China', *Studies in History, Economics and Public Law* vol.50, no.2 (Columbia University, 1912), pp.13-56.

39   T'ung-tsu Ch'u, *Law and Society in Traditional China* (Mouton, Paris, 1961), pp.201-6; Derk Bodde and Clarence Morris, *Law in Imperial China* (University of Pennsylvania

expression to Han Chinese chauvinism, and anti-foreign sentiment played a role in Chinese conflicts with both Mongols and Manchus.[40] In the latter case, secret societies kept anti-Manchu sentiment simmering for two centuries, until it surfaced again in the Taiping Rebellion (1851-64) and the burgeoning Chinese nationalist movement at the end of the century. Popular sentiment supporting these non-culturalist doctrines and movements in popular culture was evident in patriotic themes, emphasizing national history and heroes.[41]

One should not exaggerate these non-culturalist phenomena or read back into them any modern nationalistic content. The point is simply to observe that culturalism's dominance was modified or even challenged by competing views in imperial law and statecraft and in both elite and popular ideas about Chinese relations with other ethnic groups. My hypothesis is that a fuller account would show important variations in culturalism's influence over time, as well as pre-1850 periods when something like 'culturalism as a movement' developed, and throughout imperial history a greater role for issues involving ethnic differences than the culturalism-to-nationalism thesis suggests.

In the critical transition period from culturalism-to-nationalism — the late nineteenth century through the May Fourth era beginning 1919 — the thesis is at its strongest. Explicit nationalist doctrines and movements emerged accompanied by rising nationalist sentiments among educated and urban groups. By the 1920s, for most politically conscious Chinese, nationalism had replaced or at least overshadowed culturalism as the proper model for the Chinese political community. This meant that political and cultural communities should coincide, requiring efforts to strengthen the cultural as well as political unity of the Chinese state; that China should accept the norms of the international system of states, acknowledging the formal equality of other states and asserting vigorously its own territorial sovereignty; and that the Chinese state should transform its subjects into citizens, assigning them equal rights and obligations within the state, which would command their primary political loyalties.

Some aspects of this transition remain problematic, however. Accounts of both Chinese and foreign observers affirm that large sections of the

---

Press, Philadelphia, 1967), pp.168-70; and Donald Daniel Leslie, *The Survival of the Chinese Jews: The Jewish Community of Kaifeng* (E. J. Brill, Leiden, 1972).

[40] See the discussion of Wang's ideas in Etienne Balazs, *Political Theory and Administrative Reality in Traditional China* (School of Oriental and African Studies, London, 1965), pp.37-50. Varied manifestations of Chinese resistance to the Manchu are analysed in Jonathan D. Spence and John E. Wills, Jr. (eds), *From Ming to Ch'ing Conquest, Region. and Continuity in Seventeenth-Century China* (Yale University Press, New Haven, 1979); and Frederic Wakeman, Jr. and Carolyn Grant (eds), *Conflict and Control in Late Imperial China* (University of California Press, Berkeley, 1975).

[41] Yuji Muramatsu, 'Some Themes in Chinese Rebel Ideologies', in Arthur F. Wright (ed.), *The Confucian Persuasion* (Stanford University Press, Stanford, 1960), pp.241-67; and Robert Ruhlmann, 'Traditional Heroes in Chinese Popular Fiction', in Arthur F. Wright (ed.), *Confucianism and Chinese Civilization* (Atheneum, New York, 1964), pp.122-57.

population, mainly rural, remained uninvolved in political issues outside their localities. Despite all the nationalist activity and rhetoric, the country was not truly united during the period; Chinese political figures spent most of their energies fighting each other. The thesis postulates a prolonged crisis, of course, which it attributes to the trauma of exchanging culturalist for nationalist identity. The crisis was evidently real, but it is less clear that it was one of national identity.

The fact that many Chinese escaped the nationalist tide is no surprise, given the historical background and the weak development of modern education and communications in most of the country. It need not detain us here except as a cautionary footnote on tidal metaphors. The more significant limitations in the thesis lie in the problematic meaning of the transition from culturalism-to-nationalism and in the puzzle of why the crisis of modern China was (perhaps 'is') so prolonged. I suggest that the adoption of modern nationalism was a decisive break from culturalism but left unanswered some important questions about the implications of that nationalism; and that the crisis was one more of political authority than of Chinese identity.

Culturalism left an ambiguous legacy. Those elements within it that explicitly contradicted modern nationalism had to be discarded, but two of its implications were readily adaptable in the new era. Culturalism had always served as an ideology of empire, justifying Chinese rule over non-Chinese peoples as well as non-Chinese rule over the Chinese. In a sense it postulated a super-nation, a community defined by universally valid principles (though not universally accepted ones) and ruled through an imperial political system centred on China, one that transcended the specific cultural traditions of the peoples included. One need not question the sincerity or commitment of culturalists to observe that this was a very nice doctrine for emperors and their officials — that is, for anyone participating in the rule of, or benefits from, a multinational political system. It was a point of view readily transferred to state nationalism, which asserts that the state represents the true interests of its people as a whole, who constitute a nation in being or becoming, whatever their past cultural and political differences. On the other hand, the culture of culturalism's empire was Han Chinese; the principle allowed non-Chinese to enter (even rule) the community and Chinese to defect from it, but there was never any doubt that culturalism promoted a Han Chinese culture and others' participation in its practice. In effect, culturalism emphasized and extolled Han ethnicity, permitting an easy shift to cultural or ethnic nationalism — that is, political defence of Chinese culture and insistence that the Han Chinese must have their own unified state. In short, culturalism could lend its ideas to either state nationalism or ethnic nationalism, to support for a new China-centred state ruling the old empire and for a new political community among ethnic Han Chinese; one could retain its *de facto* specification of the Chinese content of the community's culture, or its more formalistic insistence that the political community rested on ideas transcending the particular ethnic identity of its members.

Culturalism's protean qualities made the transition to modern nationalism easier than the thesis suggests. The practice of the imperial state was formally brought into line with international norms in the latter part of the nineteenth century, and the transition among intellectuals was accomplished in roughly a generation. But just as culturalism had never really settled questions of ethnicity within the empire, so acceptance of modern nationalism did not resolve the possible contradictions between state and ethnic nationalism. Perhaps culturalism's capacity to tolerate such ambiguities remains its primary legacy today (as discussed later).

In any case, modern Chinese nationalism initially displayed a strong ethnic, even xenophobic, strain in opposing imperialism and Manchu rule. Turn-of-the-century ethnic nationalism placed its mark on the formative years of the Chinese Nationalist Party (KMT) and the new Republic of China, witnessed in an extensive mobilization of overseas Chinese communities in support of the anti-Manchu cause and the later granting of representation to these communities in republican national assemblies. Particularly telling was the late Qing adoption of the principle of *jus sanguinis,* confirmed in the Nationality Law of 1909, granting citizenship to all Chinese anywhere, and later allowing 'dual nationality' for Chinese subjects of another country who would also retain Chinese citizenship.[42] Nonetheless, once Nationalist and Communist states emerged from the turmoil of revolution, they asserted sovereignty over old imperial territories and saw non-Chineseness as no barrier to incorporation in a Chinese state. Like culturalism before it, modern nationalism permitted more than one definition of the Chinese nation.

A second problem involves the way the thesis construes the crisis of modern China. In a provocative study of Chinese political culture, Lucian Pye asserted that 'the Chinese have been generally spared the crisis of identity common to most other transitional systems', that 'they have little doubt about their identities as Chinese', and that 'the more they have been exposed to the outside world the more self-consciously Chinese they have become'. The primary problem, argues Pye, has been an 'authority crisis' brought on by erosion of the legitimacy of existing political authority and the search by Chinese for new forms of authority that can 'satisfy their need to reassert a historic self-confidence and also provide the basis for reordering their society in modern times'.[43] These are sweeping assertions indeed, hence subject to a variety of challenges, but I want to endorse their main thrust in the present context, which is that the culturalism-to-nationalism thesis overstates modern

---

[42]   Harley Farnsworth MacNair, *The Chinese Abroad, Their Position and Protection: A Study in International Law and Practice* (Commercial Press, Shanghai, 1925); and Chutung Tsai, 'The Chinese Nationality Law, 1909', *The American Journal of International Law,* vol.4, no.2 (April 1910), pp.404-11.

[43]   Lucian Pye, *The Spirit of Chinese Politics: A Psychocultural Study of the Authority Crisis in Political Development* (MIT Press, Cambridge, 1968), pp.5-6, passim.

China's identity crisis and directs attention away from a severe and prolonged crisis of political authority.

In the main, there has been little disagreement among twentieth-century political elites on the basic postulates of modern Chinese nationalism. Different regimes and competing elites have expressed a similar nationalist rhetoric and goals. Nonetheless, debilitating internal political conflicts have continued even as China has faced severe economic crises and international threats. This does not mean nationalist rhetoric lacks conviction or substance. Rather, it suggests that the crisis of political authority is so profound that it has overshadowed threats to national security or well-being. Except for a few brief periods (mainly 1895-98, 1919-27 and 1935-41), the integrity and survival of the nation has been a less pressing and divisive issue than how the Chinese polity should be structured, who should hold political authority, and what doctrine should guide social and economic development. I am not suggesting that the transition from culturalism-to-nationalism was painless or that the Chinese have had no problems in defining or redefining their nation. My point is that these problems have been less acute than the thesis suggests and that modern China's 'identity crisis' is difficult to separate from crises driven by elite political conflicts.

The logic of the culturalism-to-nationalism thesis suggests that Chinese nationalism entered its high-tide phase about 1919, building to the establishment of the PRC in 1949. The new regime was a product of a movement with strong nationalist credentials.[44] Its restoration of national unity and central power to a degree unknown since the mid-Qing, coupled with a strong organizational reach into the grassroots of Chinese society, enabled it to mount a vigorous development program. The resulting rise in Chinese power and international stature satisfied some nationalist aspirations and raised awareness at home and abroad of a possible Chinese pursuit of expanded nationalist ambitions. As suggested earlier, it was not difficult for observers to see nationalism everywhere in PRC history, goals and behaviour.

Once again, the thesis captures an important truth about rising Chinese nationalism while distorting or oversimplifying some of its manifestations. My discussion of the progress of nationalist doctrines, movements and sentiments suggests three points about the post-1949 period. First, a state nationalism has dominated official doctrine, placing its mark on most government statements and policies, but contradictions remain in the state's definition of citizenship and its inability or unwillingness to abandon or suppress ethnic nationalism. Second, some nationalist movements have occurred since 1949, and a powerful potential for them persists, but they have not dominated PRC political behaviour. Third, nationalist sentiments have grown among Chinese

---

[44]   The classic statement remains Chalmers A. Johnson, *Peasant Nationalism and Communist Power: The Emergence of Revolutionary China, 1937-1945* (Stanford University Press, Stanford, 1962). While aspects of Johnson's thesis are controversial, the importance of the CCP's incorporation and use of nationalism is not.

citizens, but major questions remain about the *focus* of nationalist sentiments — that is, about how the nation is defined — and the *intensity* of nationalism relative to other commitments.

State nationalism portrays the state as the embodiment of the nation's will, seeking for its goals the kind of loyalty and support granted the nation itself and trying to create a sense of nationhood among all its citizens. It is often difficult to distinguish state from ethnic nationalism in a country like China where political and cultural communities are largely congruent, both historically and today. But they are not totally congruent, now or in the past, and recognition of the difference is essential in any analysis of contemporary Chinese nationalism. The PRC is a multinational state — approximately 93 per cent of its population consisting of Han Chinese (usually referred to in this essay simply as 'Chinese'), the other 7 per cent non-Chinese divided officially among 55 minority nationalities. State nationalism asserts that the Chinese nation includes all PRC citizens irrespective of their nationality. Like culturalism, it acknowledges the ethnic differences among its population but insists that all are members of a larger nation that binds them together despite these historical ethnic differences. The state cannot deny the potential for ethnic nationalism on behalf of a particular ethnic group, or deny that many of its citizens lack strong attachments to larger political communities. Hence state nationalism requires 'nation-building'; creation of a new Chinese nation that incorporates all of its nationalities; concentration of political loyalty on the state; and repudiation of the idea that Chinese history and culture are purely a Han affair. The terms 'nationalism' and 'chauvinism' usually refer in official discourse to reactionary attachments to nationalities, whereas 'patriotism' is the desired love and support for the new China, always indistinguishable from the Chinese state and its objectives.[45]

State nationalism accords closely with conventional international norms emphasizing the indivisibility of territorial sovereignty and citizenship. PRC pronouncements usually support these norms vigorously. A key illustration has been the PRC's retreat from the principle of 'dual nationality' for overseas Chinese that had emerged during the flowering of Chinese ethnic nationalism earlier in the century. After many partial or *ad hoc* compromises on the issue from the early 1950s on, the PRC Nationality Law of 1980 explicitly rejected dual nationality, provided for naturalization of aliens as Chinese nationals, and stated that children born of Chinese nationals settled abroad could not hold

---

[45] The origins and evolution of PRC policy toward its nationalities are analysed in June Teufel Dreyer, *China's Forty Millions: Minority Nationalities and National Integration in the People's Republic of China* (Harvard University Press, Cambridge, 1976); and Thomas Heberer, *China and Its National Minorities: Autonomy or Assimilation?* (M. E. Sharpe, Armonk, 1989). For an example of Chinese assertions that the Chinese nation is actually multinational, and that 'China' *(Zhongguo)* historically included all the nationalities and their territories, see *Social Sciences in China*, vol.3, no.4 (December 1982), pp.237-8.

Chinese nationality if they had acquired foreign nationality by birth.[46] In keeping with this principle, the PRC has generally urged Chinese settled abroad to choose the nationality of their country of residence, giving up Chinese nationality.

State nationalism has met strong competition from two sources, however. One is the prominence in CCP doctrine, especially in the Maoist era, of class struggle and its impact on the real meaning of citizenship. Class-based definitions of the 'people' and recurring movements of class struggle divided the Chinese nation up to 1979, in effect revoking the citizenship of millions of its members by labelling them as enemy classes devoid of political rights. Nationalist movements frequently identify as 'traitors' members of the nation who allegedly collaborate with a foreign enemy, but CCP practice extended this act of national excommunication to vast numbers of people for purely internal political reasons, often on the thinnest of evidence. The legal and doctrinal implications of this are complex but one must recognize that it contradicts the substance of both state and ethnic nationalism, dividing the nation rather than unifying it by imposing arbitrary and shifting political criteria for membership.[47]

The other problem is ethnic nationalism's stubborn refusal to dissipate, even in some doctrinal forms. On internal issues, state nationalism has been relatively effective in resisting open espousal of Han Chinese ethnic nationalism, but it has not silenced statements of ethnic nationalism from Tibetans and some other minority nationalities. Externally, Chinese ethnic nationalism found expression after 1949 in granting overseas Chinese representation in the Chinese People's Political Consultative Conference (CPPCC) and the National People's Congress (NPC), as well as in other policies addressing this overseas group. With the trend that led to explicit renunciation of dual nationality in 1980, formal policy changed. Overseas Chinese no longer have seats in the NPC and their representatives in the CPPCC are said to be 'Chinese nationals residing abroad' — that is, not overseas Chinese who hold foreign nationality.[48] Much confusion remains in both Chinese and foreign views of this matter, however, and the PRC

---

[46] 'The Nationality Law of the People's Republic of China', *Beijing Review,* vol.23, no.40 (6 October 1980), pp.17-18.

[47] See Richard Kurt Kraus, *Class Conflict in Chinese Socialism* (Columbia University Press, New York, 1981).

[48] *Encyclopedia of New China* (Foreign Languages Press, Beijing, 1987), p.151. Key documents of the early CPPCC and NPC are found in Theodore H. E. Chen (ed.), *The Chinese Communist Regime: Documents and Commentary* (Praeger, New York, 1967). Complexities of PRC policy and terminology with respect to overseas Chinese are analysed in Stephen Fitzgerald, *China and the Overseas Chinese: A Study of Peking's Changing Policy, 1949-1970* (Cambridge University Press, Cambridge, 1972); and Wang Gungwu, 'External China as a New Policy Area', *Pacific Affairs,* vol.58, no.1 (Spring 1985), pp.28-43.

continues to assume or imply that ethnic Chinese the world over have some special bond or even obligation toward the PRC, albeit of variable intensity. Particularly significant is China's position on the nationality of Hong Kong residents, expounded in the 1984 'Sino-British Joint Declaration' and the 1988 Draft 'Basic Law', which implies that all ethnic Chinese residents are automatically Chinese nationals. The suggestion that Hong Kong's ethnic Chinese will automatically acquire PRC citizenship in 1997, whereas non-Chinese will not, contradicts the principle of state nationalism expressed in the PRC constitution and Nationality Law. If Hong Kong and Macao are Chinese territory, all their permanent residents who do not hold foreign nationality should become Chinese nationals, with the non-Chinese treated like the minority nationalities of the PRC.[49] Here, as with class struggle, there are competing doctrinal views of the Chinese nation that confuse the meaning of Chinese nationalism and qualify our evaluation of its significance.

Movements and sentiments that can be identified as reflecting both state and ethnic nationalism, often thoroughly mixed, have a prominent place in PRC history. At the broadest level, state nationalism and its nation-building aspirations invest state policy with a nationalistic tone. Development becomes a national cause, a collective effort to transform China into a newly powerful and modernized state as well as a new national community integrating all of the state's territories and peoples. If one accepts Deutsch's argument that nationalism grows with the intensification of 'complementary communications',[50] then the post-1949 expansion of surface and air transportation, postal and electronic communications, film and publishing industries, literacy and education, and the use of the national language *(putonghua)* — all accompanied by or infused with official propaganda emphasizing national unity, goals and accomplishments — must have produced a significant increase in national consciousness. From this perspective, the real nationalist revolution in China came after 1949 in the building of an infrastructure that reached all of the state's citizens and regions.

The PRC's international conflicts have also stimulated nationalist movements and sentiments. The Korean War was the prototype, with its use of force in support of state objectives, backed by a Resist America-Aid Korea campaign that mobilized popular energies for the war effort through a variety of nationalistic anti-American claims and appeals. No subsequent conflict quite matched this first one's intense concentration of military action, domestic mobilization, and popular emotion, but some mixture of extraterritorial (that is, involving areas of disputed or foreign sovereignty)

---

49   On the vagueness and inconsistency in the PRC position, see Frank Ching, 'Chinese Nationality in the Basic Law', in Peter Wesley-Smith and Albert Chen (eds), *The Basic Law and Hong Kong's Future* (Butterworths, Hong Kong, 1988), pp.288-93; and Robin M. White, 'Nationality Aspects of the Hong Kong Settlement', *Journal of International Law*, vol.20, no.1 (Winter 1988), pp.225-51.

50   Deutsch, *Nationalism and Social Communication.*

military action coupled with nationalistic rhetoric and supporting popular demonstrations can be found in the Taiwan Straits crises of the mid-1950s, the Sino-Indian border war of 1962, the Sino-Soviet border clashes of the 1960s, the Chinese invasion of Vietnam in 1979, and the Chinese seizure of the Xisha Islands (the Paracels) in 1974 followed by occasional Sino-Vietnamese skirmishes around those islands and more recent assertions of PRC claims to all the islands (primarily including the Nansha or Spratly group) in the South China Sea.[51] The continuing drama of PRC efforts to regain Hong Kong, Macao and Taiwan also ensures a steady diet of nationalistic themes in the official media. Although the primary nationalist components in these conflicts involve state pronouncements and popular demonstrations, and even external military action, they also enter popular culture as subject matter for film, drama, poetry and song. In these media they compete with more peaceful images of the nation that dwell on its history, monuments, landscape and ethnic diversity.

Because nation-building and international conflicts reflect state interests and goals, they tend to define the issues in terms of state nationalism. Nonetheless, mobilization of popular support against foreign threats often appeals to Han history and symbols and we may assume that much of the Chinese response sees the nation defended as Han, not as the multinational community portrayed in state nationalism. Is there more direct evidence of ethnic nationalism and conflict in the PRC? There is no doubt that Chinese inclinations to distinguish sharply between foreigners and themselves — an inclination I see stemming in part from culturalism's emphasis upon Chinese ethnicity — is alive and well, surfacing in Han-minority relations as well as in Chinese treatment of foreigners residing or travelling in their country. The desire to segregate foreigners is official policy, not just a popular attitude, and although the state emphasizes the Chineseness of its minority population, it also endorses a continuing sense of their distinctiveness by granting minorities various kinds of special representation and autonomy.

Ethnic consciousness in China has also become conflictual and even violent, most notably in Tibet, where ethnic nationalism has triumphed for now over the state's version of Han-Tibetan relations. Similar though less intense conflict has appeared in Han relations with the Uighurs and other Muslim nationalities, notably in Xinjiang and Yunnan. Some Red Guard behaviour during the Cultural Revolution revealed Han hostility toward Tibetan, Mongol and Islamic nationalities as well as more generalized xenophobia. More recent years have witnessed repeated incidents between

---

[51]   PRC claims in the South China Sea, which are disputed by many other states in the region, are analysed in Marwyn S. Samuels, *Contest for the South China Sea* (Methuen, New York, 1982). There was a suggestion, not approved, that the islands in question be incorporated in the new PRC province of Hainan when that large island off the southern coast was separated from Guangdong province in 1988. See *Beijing Review* (21 September 1987), p.5.

Chinese and African students, and a few more or less spontaneous demonstrations of anti-foreign, especially anti-Japanese, sentiment. The official press condemns all such nationalist, chauvinist or racist ideas and actions, which it attributes to lingering influences from China's feudal and semi-colonial past; and it continues to call for patriotism among all Chinese coupled with internationalism in their relations with foreigners. Nonetheless, like popular sentiment, official attitudes and policies toward other states continue to show the influence of the international rivalries of the past.[52]

Although the PRC has led what might be called a nationalist revolution in Chinese political behaviour and sentiment, the intensity and focus of this revolution remain uncertain. It is difficult to judge the intensity of nationalist belief in China because its profession is something like a state religion. Like professions of morality among politicians, it may tell us more about conventions of political discourse than the reality of either public behaviour or private belief. Much of our evidence on Chinese nationalism, from 1949 to the present, derives from state proclamations, state-promoted demonstrations, or state-sponsored and censored public expression. With this caution in mind, I suggest two generalizations. First, nationalism was most intense in the period between 1949 and 1969 when the Korean War, tension in the Taiwan Straits, and the Soviet threat of the 1960s made calls for defence of the nation more credible and emotional. Thereafter, Chinese leaders began their long effort to resolve the crisis left by the Cultural Revolution, and foreign enemies, in the main, became progressively less threatening. Second, the primary effect of the post-1978 reforms (so far as nationalism is concerned) has been to encourage a kind of privatization, a retreat from politics and an increasingly open pursuit of individual, family or group interests. The official gloss portraying a united people striving together for China's modernization does not jibe with the realities of Chinese behaviour. The nationalism most stimulated by the reforms was Tibetan, not Chinese.

State nationalism has not made the PRC's international behaviour particularly aggressive or inflexible, according to most observers, but rather cautious and opportunistic. China has pursued its interests vigorously, backing them with force on several occasions, but has manoeuvred and even retreated on many issues involving nationalistic concerns. In the 1970s the PRC abandoned its earlier demands for severance of American relations with Taiwan as a condition for United States-China rapprochement, accepting *de facto* relations with the United States between 1972 and 1978 even as formal American recognition of and support for the Republic of China on Taiwan continued. Some see the PRC's position on Hong Kong as nationalistic, but it

---

52   See Allen S. Whiting, *China Eyes Japan* (University of California Press, Berkeley, 1989) for a thorough analysis of Chinese images of and policies toward Japan, emphasizing the historical image of Japan as the enemy of Chinese nationalism and giving special attention to anti-Japanese demonstrations among Chinese students in 1985.

had always insisted on its sovereignty there and could hardly be expected to relinquish that claim. The formula of 'one country, two systems' for Hong Kong, Macao and Taiwan involves important concessions on matters of local autonomy, although the PRC insists on the formalities of its sovereignty over these areas.

As for popular nationalism in China, I have already suggested that it is less intense than the state would have us believe. It is also probably less oriented toward state nationalism. No doubt, most of those who are officially involved in national affairs take state nationalism seriously, with relatively full understanding and acceptance of its premises. That stance may be widely shared in more highly educated and politically conscious circles. But the evidence available suggests that for most Chinese it is the Han Chinese nation, not the PRC state, that is the focus of national sentiment. Judging from Han-minority relations, from Chinese attitudes toward foreigners, and from Chinese attitudes toward other ethnic Chinese who are not PRC citizens, this ethnic nationalism is more spontaneous, volatile and potent than the state nationalism that it often challenges. In sum, I am suggesting that state nationalism is weaker than official communications proclaim; that ethnic nationalism, among both Han and minorities, is more powerful than the state likes to admit; and that neither state nor ethnic nationalism among the Han Chinese has been particularly intense in the post-Cultural Revolution era.

Summary and Evaluation

The culturalism-to-nationalism thesis has two primary strengths. Most importantly, it identifies a fundamental change in prevailing elite belief and official doctrine about the nature of the Chinese community and its place in the world. This belief in imperial times was culturalism as defined at the outset of the preceding section. It was widely held among those educated in the Confucian tradition and it was part of the ideology of the imperial state. As orthodox state doctrine, culturalism gave way to modern nationalism under the impact of imperialism, the transition taking place between the mid-nineteenth century and the May Fourth era. The two doctrines were incompatible in three respects. First, although both doctrines recognized ethnic diversity within a broader cultural and political community of empire or modern state (both ruling much the same territory and population at times), culturalism placed primary emphasis on cultural determinants of community boundaries and membership, whereas modern nationalism defined the community as a territorial state in the process of achieving a higher degree of cultural and political integration. Second, culturalism did not acknowledge the formal equality of states in an international system of such states, nor did it see other cultural or political systems as competitors that could challenge Chinese ways, whereas modern nationalism asserted the reverse in both cases. Third, culturalism saw the common people as subjects of an absolute political authority, whereas modern nationalism insisted that all subjects would become citizens of the state, holding formally equal rights and obligations within it.

A second strength is the thesis' conceptualization of a broader pattern of intellectual change that accompanied the decline of empire and its replacement by a new kind of state. Levenson made use of the thesis as a 'heuristic device', counterposing abstractions that are 'not literally there in history'. It refers to a struggle in the minds of China's intellectual elites as they tried to resolve questions about their own and their nation's 'identity', a struggle resolved in this formulation by abandoning culturalism and adopting nationalism. By dramatizing the struggle as a confrontation between polar concepts, the thesis emphasizes the intellectual and psychological dimensions of the debate and sharpens the focus on its key issues. I hope that my efforts to respond to the broader ramifications of the thesis show that it does indeed hold value as a 'heuristic device', even though one may qualify it sharply.

The thesis' main weakness is that it exaggerates the totality and clarity of the change in question. It overstates both the dominance of culturalism and the weakness of pre-modern nationalism in imperial times, as well as overstating the eclipse of culturalism and triumph of nationalism in modern times. Contrary to the thrust of the thesis, culturalism could co-exist with other ideas about state and nation, could lend support in modern times to both state and ethnic nationalism, and hence could retain some influence on Chinese nationalism down to the present. Culturalism and state nationalism have been dominant elite doctrines in their respective eras, but neither has monopolized the field of ideas and sentiments about the Chinese nation.

These errors occur because the thesis focuses on intellectual history, elite behaviour and official rhetoric, without taking full account of popular sentiments or the realities of statecraft, and because it does not consider carefully the conceptual problems involved in the study of nationalism and ethnicity. In particular, it does not analyse closely the Chinese nation and its changing relationship to other Chinese and non-Chinese communities. The study of Chinese nationalism requires examination of the social landscape in which it operates, to supplement the thesis by linking intellectual history to an anthropology of the Chinese nation. In the concluding part of this chapter, I will try to demonstrate such an approach by a few general observations on different Chinese nations and their changing composition and significance.[53]

Changing Chinese Nations

A Han Chinese nation has existed for centuries, recognized by the Chinese and others as a distinct cultural and political community. There is disagreement on when this nation came into being — that is, when the Chinese became

---

[53]   Although I cite few titles, the discussion that follows reflects my understanding of a large literature that examines these issues in depth and provides a growing scholarly foundation for the approach I suggest.

conscious of their shared culture and began to view that cultural community as requiring its own political system. One argument dates the nation from the first imperial unification in the Qin-Han period, with its combination of cultural standardization and political centralization,[54] whereas a strict culturalist perspective can assert that it was 'impossible for such a thing as a nation' to exist in imperial China.[55] This is a dispute involving both conceptual choice and empirical evidence. My conceptual choice reveals a pre-modern nation in China but I am not qualified to assess the evidence that might date that nation's founding. It is sufficient here to observe that the Qin-Han unification established an administrative and ideological framework within which the Chinese nation evolved. Internal divisions, alien conquests, Tang cosmopolitanism, elite culturalism, peasant particularism, and Han and non-Han migrations and assimilation (in both directions) all complicated but did not block the nation's evolution. By the later dynasties, it was distinguished from other ethnic groups and nations by a sense of a common history, with myths of origin and descent; a distinctive written language and literary forms associated with it; some common folklore, life rituals and religious practices; and a core political elite, with a common education and orientation toward government service, that staffed the imperial bureaucracy, provided Chinese rule of most localities even under alien emperors, and circulated through official assignments and other travel throughout the empire.

For many reasons, however, this nation was not a continuous or even prominent focus for organization or loyalty. The imperial government's philosophy of rule, coupled with class barriers and regional differentiation, weakened its direct control of localities. Within and between regions were pronounced communal cleavages. In peripheral regions these stemmed in part from the presence of non-Han subjects, but the fundamental problem was communal divisions among the Han and a persistent tendency among commoners (and not a few elites) to attach their primary loyalties to these localized communities and organizations. Foremost among them were kinship associations, but these lower-level foci of loyalty included villages, marketing systems, religious sects, secret societies, and self-defence organizations. The largest communities within the Han nation were ethnic or sub-ethnic groups (scholars differ on the proper or least confusing term) defined by language or 'dialect', related cultural markers, and common provenance or residence. All of these communities possessed at least intermittent political organizations, including armed forces, for managing internal affairs and external conflicts. As they were the primary objects of loyalty for most Chinese, they reduced the importance of the nation in the Chinese universe of communities and were an

54   Wang Lei, 'The Definition of "Nation" and the Formation of the Han Nationality', *Social Sciences in China*, vol.4, no.2 (June 1983), pp.167-88.

55   Etienne Balazs, *Chinese Civilization and Bureaucracy,* translated by H. M. Wright, edited by Arthur F. Wright (Yale University Press, New Haven, 1964), p.22.

obstacle to nationalist movements or doctrines that demanded major sacrifices on its behalf.

Communal cleavages did not destroy the nation because of the overlay of the imperial government, which always became re-centralized after periods of disunity; the existence of a pre-modern nationalism, expressed in national history, myth and doctrine did not support political separatism for regional and ethnic (sub-ethnic) communities, and unity was preserved by the presence of political elites who constituted a true national community and tied localities indirectly to the imperial system by their participation in both local and national affairs. But the elites, too, contributed to the low salience of the nation by their belief in culturalism, which postulated a second kind of Chinese nation that could include aliens and even alien rulers, and could exclude Chinese who failed to adhere to Confucian norms. When the great Chinese emigration got underway in Ming times (it was to continue off and on to the present), a further complication arose with the overseas Chinese. Ming and Qing governments tended to assume that emigrants were unworthy subjects who had forsaken home and ancestors;[56] from the perspective of culturalism they had ceased to be Chinese. Nonetheless, as we have noted, a late nineteenth-century revisionist culturalism could view overseas Chinese as imperial subjects because they were obviously Chinese in culture. The point is that culturalism blurred the nation's boundaries, opening up the possibilities of a Chinese nation that included non-Han and one that included Chinese not really subject to the nation's political authority, both a bit different from the core Chinese nation. These different nations are more apparent today, with our norms of indivisible sovereignty and citizenship, and are politically very significant.

The Chinese nation in which modern nationalism emerged bore little resemblance to the ideal-type nation of Western theory. It was one among many communities to which Chinese belonged, and seldom the most important one to them, and even its leaders offered no explicit doctrine that we can comfortably call nationalism. But it was there and it endured, with its core territory and population relatively stable over the centuries. Charles Tilly reminds us that the construction of national states in Europe was a hazardous enterprise, despite the European political tradition that supposedly favoured such formations. Of some five hundred more-or-less independent political units in Europe in 1500, only about twenty-five were left in 1900; and even the survivors went through precarious episodes in which their integrity and future were much in doubt.[57] Something more than common culture held Chinese together, as there were ample opportunities to divide the empire along its internal regional or communal lines. The strength of the nation, including a form of pre-modern nationalism, must have been an important element here.

---

[56]   MacNair, *The Chinese Abroad, Their Position and Protection*, ch.1.

[57]   Charles Tilly (ed.), *The Formation of National States in Western Europe* (Princeton University Press, Princeton, 1975), pp.15, 38-9.

Culturalism and particularism both lowered the salience of the core nation, placing other loyalties above it, but neither challenged the idea that it was a political and cultural community that ought to remain intact. Culturalism played a particularly important role by rationalizing periods of alien rule and glorifying what was in fact the core nation's culture and tradition. Chinese attitudes toward the nation seem to have been flexible and pragmatic, enabling it to endure ruptures, discontinuities, contradictions and competing loyalties, without disintegrating.

This perspective helps explain why the rise of modern nationalism failed to produce a stable national unification. Old conceptions began to shift without crystallizing into a unitary form. The Han Chinese notion of ethnic nationalism quickly eclipsed the culturalist version, adding to the core Chinese nation those overseas Chinese who responded to its appeals. Dual nationality and representation in national political bodies gave overseas Chinese legal membership in the nation they were supporting with their funds, bodies and overseas havens. The nation of culturalism and empire that included non-Chinese did not disappear, because no Chinese government would abandon territorial claims so closely linked to national tradition and security, but it became changed in significant ways. The *de facto* separation or autonomy of most non-Han peripheral regions took them out of the mainstream of Chinese politics. Moreover, ethnic nationalism necessarily altered their relationship to the core nation. Logically, under this doctrine, the most distinct non-Chinese groups — really nations themselves — deserved formal autonomy if not independence, and some Chinese followed this logic by acknowledging that such groups were not part of the Chinese nation. Generally, however, the KMT moved toward a policy of assimilation, arguing that these territories remained Chinese and that their peoples either were, or by assimilation should become, ethnically indistinguishable from the Han. In effect, modern nationalism was pushing the Chinese state toward a formal position on how an integrated nation could emerge from the multinational empire. Ethnic nationalism encouraged assimilation of minorities into a Han nation or, less acceptably, independence or autonomy for all nationalities; state nationalism asserted that all nationalities could unite in a greater political and cultural community based on the territorial state.

Within the core Han nation, old regional and communal cleavages resisted national integration, while new classes contributed to rival political movements and ideologies that heightened the crisis of political authority. The paradoxical result became decades of rising nationalism coupled with persistent national disunity. The latter generally prevailed, postponing realization of nationalist goals, but the core nation survived and with it elite commitment to build a modern nation on the ruins of the empire. The CCP's victory in 1949 temporarily ended the crisis of political authority — it was to recur in the Cultural Revolution and the 1980s — permitting a new effort to define what an integrated modern Chinese nation could be.

For several reasons, the CCP committed itself after 1949 to state nationalism as a doctrine for creating a single Chinese nation. The outcome of World War II and the decisive military triumph of the People's Liberation Army extended PRC authority into most of the old imperial domains, so the new government immediately had to face the reality of its multinational state; and state nationalism, like culturalism before it, was an appealing doctrine for legitimating this political and cultural formation. Soviet doctrine and example provided a ready-made model for creating a new state-wide nation that included within it several more or less autonomous older nationalities, which could continue to exist as their members additionally adopted the new super-nationality. Internationally, the PRC's acceptance of formal international norms pushed it to abandon dual nationality, although this remained ambiguous until adoption of the Nationality Law of 1980. In doctrine, then, the PRC had established a single Chinese nation coterminous with the territorial state.

In practice, the issue is not resolved because four different Chinese nations continue to exist. The first is the official one of state nationalism, composed of all PRC citizens, Han and non-Han alike. The second, defined by ethnic nationalism and political reality, is the PRC's Han nation, composed of the core Han population, distinct from non-Han nations within the PRC as well as from Chinese outside the PRC who are subject to other political authorities. The third, a product of ethnic nationalism and the vagaries of Chinese political and migratory history, consists of the PRC plus the 'compatriots' or *tongbao* (in mainland terminology) of Taiwan, Hong Kong and Macao, whom both the PRC and the Republic of China on Taiwan see as part of the same nation-state even though presently under different political authorities. The fourth includes Chinese who are elsewhere around the world and who retain some idea, however attenuated, of dual nationality; this is a nation made possible by a continuing sense of Chineseness combined with the idea that residence and citizenship in another country do not preclude political as well as cultural attachment to China. The study of Chinese nationalism must include these four nations, taking into account their internal cohesion and cleavages as well as their complex relations with each other and with other nations. They are important, not because their boundaries and membership are clear-cut, but because they all contribute to Chinese nationalism and what it means for themselves and others with whom they are in contact. Because all four nations are in flux, Chinese nationalism remains an elusive and unpredictable phenomenon.

The official nation is mainly one of aspiration, not social reality. No doubt many educated Han, and some minorities, accept the idea that Chineseness is shared among all the nationalities, but most of the movement toward integration of this nation results from assimilation of the non-Han into Chinese culture. The most active nationalism within the PRC is currently Tibetan, with stirrings among the Uighurs, other Muslims, and Mongols. Ethnic nationalism among these peoples makes it clear that some may choose greater differentiation and autonomy over integration into a new PRC nation, a trend that on all sides can only strengthen awareness of the distinctiveness and dominance of the core Han Chinese nation. That core nation is also changing, as it adds new members by assimilation or by the projected infusion of Hong Kong and Macao compatriots at the end of the decade. Its earlier nationalist mobilization, which was moderated in the 1970s and 1980s, could easily revive in the face of a clear foreign threat or severe conflict with elements of other Chinese nations. Nonetheless, the core nation currently seems less involved in nationalist issues and movements than either the PRC or compatriot nations.

The third nation of compatriots is the most complex and unpredictable. For many years after 1949 the gulf between the PRC and the three territories was so great that the nation existed only as a legal fiction. Growing contacts with the mainland, first on the part of Hong Kong and Macao, then Taiwan in the 1980s, rekindled awareness that the combined territories do constitute a nation in some sense and that unification is possible. For Hong Kong and Macao, it is now a virtual certainty. The ROC shows no signs of yielding to PRC versions of reunification, but Taipei has contributed significantly to a renewed sense of nationhood by its vigorous promotion of contacts. At the same time, a contradictory trend exists in the rise of more open claims for Taiwanese self-determination or independence. Moreover, because many residents of Hong Kong and Macao object to reunification on PRC terms, or under the auspices of the current PRC regime, they, too, may push for greater autonomy or even independence, or may at least resist assimilation. In other words, this nation is in the midst of dramatic change that could lead to reunification of all the territories, to more explicit demands for independence or autonomy for Taiwan and Hong Kong, or to many other combinations in between. Whatever the outcome, it is important to note that nationalist activity in the 1980s and 1990s was more vigorous in Tibet and Taiwan, and perhaps even in Hong Kong, than in the core Chinese nation.

The fourth nation that incorporates some overseas Chinese cannot take any unified political form, as most of its external members have primary obligations to non-Chinese states. Nonetheless, the overseas compatriots have contributed both politically and economically to the PRC, Hong Kong, Macao and Taiwan, continuing to nurture the idea that important community bonds remain. The history of this association and concern about its future role make it a very sensitive political issue, especially in Southeast Asia. The fourth nation also participated in the mobilization of external Chinese in support of the 1989 Democracy Movement in China, perhaps the greatest such mobilization since turn-of-the-century support for various reformist and revolutionary activities in China. Some kind of national consciousness is obviously at work when Chinese of all the nations described here can rally around a political movement within the PRC, although one must note that the 'nationalism' of the supporters of this movement was labelled 'unpatriotic' by

PRC authorities. Nationalism continues to divide the Chinese as often as it unifies them.

How these different formations of Chinese nations will sort themselves out is difficult to foresee. We must anticipate continuing changes in their relations with each other, and with other nations, as well as in the intensity and focus of ethnic sentiments among their members. Possible changes include the escalation of new Chinese nationalisms, perhaps leading to independence movements in Taiwan, Tibet and even Hong Kong; or a reunification, on either a unitary or federal basis, that brings three of the nations — but not the overseas Chinese — into the same political system. Studying Chinese nationalism does not enable us to predict such outcomes, but it does tell us something about the limits of change. We can be sure that reunification would not remove a sense of ethnic (or sub-ethnic) differentiation among the peoples brought together, nor would independence for Taiwan or Hong Kong remove their sense of attachment to some kind of Chinese community. It seems to be a characteristic of Chinese nationalism that it permits shifting loyalties among different political authorities to co-exist with an abiding sense of Chinese nationhood.

TWO

De-Constructing the Chinese Nation

Prasenjit Duara

Most Sinologists view the Chinese nation as a relatively recent development, one that made the transition from empire to nation only around the turn of the twentieth century. This contrasts with the view of Chinese nationalists and the ordinary people of China that their country is an ancient body that has evolved into present times. This split in the understanding of the Chinese nation cannot be easily resolved by Western theories of nationalism, whose assumptions are deeply embedded in modernization theory. In this chapter, I propose a few alternative categories, inspired in part by post-modernist theories and in part by a comparative perspective, to understand both the question of the history of the nation as well as the related one about the nature of national identity.

In the problematique of modernization theories the nation is a unique and unprecedented form of community which finds its place in the oppositions between empire and nation, tradition and modernity, and centre and periphery. As the new and sovereign subject of history, the nation embodies a moral force that allows it to supersede dynasties and ruling segments, which are seen as merely partial subjects representing only themselves through history. By contrast, the nation is a collective subject – whose ideal periphery exists outside itself – poised to realize its historical destiny in a modern future.[1]

To be sure, modernization theory has clarified many aspects of nationalism. But in its effort to see the nation as a collective subject of modernity, it obscures the nature of national identity. I propose instead that we view national identity as founded upon fluid relationships; it thus both resembles and is interchangeable with other political identities. If the dynamics of national identity lie within the same terrain as other political

---

[1] The *Oxford English Dictionary* (compact edition) defines the modern philosophical meaning of the 'subject' as 'More fully *conscious* or *thinking* subject ... the thinking or cognizing agent; the self or ego'. *Oxford English Dictionary* (Oxford University Press, Oxford, 1971), vol.II, p.3120.

identities, we will need to break with two assumptions of modernization theory. The first of these is that national identity is a radically novel form of consciousness. Below, we will develop a crucial distinction between the modern nation-state system and nationalism as a form of identification. As an identification with a political community, nationalism is never fully subsumed by the nation-state and is best considered in its complex relationships to other historical identities. The second assumption is the privileging of the grand narrative of the nation as a collective historical subject. Nationalism is rarely the nationalism of the nation, but rather represents the site where very different views of the nation contest and negotiate with each other. Through these two positions, we will seek to generate a historical understanding of the nation that is neither historicist nor essentialist, and through which we might try to recover history itself from the ideology of the nation-state.

Historical Nations in China

Scholarship of modern China in the West has preferred to see nationalism in China as a modern phenomenon. Joseph Levenson observed a radical discontinuity between a nationalistic identity, which he believed came to Chinese intellectuals around the turn of the twentieth century, and earlier forms of Chinese identity.[2] The high culture, ideology and identification of the mandarin, he believed, were principally forms of cultural consciousness, an identification with the moral goals and values of a universalizing civilization. Thus the significant transition here is from a 'culturalism' to a nationalism, to the awareness of the nation-state as the ultimate goal of the community. Culturalism referred to a natural conviction of cultural superiority that sought no legitimation or defence outside of the culture itself. Only when, according to Levenson, cultural values sought legitimation in the face of the challenge posed by the Other in the late nineteenth century do we begin to see 'decaying culturalism' and its rapid transformation to nationalism – or to a culture protected by the state (politicization of culture).

As James Townsend also notes in the previous chapter, it is very hard to distinguish 'culturalism' as a distinct form of identification from ethnic or national identification. In order for it to exist as a pure expression of cultural superiority, it would have to feel no threat from an Other seeking to obliterate these values. In fact, this threat arose historically on several occasions and produced several reactions from the Chinese literati and populace. First, there was a rejection of the universalist pretensions of Chinese culture and of the principle that separated culture from politics and the state. This manifested itself in a form of ethnocentrism that we will consider in a moment. A second, more subtle, response involved the transformation of cultural universalism from a set of substantive moral claims into a relatively abstract official

---

2   Joseph Levenson, *Modern China and its Confucian Past: The Problem of Intellectual Continuity* (Anchor Books, New York, 1964).

doctrine. This doctrine was often used to conceal the compromises that the imperial state had to make in its ability to practice these values or to conceal its inability to make people who should have been participating in the cultural-moral order actually do so.

Consider the second reaction first. The Jin and Mongol invasions of north China during the twelfth century and their scant respect for Chinese culture produced an ideological defensiveness in the face of the relativization of the conception of the universal empire (*tianxia*). In the twelfth and thirteenth centuries Confucian universalists could only maintain their universalism by performing two sleights of hand: connecting individuals to the infinite (severing theory from fact) and internalizing the determination of personal values, both of which represented a considerable departure from the traditional Confucian concern with an objective moral order.[3] During the Ming dynasty, the Han Chinese dynasty that succeeded the Mongols, Chinese historians dealt with the lack of fit with the Chinese world view simply by maintaining a silence.[4] When we look at the tribute trade system, which is often cited as the paradigmatic expression of universalistic claims to moral superiority, the imperial state adapted readily to the practical power politics of the day. In the early nineteenth century, the tiny northwestern khanate of Kokand (like the Jesuits, the Russians and several others before) successfully challenged the Qing tribute system and established all but a formal declaration of equality with the Chinese empire. The Qing was forced into a negotiated settlement, but it continued to use the language of universalism – civilizing values radiating from the son of heaven – to conceal the altered power relations between the two.[5]

Thus the universalistic claims of Chinese imperial culture constantly bumped up against, and adapted to, alternative views of the world order, which it tended to cover with the rhetoric of universalism: this was its defensive strategy. It seems evident that when the universalistic claims of this culture were repeatedly compromised and efforts were made to conceal these compromises, advocates of this universalism were operating within the tacit idea of a *Chinese* universalism – which is of course none other than a hidden form of relativism. We have tended to accept Chinese declarations of universalism at face value far more readily than we do other official doctrines

---

3   Rolf Trauzettel, 'Sung Patriotism as a First Step Toward Chinese Nationalism', in John W. Haeger (ed.), *Crisis and Prosperity in Sung China* (University of Arizona Press, Tuscon, 1975), pp.199-214.

4   Wang Gungwu, 'Early Ming Relations with Southeast Asia: A Background Essay', in John K. Fairbank (ed.), *The Chinese World Order: Traditional China's Foreign Relations* (Harvard University Press, Cambridge, 1968), pp.45-46.

5   Joseph Fletcher, 'The Heyday of the Ch'ing Order in Mongolia, Sinkiang and Tibet', in John K. Fairbank (ed.), *The History of China* (Cambridge University Press, Cambridge, 1978), pp.351-408.

(perhaps because it plays a crucial role as the Other in interpretations of the encounter with the nation-states of the West).[6]

Viewing 'culturalism' (or universalism) as a 'Chinese culturalism' is to see it not as a form of cultural consciousness *per se*, but rather to see culture – a specific culture of the imperial state and Confucian orthodoxy – as a criterion defining a community. Membership in this community was defined by participation in a ritual order that embodied allegiance to Chinese ideas and ethics centred around the Chinese emperor. While this conception of political community may seem rather distant from nationalism, one should consider the fact that the territorial boundaries and peoples of the contemporary Chinese nation correspond roughly to the Qing empire, which was held together ideologically precisely by these ritual practices. A look at the ideas of Confucian modernizers writing in the late nineteenth and early twentieth centuries, such as Kang Youwei and Zhang Zhitong, reveals that the national community they had in mind was established on Confucian cultural principles that would include ethnically non-Han peoples – such as the Manchus – as long as they had accepted (Chinese) cultural principles.

This was, of course, challenged by the revolutionaries of the 1911 revolution, who saw nationhood as based on inherited 'racialist' (or ethnocentric), not cultural traits. However, it is important to note that after the 1911 revolution, the revolutionaries themselves reverted to the boundaries of the Qing empire to bound their nation. So, too, the Communist version of the nation builds upon a conception grounded in the imperial idea of political community.

Just as significantly, looking back historically, during the Jin invasion of the twelfth century, segments of the scholar class completely abandoned the concentric, radiant concept of universal empire for a circumscribed notion of the Han community and fatherland (*guo*) in which the barbarians had no place. This ethnocentric notion of Chineseness was, of course, not new. Chinese authors typically trace it to a quotation from the *Zuo Zhuan*: 'the hearts of those who are not of our race must be different'.[7] Others such as Yang and Langlois found it still earlier in the concentric realm of inner and outer barbarians found in the *Shang Shu*: pacific cultural activities were to prevail in

---

6   We are perhaps beginning to see the complex status of 'culturalism' as a concept, or more appropriately, as a representation of Chinese culture. While it obviously occupies an important role in constructing nineteenth-century China as the Other, it also plays a major part – perhaps as the centrepiece – in the intellectual apparatus of Sinology. In this respect, like the concept of 'sinicization', culturalism may, too, have reflected an 'unskeptical approach to the civil ideal in Chinese elite culture'. See Pamela Crossley, 'Thinking About Ethnicity in Early Modern China', *Late Imperial China*, vol.11, no.1 (1990), pp.1-35.

7   Tsung-I Dow, 'The Confucian Principle of A Nation and Its Historical Practice', *Asian Profile*, vol.10, no.4 (1982), p.353; and Li Guoqi, 'Zhongguo jindai minzu sixiang' [Modern Chinese Nationalist Thought], in Li Guoqi (ed.), *Minzuzhuyi* [Nationalism], (Shibao chuban gonsi, Taipei, 1970), p.20.

the inner part whose inhabitants were not characterized as ethnically different, with militancy toward the outer barbarians who appeared to be unassimilable.[8] Trautzell believes that in the Song, this ethnocentrism brought together state and people. The state sought to cultivate the notion of loyalty to the fatherland downward into peasant communities from among whom arose resistance against the Jin in the name of the Chinese culture and the Song dynasty.[9]

While we see the ethnic nation most clearly in the Song, its most explicit advocate in the late imperial period was Wang Fuzhi. Wang likened the differences between Manchus and Han to that between jade and snow, which are both white but different in nature, or, more ominously, between a horse and a man of the same colour but whose natures are obviously different.[10] To be sure, it was the possession of civilization (*wen*) by the Han that distinguished them from the barbarians, but this did not deflect Wang from the view that 'it is not inhumane to annihilate (the barbarians) ... because faithfulness and righteousness are the ways of human intercourse and are not to be extended to alien kinds (*i-lei* [*yilei*])'.[11] Although Wang may have espoused the most extreme view of his generation, several prominent scholars of the Ming-Qing transition era held on to the idea of the fundamental unassimilability of the *yi* (barbarian) by the *hua* (Chinese).[12]

Despite the undoubted success with which the Qing did in fact make themselves acceptable as the legitimate sons of heaven, they were unable to completely suppress the ethnocentric opposition to their rule either at a popular level or among the scholarly elite. The anti-Manchu writings of Wang Fuzhi, Huang Zongxi and Gu Yanwu during the early period of Qing rule together with collections of stories of Manchu atrocities during the time – *Mingji Yeshi* [Unofficial history of the late Ming] – were in circulation even before the middle of the nineteenth century.[13] Zhang Binglin, for instance, claims to having been nourished by a tradition both in his family and in wider Zhejiang society which held that the defense of the Han against the barbarians

---

8   See John D. Langlois Jr., 'Chinese Culturalism and the Yuan Analogy: Seventeenth-Century Perspectives', *Harvard Journal of Asiatic Studies*, vol.40, no.2 (1980), p.362; and Lien-sheng Yang, 'Historical Notes on the Chinese World Order', in John K. Fairbank (ed.), *The Chinese World Order: Traditional China's Foreign Relations* (Harvard University Press, Cambridge, 1968), pp.20-33.

9   Trauzettel, 'Sung Patriotism as a First Step Toward Chinese Nationalism'.

10   Li Guoqi, 'Zhongguo jindai minzu sixiang', p.22.

11   Langlois, 'Chinese Culturalism and the Yuan Analogy', p.364.

12   Hidemi Onogawa, 'Zhang Binglinde paiman sixiang' [The Anti-Manchu Thought of Zhang Binglin] in Li Guoqi, *Minzuzhuyi*, pp.207-60. Wu Wei-to, 'Zhang Taiyan zhi minzuzhuyi shixue' [Zhang Taiyan's Historical Studies of Nationalism], in Li Guoqi, 'Zhongguo jindai minzu sixiang', pp.261-71.

13   Wu Wei-to, 'Zhang Taiyan zhi minzuzhuyi shixue', p.263.

(*yi xia*) was as important as the righteousness of a ruler.[14] Certainly Han ethnic consciousness seems to have reached a height by the late eighteenth century when the dominant Han majority confronted the non-Han minorities of China in greater numbers than ever before over competition for increasingly scarce resources.[15] Thus it is hardly surprising to find resistance to the increased foreign presence after the Opium Wars through to the Boxer Rebellion of 1900 among both the elite and the general populace.[16]

At least two conceptualizations of the political community in imperial Chinese society can be discerned: the exclusive ethnic-based one founded on a self-description of a people as Han and a community based on the cultural values and doctrines of a Chinese elite. What has been described as culturalism is a statement of Chinese values as superior but, significantly, not exclusive. Through a process of education and imitation, barbarians could also become part of a community sharing common values and distinguishing themselves from yet other barbarians who did not share these values. In these terms, culturalism is not significantly different from ethnicity, because, like ethnic groups, it defines the distinguishing marks and boundaries of a community. The difference lies in the criterion of admissibility: the ethnocentric conception refused to accept as part of the political community anyone not born into the community, despite their educability into Chinese values, whereas the cultural conception did.

The social whole in historical China was conceived, in short, in a way that is not completely different from the conceptualization of the social whole of modern nationalism. Yet the impulse in modern scholarship to view the two as fundamentally different is not confined to China scholarship, but informs the most influential studies of nationalism today. Two such studies, by Benedict Anderson and Ernest Gellner, have stressed the radically novel form of consciousness represented by national identity. Both analysts identify national consciousness conventionally as the co-extensiveness of politics and culture – an overriding identification of the individual with a culture that is protected by the state. Both also provide a sociological account of how it was only in the modern era that such a type of consciousness – where people from diverse locales could 'imagine' themselves as part of a single community – was made possible. Gellner provides a full account of this discontinuity. Pre-industrial society is formed of segmentary communities, each isolated from the other, with an inaccessible high culture jealously guarded by a clerisy – Gellner's general term for literati ruling elites. With the growth of industrialism, society requires a skilled, literate and mobile workforce. The segmentary form of

---

[14]   Onogawa, 'Zhang Binglinde paiman sixiang', p.216.

[15]   Susan Naquin and Evelyn S. Rawski, *Chinese Society in the Eighteenth Century* (Yale University Press, New Haven, 1987).

[16]   Joseph W. Esherick, *The Origins of the Boxer Uprising* (University of California Press, Berkeley, 1987); and Frederic Wakeman Jr., *Strangers at the Gate: Social Disorder in South China 1839-1861* (University of California Press, Berkeley/Los Angeles, 1966).

communities is no longer adequate to create a homogeneously educated work force in which the individual members are interchangeable. The state comes to be in charge of the nation, and through control of education creates the requisite interchangeability of individuals. The primary identification with segmentary communities is transferred to the nation state.[17] In Anderson's view, the spread of print media through the capitalist market made possible a unity without the mediation of a clerisy. Print capitalism permitted an unprecedented mode of apprehending time that was 'empty' and 'homogeneous' – expressed in an ability to imagine the simultaneous existence of one's co-nationals.[18]

I believe that this claim of a radical disjuncture is exaggerated. The long history of complex civilizations such as that of China does not fit the picture of isolated communities and a vertically separate but unified clerisy. Scholars have filled many pages writing about complex networks of trade, pilgrimage, migration and sojourning that linked villages to wider communities and political structures. This was the case as well in Tokugawa Japan and eighteenth century India.[19] Moreover, even if the reach of the bureaucratic state was limited, recently developed notions of the culture-state[20] indicate the widespread presence of common cultural ideas which linked the state to communities and sustained the polity.

It was not only, or perhaps even primarily, the print media that enabled Han Chinese to develop a sharp sense of the Other, and hence of themselves as a community, when they confronted other communities. The exclusive emphasis on print capitalism as enabling the imagining of a common destiny and the concept of simultaneity ignores the complex relationship between the written and the spoken word. In agrarian civilizations this interrelationship furnishes an extremely rich and subtle context for communication across the culture. For instance, in pan-Chinese myths, such as that of Guandi, the god of war, not only were oral and written traditions thoroughly intertwined, the myth also provided a medium whereby different groups could announce their participation in a national culture even as they inscribed their own interpretation of the myth through the written and other cultural media, such

---

17   Ernest Gellner, *Nations and Nationalism* (Cornell University Press, Ithaca, 1983).

18   Benedict Anderson, *Imagined Communities: Reflections on the Origins and Spread of Nationalism* (Verso Editions and NLB, London, 1983).

19   Chris Bayly, 'The Prehistory of Communalism: Religious Conflict in India 1700-1850', *Modern Asian Studies*, vol.19, no.2 (1985); and Homi K. Bhabha, *Nation and Narration* (Routledge, London/New York, 1990).

20   See, for instance, Burton Stein's concept of the segmentary state in India in *Peasant State and Society in Medieval South India* (Oxford University Press, Delhi/New York, 1980), and Stanley Tambiah's galactic polity in the Thai kingdom of Ayutthaya in *Culture, Thought and Social Action* (Harvard University Press, Cambridge, 1985).

as folk drama and iconography.[21] These groups were articulating their understanding of the wider cultural and political order from their own particular perspective. There were large numbers of people in agrarian societies who were conscious of their culture and identity at multiple levels, and in that sense were perhaps not nearly so different from their modern counterparts.

The point is not so much that national identity existed in pre-modern times; rather, it is that the manner in which we have conceptualized political identities is fundamentally problematic. In privileging modern society as the only social form capable of generating political self-awareness, Gellner and Anderson regard national identity as a distinctive mode of consciousness: the nation as a whole imagining itself to be the unified subject of history. There is a special and restricted sense in which we can think of a unified subjectivity; we shall have occasion below to review it in our discussion of nationalism as a relational identity. But this restricted sense of unity is not unique to modern society.[22] The deeper error, however, lies in the general postulate of a cohesive subjectivity.

Individuals and groups in both modern and agrarian societies identify simultaneously with several communities that are all imagined; these identifications are historically changeable, and often conflict internally and with each other. Not only did Chinese people historically identify with different types of communities, but, as we shall see, when these identifications became politicized they came to resemble national identities. To be sure, this does not validate the claim of some nationalists that the nation had existed historically as a cohesive subject gathering self-awareness and poised to realize its destiny in the modern era. Pre-modern political identifications do not necessarily or teleologically develop into the national identifications of modern times. A new vocabulary arises within which a political system selects, adapts, reorganizes and even recreates these older identities. Nonetheless, the fact remains that modern societies are not the only ones capable of creating self-conscious political communities.

At the same time we can see that modern nations, too, are unable to confine the identity of individuals exclusively, or even principally, to the nation-state. All over the world, the nation-state faces one challenge or

---

21   Prasenjit Duara, 'Superscribing Symbols: The Myth of Guandi, Chinese God of War', *Journal of Asian Studies*, vol.47, no.4 (1988), pp.778-95.

22   Even a pre-modern village community has to be imagined. Etienne Balibar says about 'imaginary' communities that 'Every social community reproduced by the functioning of institutions is imaginary, that is, it is based on the projection of individual existence into the weft of a collective narrative, on the recognition of a collective name and on traditions lived as the trace of an immemorial past (even when they have been created and inculcated in the recent past). But this comes down to accepting that, in certain conditions, only imaginary communities are real'. Etienne Balibar, 'The Nation Form: History and Ideology', *Review*, vol.13, no.3 (1990), p.346.

another to its claim to sovereignty, whether it is in Brittany, Quebec, Punjab or Tibet. More subtle are the changing relationships between both old and new sub-groups and the nation-state, such as the waxing and waning of Scottish nationalism or southern Chinese 'regionalism'. Finally, all good nationalisms are also disposed to a trans-national ideal, whether it be anti-imperialism, pan-Europeanism, pan-Africanism, pan-Islamism, Shiism or Judaism. Sun Yat-sen and other Chinese nationalists believed that it was in the interest of Chinese minorities to join with the Han majority against the imperialists during the war-ravaged republic because of the security bestowed by numbers. When the imperialist threat faded, it became easy for these minorities to perceive the threat from precisely the numbers of the Han majority. When these political identifications are viewed in these dynamic or fluid terms, it becomes clear that what we call nationalism is more appropriately a *relationship* between a constantly changing Self and Other, rather than a pristine subject gathering self-awareness in a manner similar to the evolution of a species.

The Modern Nation-State System and the Question of History

What is novel about modern nationalism is not political self-consciousness, but the world *system* of nation-states. This system, which has become globalized in the last hundred years or so, sanctions the nation-state as the only legitimate form of polity. It is a political form with distinct territorial boundaries within which the sovereign state, 'representing' the nation-people, has steadily expanded its role and power. The ideology of the nation-state system has sanctioned the penetration of state power into areas that were once dominated by local authority structures. For instance, 'children' have come increasingly under the jurisdiction of the state as the institutional rules governing childhood were diffused to all types of nation-states over the past hundred years.[23] The term nationalism is often confused with the ideology of the nation-state which seeks to fix or privilege political identification at the level of the nation-state. The slippage in this relationship is a principal source of the instability in the meaning of the nation.

The lineage of the sovereign territorial conception may be traced to what William McNeill has characterized as the system of competitive European states. From as far back as 1000 AD, each of these states was driven by the urge to gain an edge over the others in resources, population and military technology. In their competition, these states gradually became dependent on capital markets, both externally and internally, which further propelled the

---

[23]   John W. Meyer, 'The World Polity and the Authority of the Nation State', in Albert Bergesen (ed.), *Studies of the Modern World System* (Academic Press, New York, 1980). See also John Boli Bennet and John W. Meyer, 'The Ideology of Childhood and the State: Rules Distinguishing Children in National Constitutions, 1870-1970', *American Sociological Review*, no.43 (1978), pp.797-812.

development of their economy and the competition between them.[24] In time, the Church came to sanction some of these emergent regional states by endowing them with a theory of sovereignty without at the same time obliging them to achieve universalizing empire. This was possible because of the separation of temporal and spiritual authority, or, in other words, the source of legitimacy from the actual exercise of power.[25] The culmination of this conception of the nation was first seen in the French revolution and exemplified in the idea of citizenship for all within the territory.[26]

Elsewhere in the world, competition was never institutionalized in the same way. For instance, in China during the many periods of inter-dynastic struggles, the divisions of the empire were brought to an end by a victor who established a command polity that squelched the dynamic of competition among states. Similarly, although regional successor states emerged from the disintegration of the Moghul empire in eighteenth century India, the competition between them was not institutionalized in the same way. Moreover, from the point of view of sovereignty, legitimacy in China necessarily resided in the imperial centre, in the son of heaven, and thus regional states were never able to claim any durable sovereign status. Likewise, the most powerful successor state of the Moghuls, the Hindu Marathas, strove not for territorial sovereignty but toward the Brahmin ideal of a universal ruler.[27]

However, no contemporary state is a nation exclusively in this territorial sense. Even among the early modern European states, European dynasts had to combine the theory of territorial sovereignty with ethnicity to create modern nation states.[28] While most historical nations, defined as self-aware and even politicized communities, lacked the conception of themselves as part of a system of territorially sovereign nation-states, modern nations embody both territorial and ethnic conceptions. Of course, it may legitimately be asked, 'To what extent does the (modern) nation-state system influence the political identities of its citizens?' As Etienne Balibar points out, the nation-state has doubtless developed the ability to have territorial boundaries acquire a salience and have its citizens develop powerful attachments to these boundaries.[29] Yet even these territorial identifications have to come to terms

---

24   William McNeill, *The Pursuit of Power* (University of Chicago Press, Chicago, 1982).

25   John A. Armstrong, *Nations before Nationalism* (University of North Carolina Press, Chapel Hill, 1982).

26   Geoff Eley, 'Nationalism and Social History', *Social History*, vol.6, no.1 (1981), pp.83-107.

27   Ainslee T. Embree, 'Indian Civilization and Regional Cultures: The Two Realities', in Paul Wallace (ed.), *Region and Nation in India* (Oxford University Press, New Dehli, 1985), p.32.

28   Armstrong, *Nations Before Nationalism*.

29   Balibar, 'The Nation Form'.

with historical understandings, as we shall see in the case of the Chinese republican revolutionaries. More generally, territorial identifications have to bear some relationship to an inherited sense of the 'homeland' – even if this sense is a highly contested one.

The shape and content of national identities in the modern era are a product of negotiation with historical identities within the framework of a modern nation-state system. From this vantage point the efforts by scholars – from Kedourie to Gellner – to vociferously debunk nationalist historiography for assuming an ancient history of the nation (the nation as a continuous subject gathering self-awareness) seem to miss the point. Nationalist historians engage in what all historians have to do: narrate the facts of the past in a way that is most meaningful to them.

During the years before the republican revolution of 1911 when modern nationalism took hold among the Chinese intelligentsia, the debates between them about the nature of the future Chinese nation were shaped as much by modern discourses of the nation-state (see below) as by the historical principles involved in defining community that we have traced above. The constitutional monarchists, represented by Kang Youwei, inherited the Confucian culturalist notion of community. Although Kang was influenced by modern Western ideas, the conception of political community that he retained drew on culturalist Confucian notions. We see this in his lifelong devotion to the emperor (in his founding of the Protect the Emperor Society), which in the political context of the time meant more than a nostalgia for monarchy. That the monarchs were Manchu and not Han implied that Kang was convinced that the community was composed of people with a shared culture and not restricted to a race or ethnic group (imputed or otherwise).[30]

Revolutionaries such as Zhang Binglin and Wang Jingwei articulated their opposition to this conception by drawing on the old ethnocentric tradition, which acquired new meaning in the highly charged atmosphere of

---

[30] In his debates with the republican revolutionary Zhang Binglin, Kang cites Confucius in *The Spring and Autumn Annals* to argue that although Confucius spoke of barbarians, their barbarism was expressed in their lack of ritual and civilization. See Onogawa, 'Zhang Binglinde paiman sixiang', p.245. If indeed they possessed culture then they must be regarded as Chinese. Since the Manchus had culture they were Chinese. Appealing to history, Kang declared that during the Warring States period, Wu and Chu had been different countries, but had become part of China by the time of the Han. Similarly, although the Manchus were barbarians in the Ming, by now they had become Chinese. Kang asked whether it was necessary for China to get rid of the Manchus in order to build a new nation or whether the nation could embrace all ethnic groups on a harmonious basis, including the Manchus, Hans, Miaos and Muslims, as well as the Tibetans? His disciple Liang Qichao developed this argument further, alleging that the revolutionaries deliberately confused bad government with racism. What was important was that the government was badly run; whether it was run by Manchus or Han was beside the point. There was no reason why China could not be rebuilt on a multi-racial basis. See Onogawa, 'Zhang Binglinde paiman sixiang', p.249.

the 1900s. To be sure, Zhang was a complex figure whose thought can scarcely be reduced to any single strain. But he and his associate, Zou Rong, succeeded in articulating an image of the new community that was persuasive to many in his generation. At the base of this reformulation of the old ethnocentrism was a dialectical reading of Wang Fuzhi's notions of evolutionism plus a new Social Darwinist conception of the survival of the fittest races. The complex architecture of Zhang's ideas of the nation seem as much to use modern ideas to justify an ethnocentric celebration of the Han as it was a selective use of the past to ground the present. Modern nationalists like Kang and Zhang were each engaged in dialogues with disputed legacies that were, nonetheless, authentic and by no means completely assimilable by modern discourses.

This same type of critique in scholarly writings on nationalism is misplaced because it slights the strong contrary urge within nationalism to see itself as a modern phenomenon. While on the one hand nationalist leaders and nation-states glorify the ancient or eternal character of the nation, they simultaneously seek to emphasize the unprecedented novelty of the nation state, because it is only in this form that the 'people' have been able to realize themselves as the subjects or masters of their history. The discourse of the people as sovereign, which the nation-state promotes (without always questioning too closely the fact of the nation-state's representation of this sovereignty), remains the single most important source of legitimacy of the nation-state within the nation.

There is thus a built-in ambivalence in modern nationalist ideology toward the historicality of the nation, which we can sometimes see in the writings of a single figure. In the writings of Sun Yat-sen, the ambiguity is concealed through a political attack on his enemies. Sun argues that China, which for him is the Han nation, is the world's most perfectly formed nation because the people are bound together by all the five criteria that (for him) it took to form a nation: blood/race, language, custom, religion and livelihood. At the same time, Sun is unclear on whether the nation is already fully awakened or whether national consciousness needs to be further aroused. He is torn between these options, because, on the one hand, nationalists like himself could fulfil their mission only if the Han people still suffered from a 'slave mentality' with no national consciousness. On the other hand, the pre-existing fullness of China as a nation was necessary for the legitimacy of any nationalist rhetoric. Initially, Sun maintained both positions by arguing that the awakening was also a re-awakening. There had been difficult historical periods when the Han people had risen to the occasion and revealed the fullness of their national being, as during Han resistance to the Jurchens or the Mongols.

Ultimately, Sun concealed this ambiguity by transforming it into a problem inherent in Confucian cosmopolitanism: the original spirit of Han independence had been weakened by a cosmopolitanism which accepted alien rulers like the present Manchu regime as rulers of the Chinese people. This was, of course, precisely the cosmopolitanism advocated by his reformer enemies, who advocated a China composed of all of the ethnic groups of the old empire. Sun and the republican revolutionaries sought to mobilize a particular history not only to serve as the foundation of the new nation-state, but to de-legitimate the ideological core of the alternative territorial and culturalist conception of the nation. Thus ambivalence between the old and the new presents us with a window to view history, not as something merely made up, but as the site of contestation and repression of different views of the nation.[31]

The ambivalence about the historicality of the nation reveals a fundamental aporia for nationalists: if the people-nation had always been present historically then on what grounds can the present nation-state make a special claim to legitimacy as the first embodiment of the people-nation? We have seen the elaborate rhetorical strategy that Sun employed to address this ambiguity. In other cases, such as in Israel or India, the tensions between the claim for an ancient and pristine essence of the nation and the claim for the new and modern cannot be contained by the rhetoric of nationhood, and erupts into political conflict. An important aspect of the ideological struggle between the CCP and the KMT – both ardent nationalists – centred upon how much of the 'historical' nation (or which historical nation) needed to be transformed or revolutionized. Thus nationalists have not been able to fully control the meaning of the nation's history. The real significance of this aporia lies in the possibilities it generates for contested meanings of the nation. Modernist and post-modernist understandings of the nation tend to view history epiphenomenally – as the space for forgetting and recreating in accordance with present needs. A more complex view of history suggests that if the past is shaped by the present, the present is also shaped by the past as inheritance, and the most fertile questions lie in understanding how this dialectic is articulated in the contest over the significance of national history.

Toward an Analytics of National Formations: Identity and Meaning

Social science explanations of political identity – ethnic and national – have centred around the debate over whether these are primordial or instrumentalist. Neither has much use for historical process since the primordialists simply assume an essential and unchanging identity, whereas the instrumentalists, who usually attribute the creation of such identities to

---

31   The discussion is reproduced in the third lecture of nationalism in Sun's *Three People's Principles* delivered in 1924. The attack against cosmopolitanism is also directed against the cosmopolitan strain in the May 4 'new culture' movement. Incidentally, the English version of this lecture contains yet another level of repression for it leaves out the vitriolic racialist language characteristic of the original Chinese text and omits many of Sun's references to his debates with the reformist cosmopolitans in the early years of the century. Sun Yat-sen, *Sanminzhuyi* [The Three People's Principles] (a reprint) (Zhongyang wenwu gongyingshe, Taipei, 1986), pp.41-2.

manipulation by interested elites or others, often find the past to be irrelevant. What remains unclear in the instrumentalist view pertains to what it is that is being manipulated. More recently, the instrumentalist position is being revisited by scholars influenced by post-structuralism and discourse analysis, who are extremely suspicious of historicist or even historical explanations, preferring to see identities as 'constructed' by the discourses of the era.

The alternative strategy that I have been proposing in this essay posits a plurality of sources of identifications in a society – which do not necessarily harmonize with one another. Thus while a nationalist identity may sometimes be entirely invented, more often than not its formulators are able to build it upon, or from among, pre-existent loci of identification. Building this identification, of course, entails obscuring and repressing other expressions of identity, whether these are historical vestiges or whether they evolve as oppositional forms. In this way, historical agents are constantly in dialogue with a past that shapes but does not determine them. Moreover, since it is a history rather than History, it has the authority of authenticity at the same time as it is manipulated.

Identifying the processes by which nationalisms and nation-views are formed and repressed, negotiated and de-legitimated is a complex problem that has had to relink issues that the study of nationalism had considered separate, such as ethnicity and nationality, and empire and nation. Consider now the more subtle relationship between identity and meaning. The argument is often made about nationalism that while one can have different ideas of the nation, the sense of identification with the nation overrides the differences. It is doubtless true that there are times when one simply feels Australian or Chinese, and indeed, when faced with a common outside threat, differences about what it means to be an Australian or Chinese are often temporarily submerged. This is what we have meant by nationalism as a relational identity. But the strength of the feeling for the nation – which is also exactly what passionately divides fellow-nationals – derives from what it *means* to be Australian or Chinese. Identities are forged in a fluid complex of cultural signifiers: symbols, practices and narratives. How are the central reference points of this complex fixed, authorized, contested and changed over time and space?

For analytical purposes, I will separate 'meaning' – what the nation means to the people – into two areas: 1) discursive meaning, and 2) symbolic meaning. In the first realm, I include such subjects as language-as-rhetoric and ideology – subjects that have traditionally fallen within the scope of the intellectual historian. In this sense, the nation is a product of the rhetoric and ideas of nationalist intellectuals and pamphleteers. In the realm of symbolic meaning, I include the ensemble of cultural practices of a group such as rituals, festivals, kinship forms, and culinary habits – traditionally subjects of the social historian or anthropologist. In this sense, the nation is an embodiment of the cultural marks of its distinctiveness. While, of course, the two realms are inseparable in the way the nation is imagined by the people, it is useful for the historian to be able to separate and subsequently recombine them in order to better conceive the formation/repression process.

In the discursive realm, the meanings of the nation are produced mainly through linguistic mechanisms. These are the narratives,[32] the signifying chains of metaphors, metonyms and binary oppositions that give meaning to the nation and vice-versa (cross-referentially).[33] Among narratives of the nation are not only the historical narratives of individual nations such as those of Nehru and Sun Yat-sen, but also narratives of the present and future with which these historical narratives have to engage. One such narrative by which early twentieth century Chinese nationalists constructed their understanding of modern nations and the nation-state system was the story of evolutionary ranking and competition as the road to success drawn in major part, but not exclusively, from Western Social Darwinism. This narrative also drew its sustenance from Chinese evolutionary thought, most notably from the writings of Wang Fuzhi. It was a narrative in which the meaning of a 'civilized' nation derived from the model of Western nation-states. Subsequently, this narrative was both countered and intertwined with a narrative of victimization and redemption: the narrative of anti-imperialism. By the 1920s, the writings of Sun Yat-sen indicated that it was not enough for China to aspire to the goal of an industrial civilization. China would fulfill its 'sacred mission' by supporting weak and small nations and resisting strong world powers. It would do so by transcending Western goals of materialism and violence and seek to realize its own cultural destiny in the way of the sage kings (*wang dao*) of ancient China.[34]

Generally around the world, the nation is a linguistically gendered phenomenon, evident from the simple fact that its most common signifier is fatherland or motherland. The master metaphor of the nation as family in turn yields a variety of strategies and tactics for incorporating women into the nation. Historically in China, the purity of the woman's body has served both

---

[32]   Homi K. Bhabha, 'DissemiNation: Time, Narrative and the Margins of the Modern Nation', in Bhabha, *Nation and Narration*, pp.291-322.

[33]   For a good example of a binary opposition defining the national identity of Australian settler culture, see Patrick Wolfe, 'On Being Woken Up: The Dreamtime in Anthropology and in Australian Settler Culture, *Comparative Studies in Society and History*, vol.33, no.3 (1991), pp.197-224. Australian settlers adapted the anthropological notion of 'dream time' and the Dreaming complex – the pre-contact idyll in which the aborigines lived – as timelessness and spacelessness and counterposed it to their own idea of 'awakenment' embodied in the doctrine of progress and legitimation of colonization. By doing so, they were able to establish a claim to the land by romanticizing and thus excluding the 'dreaming' aborigines from any terrestrial claims.

[34]   Lev Delyusin, 'Pan-Asiatic Ideas in Sun Yat-sen's Theory of Nationalism', in Lev Delyusin (ed.), *China, State and Society* (Social Sciences Today Editorial Board, USSR Academy of Sciences, Moscow, 1985), p.190.

as metaphor and metonymy of the purity of the nation.[35] The bodies of Chinese women raped by foreign invaders – Mongol, Manchu or Japanese – were both symbol and part of the national body violated by these foreigners. However, as Lydia Liu has recently shown, at least some women registered a strong ambivalence and, in the case of the writer Xiao Hong, a rejection of nationalism's incorporation of women. In Liu's analysis of Xiao Hong's *Field of Life and Death*, nationalism 'comes across as a profoundly patriarchal ideology that grants subject-positions to men who fight over territory, possession and the right to dominate. The women in this novel, being themselves possessed by men, do not automatically share the male-centred sense of territory'.[36] In a deliberate subversion of the trope of the raped woman in nationalist discourse, Xiao Hong's protagonist turns out to have been raped by a Chinese man. As Liu notes, 'The novel resists the appropriation of the female body by nationalist discourse and chooses to present nationalism from a woman's point of view'.[37]

In most modern nations, the family was valorized as embodying national morality and the obligation to educate and 'emancipate' women, derived from the imperative to produce more efficient mothers.[38] Tani Barlow and Wendy Larson have revealed that in China there existed another strategy among the May Fourth generation of cultural iconoclasts whereby women were incorporated into the modern nation. These radicals sought to absorb women directly as citizens of the nation (*guo*) and thus force them to reject their kin-based gender roles in the family or *jia*. The vitriolic May Fourth attack on the family as site of the reproduction of hierarchy in society may have been the reason why the radical intelligentsia found it almost impossible to 'identify women's role within the *jia* as a position from which to initiate a positive re-theorization of "women".[39] In doing so, they de-gendered women (who were to be just like male citizens of the nation), and many important women writers like Ding Ling ultimately abandoned writing about the problem of gender. Nonetheless, Larson observes a kind of resistance among some women writers to this mode of incorporation as they began to reject 'nation' as an overarching concept within which to frame 'woman'.[40]

---

[35]   Keith R. Schoppa, *Xiang Lake: Nine Centuries of Chinese Life* (Yale University Press, New Haven, 1989).

[36]   Lydia Liu, 'The Female Body and Nationalist Discourse: The *Field of Life and Death* Revisited', in Inderpal Grewal and Karen Caplan (eds), *Scattered Hegemonies: Postmodernity and Transnational Feminist Practices* (Minneapolis: University of Minnesota Press), p.58.

[37]   Ibid., p.45.

[38]   Wendy Larson, 'Definition and Suppression: Women's Literature in Post-May 4th China', Paper presented at the Association of Asian Studies Annual Meeting, New Orleans, 11-14 April 1991.

[39]   Ibid., p.11.

[40]   Ibid., p.13.

Thus while rhetorical structures *par excellence* generate meanings of the nation, these structures are by no means closed universes. In every case we see how language offers the means to construe the nation differently. Even where this variety is still restrictive, as for the women writers above, they were able to refuse to participate in the dominant and dominating metaphors of the nation. But there are other subtler means of registering difference by inflecting and improvising upon the language.

For instance, the Social Darwinist narrative had provided the categories for Chinese nationalists like Yan Fu to conceive of national survival in a struggle of the fittest nations by arguing for pursuit of the wealth and power of the nation-state. However, the young republican revolutionaries, who had become committed to the idea of a racially pure Han China, derived from this same rhetoric the necessity for the survival of races and the expulsion of Manchus and other 'races'.[41] Yet another improvisation upon this authoritative narrative was performed by the advocates of an emergent, province-based nationalism, such as Ou Qujia, to validate their view of the nation. Ou argued that the unity of China's vast, ancient land instilled a sense of security that prevented a healthy competition among its provinces, which in turn inhibited contact, knowledge and ultimately a sense of closeness among the different provinces. Since love for the nation was not as intimate as love for the province in which one was born, he urged Chinese to invest their energies in developing the competitiveness and independence of the province. In the strivings and competition of the provinces, those which were unable to establish their own independence would be merged with (*guibing*) the successful ones, and on the bases of these strong independent provinces could be built a federated independent China.[42]

I have highlighted the openness of language to strategic appropriations because traditional writings about nationalist rhetoric all too easily accept its closures. These appropriations also reveal that language can only be mapped upon social reality through the mediation of ideology. Having made this point, I would emphasize that it is not infinitely manipulable and the limits imposed by the meanings of words reflect not the unerasable truth of some historical reality, but powerful political forces bent upon nipping in the bud certain deployments of language. The limits of linguistic appropriation are illustrated by the narratives of history employed in the contest between centralizers and federalists in the first twenty years of the twentieth century. Most nation-builders in republican China shared more with the imperial state than we have recognized: i.e., the depiction of the telos of Chinese history as the maintenance of unity under the centralized state. Their opponents, the above-

---

41   James Reeve Pussey, *China and Charles Darwin* (Council on East Asian Studies, Harvard University, Cambridge, 1983), p.327.

42   Ou Qujia, 'Xin Guangdong' [New Guangdong], in Zhang Yufa (ed.), *Wan qing geming wenxue* [Late Qing Revolutionary Literature] (Xinzhi zazhishe, Taipei, 1971), pp.2-3.

mentioned federalists, sought to build a federated structure from the bottom-up, with autonomous provinces determining the nature of the federal state.[43]

The federalists fought a hard political battle for their cause, especially in the provinces of Hunan, Guangdong and Zhejiang, but were ultimately defeated in the northern expedition by the combined centralizing forces of the CCP and the KMT in 1926-27. Yet one could argue that the greatest failure of the federalists lay in their ultimate inability to appeal to a historical narrative that would legitimate their cause. Thus they were always subject to the charge made by the centralizers that a federalist polity represented a veiled program for the 'feudalization' of China and the violation of its historically sacrosanct unity. Yet the federalists could have appealed to an alternative history if it were not for the way in which language had closed off this possibility. In imperial China – especially in the hands of such statesmen as Gu Yanwu and Feng Guifen – the word *fengjian* [feudalism] had developed a historically critical role as a check upon absolutist power.[44] By the 1910s, the same signifier returned by way of Japan to denote a completely different sense of the referent. Now *fengjian* and its associated vocabulary in China came to carry the more familiar negative meaning as the Other of modernity and the Enlightenment that grew out of the history of Europe. This transformation of the sense of the word *fengjian* cost the federalists dearly, for it effaced an entire tradition of political dissent with which they may have been able to associate themselves. It also deprived them of a rhetorical strategy whereby they could claim to be the legitimate successors to this tradition and thereby mobilize history on behalf of their cause.

These narratives and the rhetoric of nationhood – particularly historical narratives that are able to speak to present needs – are only one means of articulating the nation: the discursive means. Of course, for some individuals a historical narrative may itself be sufficiently powerful to command identification even where no other cultural commonalities exist. This is the case with non-practising, non-believing Jews who might nonetheless make great sacrifices for the historical narrative that legitimates the present nation-state of Israel. More commonly, the coming into being of a nation is a complex event in which an entire cultural apparatus – the realm of symbolic meaning – is mobilized in the task of forming a distinctive political community. And this mobilization must be performed by, and in accordance with, the narratives we have outlined above. In turn, these narratives derive depth only when they are embodied in a culture. The intellectual historian must don the cap of the social historian.

---

43 Prasenjit Duara, 'Provincial Narratives of the Nation: Centralism and Federalism in 20th Century China', in Harumi Befu (ed.), *Cultural Nationalism in East Asia* (Institute of East Asian Studies, University of California, Berkeley, 1992).

44 Philip A. Kuhn and Timothy Brook (eds), *Tu-ki Min, National Polity and Local Power: The Transformation of Late Imperial China* (Council of East Asian Studies, Harvard University, Cambridge, 1989), pp.92-112.

Thus the manner in which a nation is created is not the result of a natural process of accumulating cultural commonalities. Rather it is the imposition of a historical narrative or a myth of descent/dissent upon both heterogeneous and related cultural practices: a template by which the cultural cloth will be cut and given shape and meaning. When a mytho-historical narrative is imposed upon cultural materials, the relevant community is formed not primarily by the creation of new cultural forms – or even the invention of tradition – but by transforming the perception of the boundaries of the community. However, this is not only a complex process, it is also fraught with danger. Narratives, as we have seen, are necessarily selective processes which repress various historical and contemporary materials as they seek to define a community; these materials are fair game for the spokespeople of those on the outs or on the margins of this definition who will seek to organize them into a counter-narrative of mobilization.

Hard and Soft Boundaries

An incipient nationality is formed when the perception of the boundaries of community are transformed: when soft boundaries are transformed into hard ones. Every cultural practice is a potential boundary marking a community. These boundaries may be either soft or hard. One or more of the cultural practices of a group, such as rituals, language, dialect, music, kinship practices or culinary habits, may be considered soft boundaries if they identify a group but do not prevent the group from sharing and even adopting, self-consciously or not, the practices of another. Groups with soft boundaries between them are sometimes so unconscious of their differences that they do not view mutual boundary breaches as a threat and could eventually even amalgamate into one community. Thus, differences in dietary and religious practices may not prevent the sharing of a range of practices between local Hui muslim and Han communities. The important point is that they tolerate the sharing of some boundaries and the non-sharing of others.

When a master narrative of descent/dissent seeks to define and mobilize a community, it usually does so by privileging a particular cultural practice (or a set of such practices) as the constitutive principle of the community – such as language, religion or common historical experience – thereby heightening the self-consciousness of this community in relation to those around it. What occurs, then, is a hardening of boundaries. Not only do communities with hard boundaries privilege their differences, they tend to develop an intolerance and suspicion toward the adoption of the other's practices and strive to distinguish, in some way or the other, practices that they share. Thus, communities with hard boundaries *will* the differences between them. It will be noted that the hardening of boundaries is by no means restricted to the nation or to the era of the nation-state, but the principle of national formation necessarily involves the closing off of a group whose self-consciousness is sharpened by the celebration of its distinctive culture.

Because a narrative privileges certain cultural practices as the constitutive principle of a community, it shapes the composition of the community: who belongs and who does not, who is privileged and who is not. Thus if a common history is privileged over language and race (extended kinship), language and race always lie as potential mobilizers of an alternative nation that will distribute its marginals differently. Therefore, within the hard community there will always be soft boundaries which may potentially be transformed into hard boundaries, or new soft boundaries may emerge and transform into hard ones. Moreover, boundaries between communities exist along a spectrum between hard and soft poles and are always in flux. This is as much the case in the modern nation as in pre-modern societies. Thus the growth of group self-consciousness does not entail the equal rejection of all others. A community may occupy a position on the harder side of the spectrum with respect to community A than community B, and these positions may change over time as well. Not only do soft boundaries harden, but hard boundaries soften as well, as when a prolonged conflict against a common enemy submerges the differences between two erstwhile foes now united in their common opposition.

This mode of analysis challenges the notion of a stable community that gradually develops a national self-awareness. It is true that there must be some prior agency which gives meaning to a cultural practice which in turn will effect the closure of the collectivity relative to a variable other. But of equal significance is the fact that the group is only constituted when certain cultural practices begin to function as markers. So what is the nature of the collectivity before it is marked? It is precisely a group with multiple orientations and identifications – the hardening of its boundaries represents the privileging of one of these identifications, but in time too the privileged practices that organize this identification will change.

Consider the relations between Manchu and Han in late imperial China. The ruling Qing dynasty (1644-1911) derived from a Manchu ethnic community that maintained an ambivalent attitude toward the dominant Han culture that it ruled. In the early stages of its rule it actively sought to maintain Manchu distinctiveness through a variety of means, including a ban on inter-marriage and on Han migration to Manchuria, and the fostering of different customs. In time, however, not only was the ban on migration and inter-marriage ignored, but the Manchu embrace of Chinese political institutions caused it to blur the distinctions between it and the communities it ruled. More importantly, and unlike the Mongols, the Manchus recognized early the roots of politics in culture and rapidly became the patrons of Han Chinese culture. I refer here not merely to its patronage of classical Confucian learning, but its efforts to reach into local communities through the institutions of popular culture, especially those of religion and kinship. Local communities that had patronized popular gods and heroes such as Guandi, Yue Fei and Mazu, encountered versions of their gods and myths revised by the imperial state and its orthodoxy, which these communities in turn adapted to their own purposes.

In this process, although groups managed to sustain their own versions of the god, a shared cultural format of communication emerged that did much to soften the boundaries between the Manchus and the Han.[45]

The history of the Manchu community in China from the eighteenth to the twentieth centuries furnishes a good example of the multiplicity and changeability of identity that we have been speaking of. There is no question that by the eighteenth century, in terms of their social and cultural relations, the Manchu communities resident in the hundreds of garrisons outside of their homeland in the northeast were melding into the general Han populace. Not only were they violating the ban on inter-marriage; Manchus were losing their ability to speak and read Manchu as well as losing contact with the folk traditions of their clans. Indeed, the hero of Manchu children in Hangzhou was Yue Fei, a symbol of Han opposition to the Jurchen, the purported twelfth century ancestors of the Manchus themselves.[46] At the same time, though, powerful counter-tendencies worked to shore up – or reconstruct – a Manchu identity. Most noteworthy, if not the most effective, were the efforts of the Qing court, especially those of the Qianlong emperor (1736-95), to introduce the idea that race should be the constitutive principle of the peoples of the empire. In part, this was motivated by a fear on the part of the emperor of total cultural extinction of the Manchus. But it was also part of a grand narrative of rule which eschewed, or rather encompassed at a higher level, both ethnic exclusivism and cultural universalism as principles defining Chinese community.

Crossley suggests that the Qianlong emperor imposed a novel cultural structure upon the polity which attempted to harmonize 'race' and culture with the emperorship as its integrating centre. In this structure, every 'racial' group – Manchus, Mongols, Tibetans, Han, the various gradations of acculturated and unacculturated Chinese from the northeast, the central Chinese, the Turkic peoples of Central Asia – all had their proper status according to their race (not culture). The Manchus as a race were seen to reflect the culmination of an imperial tradition and civilization dating to the Jin in the northeast that was independent of the Chinese tradition. These different races bore a relationship to the emperor set by the historical role of their ancestors in the creation and development of the state.[47] Thus, in this conception, universal emperorship

---

45   See Prasenjit Duara, 'Superscribing Symbols: The Myth of Guandi', pp.778-95; and James Watson, 'Standardizing the Gods: The Promotion of T'ien Hou [Empress of Heaven] Along the South China Coast, 960-1960', in David Johnson et al. (eds), *Popular Culture in Late Imperial China* (University of California Press, Berkeley/Los Angeles, 1985).

46   Pamela Crossley, *Orphan Warriors: Three Manchu Generations and the End of the Qing* (Princeton University Press, Princeton, 1990), pp.3, 30.

47   Pamela Crossley, '*Manzhou yuanliu kao* and the Formalization of the Manchu Heritage', *Journal of Asian Studies*, vol.46, no.4 (1987), p.780.

required 'not the attenuation but the accentuation and codification of cultural, linguistic and racial sectors of the population'.[48]

While this conception would have long-term implications in the way it endorsed race as a constitutive principle of community, it was not the principal cause for the tragic flowering of Manchu identity in the nineteenth century. Manchu identity grew in large measure as a reaction to a Han ethnic exclusivism that became most evident during the years of the Taiping Rebellion. We have observed how Han ethnic consciousness was probably heightened by increasing settlement of peripheral areas inhabited by non-Han in the late eighteenth century and how Han anti-Manchuism had been kept alive throughout the period at both the scholarly and popular levels. In the days before the British attack on the lower Yangzi city of Zhenjiang during the Opium War, the tension in the city led to hostility between the Manchu soldiers in the garrisons and the civilian Han populace in which countless Han were slaughtered by Manchu soldiers on the allegation that they were traitors. Mark Elliot shows that the entire event was interpreted as ethnic conflict by both survivors and local historians.[49] This simmering tension culminated in the horrifying massacres of Manchu bannermen and their families during the Taiping Rebellion and again in the republican revolution of 1911.[50] Manchus in the republican era sustained their identity only by hiding it from public view and by quietly teaching the oral traditions to their children and grandchildren within their homes. Today Manchu identity finds expression not only in their status as a national minority in the PRC but, as Crossley observes, in such forms as the Manchu Association formed in Taipei in 1981.

And yet it would be wrong and untrue to the mode of analysis I have tried to establish here to posit an essentializing evolutionary trend in the growth of Manchu identity and the worsening of Han-Manchu relations. Crossley herself is sensitive to the ambivalences of Manchus toward this identity and we have seen how important leaders of the Confucian intelligentsia were committed to a cosmopolitanism in their nationalism that included the Manchus as Chinese. Perhaps least appreciated in this regard are the Boxer 'rebels' of the turn of the century, who actually sought to support the Qing court – as the representative of Chinese culture – in the effort to expel the hated foreigner. The Boxer

---

[48]   In this view of the community, it is not shared cultural values that govern admission but relationship to the emperor. Different peoples were to retain their unique traditions, but were held together by the institution of emperorship. The universal emperor expressed his universal sovereignty by assuming the manifestation appropriate for each group. It is, for instance, in this context that we can understand how the emperor portrayed himself in the nomadic world as a boddhisatva ruler: as the reincarnation of Manjusri, blending the Tibetan theory of the ruler as incarnation and the Chinese Manjusri cult of Mt Wutai in Shanxi. Naquin and Rawski, *Chinese Society in the Eighteenth Century*, p.29.

[49]   Mark Elliot, 'Bannerman and Townsmen: Ethnic Tension in Nineteenth Century Jiangnan', *Late Imperial China*, vol.11, no.1 (1990), p.64.

[50]   Pamela Crossley, *Orphan Warriors*, pp.130, 196-7.

movement not only gives the lie to the dichotomy between a populist racist nationalism and a more enlightened, elitist one – it was arguably less racist than the violent anti-Manchuism of the republican revolutionaries – but even reveals the appeal of the assimilationist, culture-based nationalism among the populace as well.

The Manchu search for its own separate identity may be traced back to a narrative which privileged 'race' as the definer of community. This was a contribution of both the Qing court's ingenious discovery of race as well as the resurfacing of Han racial nationalism. The tragedy of it was that this rhetoric forced a highly, if ambivalently, assimilated people to turn their backs on what had, after all, become their culture. But the effects of the emphasis upon race was not to end with the Manchus alone. Partly as a result of the Qianlong ideology of rule, most of the large minority communities viewed their incorporation into the Qing empire as being on a par with the enforced incorporation of the Han; they did not equate the Qing empire with *Zhongguo* (China). The overthrow of the Qing in 1911 created for them the possibility of independence: the hardening of boundaries that was, of course, encouraged by the revolutionaries' rhetoric of racialist nationalism. The growing Mongol independence movement, the establishment of an independent Mongolia in 1911,[51] and the threatening situation in Tibet and Xinjiang could not persuasively be countered by the republican revolutionaries, since they too had espoused the principle that the nation was to be constituted by race. It was in these circumstances that Sun Yat-sen and the leaders of the new republic sought to quickly switch to the narrative of the nation espoused by their enemies – the reformers and the Qing court itself. The Chinese nation was now to be made up by the 'five races' (Manchu, Mongol, Tibetan, Muslim and Han) and so it happened that the boundaries of the Chinese nation came to follow the outline of the old Qing empire. Later, the principle of race as constitutive of the nation would be submerged (though not very effectively) in a larger nationalist narrative of the common historical experience against imperialism.

Our effort to link narratives of descent/dissent to the self-definition of a group by way of the transformation of its social and cultural boundaries is relevant not only for ethnic nationalisms such as those of the Manchu or Mongols, but also for the nation-views of less visible communities. These include regional and provincial groupings within the Han such as the Cantonese, the so-called sub-ethnic groups such as the Hui and the Hakka,[52]

---

51   Tatsuo Nakami, 'A Protest Against the Concept of the Middle Kingdom: The Mongols and the 1911 Revolution', in Eto Shinkichi et al. (eds), *The 1911 Revolution in China* (Tokyo University Press, Tokyo, 1984).

52   In the mid-nineteenth century, the Hakkas discovered a narrative of descent/dissent in a version of Christianity which depicted them as a 'chosen people' and gave them a mission in their protracted, dreary battle against the original settlers in south China. It also caused them to celebrate their own distinctive traditions over those of the larger Han

marginals such as the boat people (*tanka*) and the 'mean people' (*jianmin*) and other immigrant and sojourning groups who encounter cultural barriers among the 'host' or dominant communities they are forced to live with. Take for instance the way in which the boundaries harden around a marginal, immigrant, regional group in Shanghai, the Subei people, during a period of intense nationalism. Emily Honig writes of the enduring prejudice against the underclass Subei people of northern Jiangsu in Shanghai, where a common curse is 'Subei swine'. After the 1932 Japanese attack on Shanghai, the Subei people became identified as Japanese collaborators, and during the occupation of 1937-45 the expression '*Jiangbei* (*Subei*) traitor' and accompanying hostility toward them became widespread. While there may have been an element of truth to the accusations of collaboration, Honig observes that other people who collaborated were not targeted in the same way. It was the prejudice against them that easily incorporated them into the category of traitor. One Subei native complained in 1932 that 'when I walk on the street and hear people making fun of us it feels worse than being a Chinese in a foreign country'.[53] The hardening of boundaries had excised the Subei folk from the nation.

Conclusion

I began this chapter by exploring the gap between the Chinese nationalist view and the Sinological view of Chinese nationality. Although it is easy to debunk the teleological nationalist view that posits a national subject gathering self-awareness, the Sinological analyses of Chinese nationalism were too deeply embedded in the modernist problematique to be able to see that their own position regarding the novelty of the nation corresponded precisely to a need within nationalist ideology to view itself as a uniquely modern phenomenon – a need as powerful as the one which seeks to view itself as an ancient essence.

The question of the historical nature of the Chinese nation is intimately tied to the question of national identity. When the nation is viewed as a subject which ultimately transcends all differences, it must necessarily have a single history which evolves into the cohesive, transcendent ideal. Framed in this way, nationalists seek to suppress or conflate the multiple histories of the peoples who inhabit a geographical expanse into the history of the 'people-nation-state'. It is also the reason why even those who see the nation as a

---

community of which they were a highly ambiguous part. This movement of the 'god-worshipping society' would go on to become the cataclysmic Taiping Rebellion in which the original animus against the neighbouring Punti community was transformed into an anti-Manchu zealotry. Philip A. Kuhn, 'The Origins of the Taiping Vision: Cross Cultural Dimensions of Chinese Rebellions', *Comparative Studies in Society and History*, vol.19, no.3 (1977), pp.350-66.

[53]   Emily Honig, 'Subei People in Republican-Era Shanghai', *Modern China*, vol.15, no.3 (1989), p.269.

recent development still cannot break with the evolutionary model of understanding the nation.

At the same time, the idea of a single, radical break in self-consciousness is hard to sustain, because it effectively denies history. By stressing the multiplicity of identities that is correlative with the variety of histories, I have suggested that the nation be understood through different, contested narratives both historically and within the framework of the new nation-state system. Only thus can we see the continuities (and discontinuities) without falling into the trap of the evolutionary model of the continuous nation. The construction of a narrative of political community which endows the nation with meaning is inevitably also a repressive activity. Thus the old model of a movement toward the ideal of a unified communal subject must instead be understood as a specific mobilization toward a particular source of identification at the expense of others/Other(s). At no other time is this multiplicity of political identities, with its ambivalences and conflicts, clearer than in our own confused time, when the nation-state is as much in the ascendant as it is in decline.

THREE

The Nationless State:
The Search for a Nation
in Modern Chinese Nationalism

John Fitzgerald

> These people are so shameless and so quick of hand that at any time they can proclaim themselves *representatives* of some group or other. Louis XIV said 'We are the State', they say 'We are the Nation'.

> Liang Qichao, May Day, 1925[1]

The history of modern China, in the round, is recounted as a struggle for national reunification and liberation traced through the rise and fall of successive state formations in the imperial, the early Republican (1912-27), Nationalist (1928-49) and Communist periods. What lends continuity to this history from one regime to the next is the motif of a unitary state reconstituting itself from the rubble of a disintegrating empire. Continuity derives as well from an implicit identification of the unitary state with the nation on whose behalf the state is presumed to act: the ideal of the unitary state is linked with the idea of a national people, firstly in the story of their common struggle and secondly in the assumption that the one, the state, 'represents' the other, the nation. The nation is presumed to be as continuous as the hoary ideal of the unitary state itself — despite the relatively recent vintage of the concept of the nation in China, despite the equally recent genesis of the idea that the state should represent anything at all, and despite

---

[1]   *Wuchan jieji yu wuye jieji* [The Property-less Class and the Unemployed Class], in Li Xinghua (ed.), *Liang Qichao xuanji* (Shanghai renmin chubanshe, Shanghai, 1984), p.853. Emphasis added.

the extraordinarily abrupt and violent moments of transition from one state formation to the next.

Certainly, the disjuncture between state formations is consistent with a sequential history of the regeneration of the state. Particular regimes may come and go, but China is still China. The assertion of *national* continuity, however, rests uneasily alongside the distinctive and often competing definitions of the nation which have been put forward by each state-building movement in its turn. Can the composition of the Chinese people change from one era to the next and the Chinese nation still be counted the same nation? Put simply, each of the major state movements of the past century has advocated a distinctive and mutually exclusive definition of the national self: Confucian reformers associated the collective self with a distinctive civilization; liberal republicans conceived of the nation as a body of citizens; Nationalist (Kuomintang) revolutionaries thought of a Chinese race; and China's Marxist-Leninists have qualified citizen and race by reference to social class. The uneasy fit between the asserted continuity of the unitary state and these sharp discontinuities in the definition of the nation raises the question I wish to pursue here. Who or what was the nation to which constitutional reformers, republican revolutionaries, May Fourth activists and the theorists of the Nationalist and Communist parties all referred when they resolved to 'save the country' (*jiuguo*)? By what procedures was it defined? Most particularly, was it ever more than a floating referent of the state, which signified the nation by 'representing' it?

I propose to explore the relationship between state and nation in the Chinese revolution by introducing recent theoretical writings on post-colonial nationalism, drawing comparisons with other nation-building movements and isolating a number of common elements among the discontinuities in national self-representation in the Chinese case — chiefly the ideal of the unitary state, the political struggle to give it particular form and associated attempts to reconfigure the nation on the part of the successive state formations that have sought to represent the nation to itself and to the world. My purpose is not to establish the continuity of nationalist thought itself, which is properly the task of nationalist histories, but to focus on its disjunctures, and to suggest that the appearance of a continuous history derives less from the preservation of a Chinese nation than from the ideal of the unitary state which transcends all state formations and is made identical with the idea of China itself. The state which *is* China has, I believe, no given nation. Instead the Chinese nation has been created and recreated in the struggle for state power, and it has ultimately been defined by the state as a reward of victory. The state's search for a nation need not imply that there was no nation out there, so to speak, waiting to be found. It means only that the people encountered by state-building movements did not quite match up to the kind of nation the revolutionaries were looking for to help build their sovereign and unified state.

The Nationless State

The phrase I have chosen to denote the problem, 'nationless state', requires some elaboration. The more familiar term, 'stateless nation', is grounded in an assumption that nations are out there in the world striving to realize their destiny as nation-states, even if only a small proportion ever succeed in crystallizing around states. Ernest Gellner estimates that for every nation which has established its own state there are perhaps nine whose aspirations to statehood remain (and will remain) unrealized.[2] The emphasis on the objective existence of the nation implied by the term stateless nation is nevertheless compromised by its general usage. In common parlance, a nation which cannot boast a state barely merits recognition at all unless its aspirations for statehood happen to threaten the stability of its parent state or to complicate relations among its neighbours. It is under these circumstances that the term generally makes its appearance; that is, when a self-defined nation fights for its independence and sovereignty and places a stable international system under threat.

The term employed here, nationless state, suggests something else again. In the first place, it focuses attention on the state in an analysis of the historical development of nationalism, and implies that the nation is an essentially-contested concept in a political discourse concerned with the assertion of state unity, sovereignty and independence within the international state system.[3] In the case of China, as Prasenjit Duara has pointed out, state-building has proven quite inseparable from nation-building.[4] The term nationless state implies an additional measure of scepticism about the existence of a Chinese nation outside the state framework. It asks us to stand at a critical distance from the state's own presumption that the nation it represents is an autonomous entity which could conceivably exist in the forms in which the state has chosen to represent it but *independently of the state*. By nationless state, in other words, I am referring to the historical development of a state or proto-state formation which operates in the name of an indeterminate nation that the state itself identifies and summons into being.

In the Chinese revolution, the state was not just midwife at the birth of the nation but in fact its sire. So the founder of the Nationalist Party, Sun Yat-sen, is appropriately remembered as the 'father of the country' (*guofu*). The state not only delivered the nation into the world but determined what form it should take, and nationality (or ethnicity) was only one of the factors which state-builders took into consideration. In fact, the state set out to create a

---

2   Ernest Gellner, *Nations and Nationalism* (Cornell University Press, Ithaca, 1983), p.45.

3   I use the terms 'essentially-contested concept' and 'discourse' in the senses elaborated by William Connelly in *The Terms of Political Discourse*, second edition (Martin Robertson, Oxford, 1983).

4   Prasenjit Duara, *Culture, Power and the State: Rural North China, 1900-1942* (Stanford University Press, Stanford, 1988), pp.2-4.

nation after its own likeness and selected only those national attributes (ethnic, geographic, cultural and social) which happened to suit the attainment and retention of state unity, sovereignty and independence in a world of nation-states. Inclusion on equal terms in this international system was the final measure of the attainment of nationhood, and hence the nation assumed forms suited to the achievement of statehood. The nation was, in other words, a desideratum of state-building, its forms determined by nothing so much as the need for the state to represent something other than itself. It took shape as a correlative of the state, gradually and incrementally, and mirrored the shape of the particular state formation which acted to represent it. In employing the term 'nationless state', I wish in the first instance to draw attention to this process of representation, or nation-defining, in state-building, and to invite closer inspection of this process.

But my aim is not simply to describe a process. A second purpose is to relocate arguments about nationalism and Marxism in anti-imperialist movements, and more particularly in the Chinese revolution, outside of orthodox Marxist and anti-Marxist frameworks of analysis. As we follow the search by the post-colonial state for a nation it can call its own, we find that one of the many ways in which the state conceives of its national constituency is in terms of social class. At this point state-builders come into contact with Marxism and have to deal with it. I shall propose an alternative method of analysing this contact between the newly emergent state-formation and Marxism, centred on the idea of the class-nation.

Nationalism, Socialism and National Liberation in Comparative Perspective

National and social revolutionaries both seek 'to assert and make good their claims to state sovereignty'.[5] Since sovereign states are, by their nature, nation-states, the claim to state sovereignty may be said to make nationalists of national and social revolutionaries alike. What is more, the revolutionary who struggles for state sovereignty in the name of a nation allegedly under threat generally assumes that the struggle to liberate the state is *identical with* the salvation of the nation. What then distinguishes the social from the national revolutionary in national-liberation struggles is neither the arena in which the struggle takes place nor the trophy for which they compete. The arena is inevitably a national one and the prize is state power. Rather, what distinguishes the one from the other is the identity of the national self which each state formation seeks to represent in asserting its sovereignty.

---

5   Theda Skocpol, *States and Social Revolutions: A Comparative Analysis of France, Russia and China* (Cambridge University Press, Cambridge, 1979), p.164.

Identifying this national self is one of the functions of nationalist thought.[6] Nationalist thought, although nothing if not particular, generally develops along fairly predictable lines and the terms in which nationals identify and celebrate their singularity have a banal familiarity about them. Americans sing of their fruited plains, Australians sing of their sweeping ones. Much the same applies to the development of nationalist thought among colonial elites, although in this case nationalism is channelled into fixed and related problematics by the elite's confrontation with imperialism. Anti-colonial nationalism has been described as a 'derivative discourse' of Orientalism, drawing closely upon the style of thought in which the dominant imperial powers characterize their 'oriental' subjects. But, notes Partha Chatterjee,

> the problematic in nationalist thought is exactly the reverse of that of Orientalism. That is to say, the 'object' in nationalist thought is still the Oriental, who retains the essentialist character depicted in Orientalist discourse. Only he is not passive, non-participating. He is seen to possess a 'subjectivity' which he himself can 'make'.[7]

In anti-colonial nationalism, men and women of colonized societies assume an active role in deciding their own fate, but within an essentialist style of thought that is appropriated from their colonial oppressors.

Nationalist thought develops in association with the struggle for state power among nationalist elites and between nationalists and the colonial powers. Chatterjee identifies a number of stages in this progression, or what he calls 'programmatic phases . . . [each] marked by innovations in political objectives, in strategy and tactics, in selecting the types of issues on which to focus its ideological sights and concentrate is polemical attack'. The term 'programmatic phases' assumes a goal toward which each stage is moving, or at least a line along which evolution is taking place.[8] The goal of nationalist thought is the creation of a sovereign national subject which parallels the struggle for sovereign state power taking place in the political field.

Chatterjee himself offers one model of such evolution based on his reading of Gramsci and Indian history. The first phase of nationalist thought seeks to combine the 'superior material qualities of Western cultures with the [presumed] spiritual qualities of the East'. Nationalist thought starts out as a defence of a so-called national tradition which is thought to be under threat from the imperialist powers and their colonial state, and yet the defence of this 'tradition' is caught in a paradox between alternating impulses to destroy and to preserve the traditional. Nationalist thought is characteristically self-contradictory. As Dipesh Chakrabarty has noted of India, the impulse to distinguish between the 'national' culture and that of the West 'is combined

---

6   Partha Chatterjee, *Nationalist Thought and the Colonial World: A Derivative Discourse* (Zed Books, London, 1986).

7   Ibid., p.38.

8   Ibid., pp.42-3.

with an aspiration to modernity that can be defined only in terms of the post-Enlightenment rationalism of European culture'. As a result of these contradictory impulses, it is felt at each phase of the development of nationalist thought that if imitation goes too far the identity of the nation will be surrendered. By way of coping with this contradiction, nationalist thought attempts to define, once and for all, an ultimate self-referent which is beyond dispute; that is, it feels compelled to draw a line in defining the nation beyond which any concession is tantamount to treason against the 'nation'.[9] The only constant in this process is the attempt to draw a line, not the actual placement of it: the line which defines the boundary of the nation moves slowly but surely, from one phase to the next, along a course charted through nationalist debate but propelled by concern for asserting state sovereignty and independence. The line moves further in the direction of the state in Chatterjee's account of subsequent stages of nationalist thought. The second phase, well illustrated in the career of Gandhi, attempts to mobilize people in the cause of an anti-colonial struggle while distancing them from the structures of the state. The third phase is concerned above all with 'the rational organization of power', exemplified in Nehru's equation of nation, people and state, in particular his overriding concern to relate all other social and economic issues to the political goal of creating a sovereign state.[10]

The parallel between each of Chatterjee's phases and the development of modern Chinese nationalism is striking, despite significant differences in the character of the state in India and China. The first of Chatterjee's phases recalls the 'culturalism' of nineteenth-century Chinese reformers, which is customarily distinguished from nationalism in Western historiography. Indeed, we generally presume later developments in nationalist thought — specifically the twentieth-century identification of the nation as the race or the whole people — to be the definitive form of nationalism. But if we consider nationalist thought more broadly as a series of evolving problematics within a single discourse, in the manner of Chatterjee, then nineteenth-century culturalism may be reclaimed as a phase of modern nationalism. Even culturalism is profoundly concerned with the preservation of the nation, the difference lying in the conception of the nation it seeks to preserve. More to my present purpose, this perspective also frees us from assuming that the nation as 'race' is the unique or final form of nationalism beyond which nationalist thought cannot proceed without turning into something else again — something we might perhaps mistake for socialism.

The second of Chatterjee's phases, associated with Gandhi's mobilization of popular resources outside state structures, seems to have had no parallel in China. Mass resistance would have waited in vain for a stable colonial state in

---

9   Dipesh Chakrabarty, 'Towards a Discourse on Nationalism', *Economic and Political Weekly* (Delhi), 11 July 1987, p.1137. I am indebted to Chakrabarty for the metaphor of the 'moving line'.

10   Chatterjee, *Nationalist Thought*, p.51.

Beijing.[11] In any event China had no Gandhi. The third phase, nationalism's 'moment of arrival' under Nehru, has much in common with the nationalism of the Chinese Nationalist Party, the Kuomintang. Cultural tradition still plays a part in identifying the nation in this phase but a part subordinated to the idea of a national 'people'. Nehru recalled in his book, *The Discovery of India* (1945), that when he toured the countryside he would frequently be greeted by cries of 'Victory to Mother India', and would turn and ask the crowd 'who [is] this Bharat Mata, Mother India, whose victory they wanted? My question would amuse them and surprise them'. The people were understandably puzzled, not about the object but about the subject of their quest for national emancipation. Who or what *was* India? Nehru would then set them at ease, pointing out that 'what counted ultimately were the people of India, people like them and me, who were spread out all over this vast land. Bharat Mata, Mother India, was essentially these millions of people, and victory to her meant victory to these people'.[12] The tone of Nehru's lectures would have been familiar to any audience in China exposed to the uplifting speeches of Sun Yat-sen and members of his Nationalist Party. Nehru and Sun Yat-sen both tried to teach the people that they made up the nation and that, for all their differences, the nation made them one. In the meanwhile, the Congress Party of India and the Nationalist Party of China offered the only concrete evidence of the existence of a single people in India and China. Before the people had come to a realization of their unity as a nation, each of the parties would substitute for the nation by representing it as a unified state.

While there were certainly close parallels between Nehru's pedagogical nationalism and the nationalism of the Chinese Nationalist Party, the Nationalist Party phase did not mark nationalism's 'moment of arrival' in China as it did in India. Nationalist thought could not settle comfortably into a sense of national self bounded by culture or people in China because events gave it little cause for complacency. The early Republican government showed scant inclination to represent the mythical people and, more to the point, even less capacity to assert national sovereignty. And unlike India, where the nationalist movement had essentially one foreign state to contend with, Chinese nationalists confronted a dozen powers exercising varying degrees of influence on Chinese soil. Their authority was not always formalised in treaties, and their influence reached far beyond the isolated

[11]   Perhaps the nearest equivalent to this phase in China was the anarchist movement. See Arif Dirlik's three recent works, *The Origins of Chinese Communism* (Oxford University Press, Hong Kong, 1989), *Anarchism in the Chinese Revolution* (University of California Press, Berkeley and Los Angeles, 1991) and, with Ming K. Chan, *Schools into Fields and Factories: Anarchists, the Guomindang, and the National Labor University in Shanghai, 1927-1932* (Duke University Press, Durham, 1992).

[12]   Jawaharlal Nehru, *The Discovery of India*. First published 1945 (Anchor, New York, 1960), p.29. See also Sanjay Seth, 'Identity and "History": Nehru's Search for India', *Thesis Eleven*, no.32 (1992), pp.37-54.

concessions and leased territories which presented relatively easy targets for nationalist attack. The diffusion and formal insubstantiality of the foreign presence in China, relative to India, made imperialism more difficult to conceptualize and much harder to sell as the target for a popular movement. The enemy of the nation was not the English, nor the Japanese or the Americans, but 'imperialism'.

China, what is more, enjoyed nominal sovereignty throughout the Republic and, with the exception of the foreign concessions, was under the rule of native administrations. In appearance and in fact, Chinese were ruling Chinese. Indian nationalism could achieve its objective of state independence and sovereignty by the seizure of state power — setting up an Indian national state in place of an effective colonial one — but in China the lack of an effective native state and the persistence of foreign intervention in domestic affairs left nationalists with the task of creating an entirely new kind of state. This state-building project made China a far more volatile setting than India for the introduction of class into nationalist thought. Once conceived in terms of class, the multi-layered linkages between domestic and foreign political, social and economic interests could become targets of class struggle conceived in the language of state nationalism. Such a prospect is not anticipated in Chatterjee's account of the Indian case.

Abdullah Laroui deals with class and nation more explicitly in his work on intellectual elites in the Islamic world. Like Chatterjee, Laroui classifies the development of nationalist thought into phases, or evolving problematics, but he finds a definitive place for class in the most highly developed form of nationalism. Laroui neglects mention of the second of Chatterjee's phases, which may be peculiar to India (or to Gandhi), but adds a further third phase which he terms 'class nationalism'.

> Where, in confrontation with Europe, the fundamentalist opposed a culture (Chinese, Indian, Islamic) and the liberal opposed a nation (Chinese, Turkish, Egyptian, Iranian), the revolutionary opposes a class — one that is often extended to include all that part of the human race exploited by the European bourgeoisie. One may refer to it as class nationalism that nevertheless retains many of the motifs of political and cultural nationalisms; hence the difficulties experienced by many of the analysts who have attempted to define it.[13]

---

13   Abdullah Laroui, *The Crisis of the Arab Intellectual* (University of California Press, Berkeley, 1976), pp.121-2. I am grateful to Brenda Sansom for bringing this work to my attention. See Brenda Sansom, 'Minsheng and National Liberation: Socialist Theory in the Guomindang', PhD Dissertation, University of Wisconsin-Madison, 1988. See also Arif Dirlik, *Culture, Society and Revolution: A Critical Discussion of American Studies of Modern Chinese Thought* (Asian/Pacific Studies Institute, Durham, 1985). It is important to distinguish here between Laroui's 'class nationalism' and the term 'class nation' as sometimes used to describe the isomorphism between ethnicity and social class in particular historical communities. The Hungarian gentry and German traders of

In so far as Nehru and Sun Yat-sen set 'the people as nation' in opposition to the West, they may loosely be classed among Laroui's liberals. Similarly, early Indian and Chinese Marxists who counterposed a 'national class' to European imperialism may be considered among Laroui's class 'revolutionaries'. Nation and class are by no means identical concepts, but Asian Marxists imagined them as in fact co-extensive: the Indian, the Indonesian and the Chinese peoples were national proletariats within a world system governed by the European bourgeoisie.[14] This is, however, a deceptive example which illustrates no more than the point of transition between liberal and class nationalism. Elementary ideas of class and class interest also featured in Laroui's liberal nationalism and in Chatterjee's state nationalism. Nehru himself made the uncompromising observation that 'economic interests shape the political views of groups and classes. Neither reason nor moral considerations override those interests'.[15] In the Chinese revolution even Communists have been reluctant to make such ambitious claims for class interest or have at least tried to make allowance for reasoned persuasion among the 'wavering' classes. In the course of its development, however, Chinese nationalism reached and exhausted Laroui's final phase of class nationalism because it articulated class differences within society in pursuit of the goals of the nation state. Chinese Marxists did not stop at defining the national people as an underprivileged class in a world capitalist system. They went on to divide their own society into revolutionary and counter-revolutionary classes, and to identify the nation exclusively with classes whose interests appeared consistent with achieving the state goals of unity and independence. The nationalist movement targeted a colonial state in India, but in China it inspired a civil war. The state, in this case, uncovered a very different kind of nation from any that had come before in the post-colonial repertoire.

Even here an Indian Marxist, M. N. Roy, anticipated later developments in China. Reflecting with some irony on the much-proclaimed spiritual essence of India, Roy wrote that the 'peculiarity' of India 'does not lie in the spiritual character of its people *but in the reactionary character of its bourgeoisie*'. Why was the bourgeoisie reactionary? Not on account of its resistance to proletarian socialist revolution but because its material interests rendered it, in Roy's words, 'historically incapable of . . . lead[ing] the nationalist movement'.[16] To Roy, domestic bourgeois ties to international

---

the Habsburg empire are termed 'class nations', in this different sense, in A. J. P. Taylor, *The Habsburg Monarchy 1809-1918* (Hamish Hamilton, London, 1948).

[14]   Maurice Meisner, *Li Ta-chao and the Origins of Chinese Marxism* (Harvard University Press, Cambridge, Mass., 1967).

[15]   Cited in Chatterjee, *Nationalist Thought*, p.140.

[16]   Cited in Sanjay Seth, 'Marxism and the Question of Nationalism in a Colonial Context: The Case of British India', PhD Dissertation, Australian National University, Canberra, 1989, p.114.

capital prejudiced the struggle for state sovereignty, and hence the bourgeoisie did not deserve inclusion in the nation. Nehru's nation, 'the people of India . . . who were spread out all over this vast land' as Nehru described them, became in Roy's hands *some* of the people of India, whose interests happened to coincide with those of the state movement for unity and independence. But the Indian nation did, in the end, more closely approximate Nehru's 'people of India' than it did Roy's proletariat. Why was it in China that Roy's more selective class-nation took hold?

China the State, China the Nation

We have noted some of the historical reasons why China should have been the site of a class war conducted in the name of the nation. Paramount among these was the history of China as a unitary state. Hegel gave this observation priority in his comparisons of the civilizations of China and India: 'This is the first point to be observed: if China may be regarded as nothing else but a State, Hindu political existence presents us with a people, but *no State*' (Hegel's emphasis).[17] Even conceding that Hegel's ideal of the state effectively excluded the principalities of India — and that he was inclined to reduce China to nothing but a state — his more general point that China's identity took the form of historical consciousness of a unitary state remains quite valid. He need not have confined his sights to history. The universal written language and the high culture of imperial China corresponded closely with the reach of the state and lived on in the performance of state functions. Confucianism was a state ideology. Hegel might confidently have predicted, even if he could not have known, that while Hinduism would thrive in twentieth-century India, Confucianian civilization would not survive the destruction of the imperial Chinese state.

Yet the Chinese state could survive the death of Confucianism. Conservative nineteenth-century Chinese scholars foresaw the decline and disappearance of Confucianism with some clarity, and feared that China would disappear as a state as well.[18] On this point they were wrong. While Confucianism did not survive the transformation of the state, the state survived precisely because it was transformed. China survived the death of

---

[17] Georg Wilhelm Friedrich Hegel, *The Philosophy of History* (translated by J. Sibree) (Wiley Book Co., New York, 1944), p.161. Compare Von Schlegel's comment, made at roughly the same time: 'In China, before the introduction of the Indian religion of Buddha . . . the state is all in all'. See Frederick Von Schlegel, *The Philosophy of History* (translated by J. B. Robertson) (Henry G. Bohn, London, 1847), p.124.

[18] So Yu Yue, 'As I look at the situation of China today, there are three things I am most fearful about. One is that the name of China or "Central Nation" will be changed . . . China can remain China or 'Central Nation' as long as she does not communicate with any of the other eight continents. My second fear is that Confucianism will be undermined and eventually destroyed . . .' Cited in Dun J. Li, *China in Transition 1517-1911* (Van Nostrand Reinhold Co., New York, 1969), p.163.

Confucianism and much else besides because the idea of China was attached to the ideal of a unitary state rather than to the ideology of a particular regime. Indeed, nationalist thought generally assumed that the danger to which China was most vulnerable in the twentieth century was the destruction neither of ideology or culture, nor even of a national people, but the disappearance of the unitary state. Not unreasonably, the great dread of Chinese nationalists from nineteenth-century modernizers to twentieth-century Communists has been the collapse and disappearance of the unitary state, a fear well captured in the phrase 'the death of the state' (*wang guo*).

In early usage the term 'death of the state' referred to little more than the downfall of a dynasty and, as one dynasty was generally replaced by another in the older cyclical view of history, it implied little more than an historical transition between ruling houses. Nothing stood to die out — neither people nor race, tradition nor state — apart from a particular imperial line of succession. But once history had shifted from a cyclical to a secular route and appeared to set its sights on progress, the phrase 'death of the state' implied a threat of far graver proportions. Progress offered little reassurance on its relentless forward march that the collapse of a recognizably Chinese state would yield another in its place, or even that the 'Chinese people' would survive the collapse of the state.[19] The survival of the people was thought to be linked irrevocably to the survival of the unitary state, and the term 'loss of the state' summoned up morbid fears of genocide.[20]

But who, after all, would die if the state were lost? More to the point, who would be saved along with the country if it were saved (*jiu guo*)? The idea of a distinctly Chinese people had some precedent in the public life of the empire but exactly which Chinese people would be rescued along with the state had to be discovered in the act of national salvation. There is no one word in the Chinese language referring to 'nation', as distinct from state (*guo*), and the want of a definitive name has encouraged state-builders to define the nation in ways consistent with their state-building efforts. The variety of terms which have been used where we might expect to find 'nation' give a fair indication of the range of options open to various state actors in their efforts to find a people whom they might represent. Words in common usage have included 'citizen' (*guomin, gongmin*), 'people' (*renmin*) and 'race' (*minzu*), along with the derivatives 'Han race' (*Hanzu*) and 'Chinese race' (*Zhonghua minzu*). Each implies a different nation. Precisely which word most accurately reflected the nation was to be discovered in the act of saving the state: the nation was neither more nor less than those people who would be represented when the state saved itself.

This particular problem of terminology reflects, in a broader sense, difficulties of conceptualization that hounded nationalists at every turn in their attempts to conceive of the national project in an ethical language which

---

19   Meisner, *Li Ta-chao*, p.19.

20   Frank Dikötter, *The Discourse of Race in Modern China* (Hurst & Co., London, 1992).

distinguished in most unrepresentative fashion between rulers (*jun*) and ruled (*min*), and which was grounded in an ethical-cyclical rather than secular conception of time. So the identity of the people raised ethical and historical questions as well as political ones. Indeed, there was not even a serviceable word for the historical and ethical community of 'China'. Among the many faults which Liang Qichao attributed to the 'Chinese people' was their inability to put a name to their own country: 'Hundreds of millions of people have maintained this country in the world for several thousand years', Liang complained in 1900, 'and yet to this day they have not got a name for their country'.[21] Liang repeated the same claim in several of his essays and always in the same tone of astonishment.[22] China had, it was true, been given a name in recent times but not by the Chinese themselves. Even the word 'China' (*Zhongguo*) 'is what people of other races call us. It is not a name the people of this country have selected for themselves'.[23] The Chinese custom of referring to their historical community by dynasty (*chaodai*) rather than by country (*guojia*) implied that there was in fact no Chinese nation at all. But in Liang's view the want of a name was not so much an indication of the want of a nation as an indictment of the cultural and intellectual immaturity of a people who had consistently failed to recognize that they constituted a nation. There was a nation, he asserted, and the lack of a name was no more than a 'conceptual' error 'lodged in every person's brain'. The act of *naming* the people would make a nation of them.[24]

At the same time, the name chosen to define the people would determine who should be counted among them and how they should be expected to behave as a nation. Liang Qichao himself opted for the ideal of the citizen. He believed that the term race could not be applied to the Chinese nation. There was no necessary correlation between ethnic groups and states in the composition of nation-states, and a racial definition of the nation might well

---

21   Liang Qichao, 'Zhongguo jiruo suyuan lun' [On the Source of China's Weakness], 1900, in *Yinbingshi wenji* [Collected Essays from the Ice-Drinker's Studio] (Zhonghua shuju, Shanghai, n.d.), vol.2, coll. 5, pp.12-42, esp. p.15.

22   See also 'Zhongguo shi xulun' [Preface to A History of China], 1901, in *Yinbingshi heji*, [Collected Works from the Ice-Drinker's Studio] (Zhonghua shuju, Shanghai, n.d.), vol.3, coll.6, p.3.

23   Liang Qichao, 'Zhongguo jiruo', p.15. The term *Zhongguo* was certainly in use in China before the modern period but it designated neither the country nor the state itself. *Zhongguo* referred only in the most general of terms to the place of the emperor at the centre of the world. It first appearance in the formal designation of state was in the attenuated form of *Zhonghu minguo* [Republic of China] in 1912. But old habits die hard. Not far from the capital, locals coped with the collapse of 'The Great Qing State' (*Da qing guo*) by referring to their country simply as 'The Great State' (*Da guo*) into the 1930s. See Reginald F. Johnstone, *Twilight in the Forbidden City* (D. Appleton-Century Company, New York, 1934), p.115.

24   Liang Qichao, 'Zhongguo jiruo', p.14.

prove a barrier to state-building in a multi-ethnic community such as China. In China, he continued, the interests of state required nationalists to sever the connection between ethnicity and national identity in order to maintain the territorial integrity of an empire which was home to many ethnic groups. Liang invented the term 'broad nationalism' (*da minzu zhuyi*) to distinguish his ideal of corporate national identity, focusing on the nation-state, from the 'narrow nationalism' (*xiao minzu zhuyi*) which focused on ethnicity. He defined ethnic identity (*minzu*) using customary distinctions of common territory, ancestry, language, religion and custom, but defined the citizenry subjectively as a group whose consciousness of their corporate identity bestowed upon them individual identities as citizens. Ethnicity was a birthmark people carried in their sleep, in contrast to citizenship, which was a graduate diploma from the state granted to those who had awakened as citizens. Liang then devised an ethics of national citizenship which linked the awakened self with the community of the nation-state through the ideal of the 'citizen'. In time, he came to use the terms citizen and state (*guojia*) interchangeably and to press for their simultaneous awakening. The awakening of the nation, for Liang, was coterminous with the manufacture of an awakened citizenry.[25]

Revolutionary nationalists, however, identified the nation with the idea of race. Sun Yat-sen repudiated the 'Western' model of the nation-state favoured by Liang Qichao, in which citizens relate directly to the state as individuals, but his concept of 'race' was no less state-oriented in its origins and its orientation.[26] Certainly, Sun's personal self-awakening was bound up with an acute consciousness of skin colour and facial features, and with a heightened sensitivity to etiquette rather than to ethics. But his concern for the race was inseparable from his fear of the 'death of the state'. The fate in store for China was likely to be far worse than that endured by the Koreans and Vietnamese, he counselled, who were already 'slaves who had lost their states' (*wang guo nu*). The people of China, however, would not even be preserved as slaves because in China the loss of state threatened the 'destruction of our race'.[27]

Making a virtue of necessity, Sun insisted that observations such as Liang Qichao's on the lack of distinction between nation and state in the Chinese language was a logical corollary of the identity of race and state in China's history. Other countries were obliged to draw appropriate distinctions between the state and the nation because they were historically benighted by the coexistence of several 'races' under the one state, or by the division of one

---

[25]   Hao Chang, *Liang Ch'i-ch'ao and Intellectual Transition in China, 1890-1907* (Harvard University Press, Cambridge, Mass., 1971), pp.260-1.

[26]   Sun Yat-sen, *San Min Chu I, The Three Principles of the People* (translated by Frank W. Price and edited by L. T. Chen) (Ministry of Information, Chungking, 1943), p.115.

[27]   Sun Yat-sen, *San Min Chu I*, pp.12, 38. On Sun's concern with etiquette, see my book, *The Irony of the Chinese Revolution: The Nationalist Revolution and the 'Awakening' of Modern China* (Stanford University Press, Stanford, 1995).

'race' among many states. China, Sun argued, was singularly favoured in this respect:

> China, since the Qin and Han dynasties, has been developing a single state out of a single race, while foreign countries have developed many states from one race and have included many nationalities within one state.[28]

Not surprisingly, Sun concluded that his own Principle of Nationalism was equivalent to the 'doctrine of the state'.[29] His candid identification of nationalism as a state doctrine rested, nevertheless, on an assertion of the racial unity of the Chinese people which seemed to defy the evidence of the senses. In fact, his definition of the Chinese race was heavily qualified by his understanding of the nature, limits and function of the state itself. When Sun insisted that the Chinese people were racially distinct from all other 'races' of the world, he drew the boundaries of the race along the borders of the Chinese state and would allow no comparable ethnic distinctions to be drawn within China itself. The gene-pool of the race, in other words, happened to coincide with the borders of the state. Minority peoples were asked to adjust their belief and behaviour accordingly if they wished to be counted among the 'Chinese people'. In time, the Nationalist government prescribed an elaborate cultural regimen to assist the people of Tibet, Mongolia, Manchuria, Xinjiang and the Han regions to achieve a thorough comprehension of their common racial identity and to recover the sentiment of 'central loyalty' toward the Nationalist state.[30]

Others held different notions of what the threat of the 'death of the state' implied for the nation, arising in part from differing conceptions of the nation itself. Two of the leading intellectuals who were to found the Chinese Communist Party, Li Dazhao and Chen Duxiu, engaged in a novel debate on the prospect of the collapse of the state some years before turning to Marxism for answers to the question. For Li Dazhao, the death of the state did not threaten racial genocide but involved instead a grave risk of loss of territory, cohesion and national identity. Still, the prospect of its loss filled him with an equal sense of dread: whether it was thought to entail loss of race, territory or

---

28 Sun Yat-sen, *San Min Chu I*, p.6.

29 Ibid., p.4.

30 Chiang Kai-shek presented a similar argument at a much later stage, the better to illustrate the point that the Chinese people 'constitute not only one nation, but one race'. See Chiang Kai-shek, *China's Destiny*, first published in 1943 (translated by Wang Chung-hui) (The Macmillan Company, New York, 1947), pp.10-13. Two of Chiang's closest associates, the Chen brothers, implemented this vision in a language-reform program in the 1930s and 1940s. Chen Guofu believed that 'China's ability to achieve unity is entirely dependent on having a unified written language', and his brother, Chen Lifu, put forward a plan for compulsory instruction in Chinese script for all minority peoples on the frontiers. See John De Francis, *Nationalism and Language Reform in China* (Princeton University Press, Princeton, 1950), p.83.

political identity, the loss of the state was counted the greatest loss of all.[31] Nevertheless, the identification of the nation was confounded by the task of evaluating *particular* state formations in China's history as a unitary state. Li Dazhao had only recently expressed his dread of 'loss of the state' when his friend, Chen Duxiu, published an article on the subject in 1913. A state which failed to inspire patriotism was, in Chen's view, not a state at all, because a true state was one which inspired a national people to achieve the ends of the state itself. 'Once the meaning of the state has been cleared up', Chen proclaimed, ' . . . one can even go so far as to say that we Chinese have never as yet set up a state'.[32] From these reflections, Chen Duxiu derived the radical conclusion that the collapse of the Republican state, as it was presently constituted, would be a matter of little moment to those who professed concern for the 'death of the state'.

In conceiving of patriotism as love of the state, Chen Duxiu was led inevitably to the conclusion that a state-directed patriotism was bound to fail in the absence of a perfect state. Li Dazhao then proposed a corrective, in the form of a particular kind of relationship between citizen and state: patriotism could be expressed in the act of *perfecting the state*, and made universal by extending the authority of the state over all its citizens.[33] The nation, in turn, consisted of all those who loved their state. Once patriotism had been channelled into the rhetoric of state ideology and came to be expressed exclusively in the iconography of the state, the problem of Chinese nationalism resolved itself into a choice among state formations competing for the love and loyalty of the Chinese people. Conversely, once people had been offered a choice of regimes, then those who declined to love a particular state forfeited their right to be counted among those it represented; that is, to be counted among the 'Chinese people'.

---

[31]   Li cited in illustration of 'loss of state' the case of the Jews, 'a lost people who dream about recovering their country', as fair warning of the fate in store for the Chinese people should they fail to preserve their state. Meisner, *Li Ta-chao*, p.19.

[32]   Chen Duxiu, 'Patriotism and Consciousness of Self', *Jiayin zazhi* [Tiger Magazine], vol.1, no.4 (10 November 1914). Chen's article is excerpted and translated, along with Li Dazhao's reply 'Pessimism and Consciousness of Self', *Jiayin zazhi*, vol.1, no.8 (10 August 1915), in Hélène Carrère d'Encausse and Stuart R. Schram, *Marxism and Asia: An Introduction with Readings* (Penguin Press, London, 1969), pp.204-8. The present translation is adapted from p.205.

[33]   Li Dazhao, 'Pessimism and Consciousness of Self', in Carrère d'Encausse and Schram, *Marxism and Asia*, pp.207-8. Li Dazhao's emphasis on the will in his rebuttal of Chen Duxiu was seminal. Maurice Meisner has noted that Li's stress at this point 'on the ability of conscious, active men to shape events' was a radical departure for Li himself and marked the source of an original and indigenous strain of Marxism which was to develop under his tutelage in China. Chen Duxiu's rather different emphasis on the limitations imposed by 'objective' conditions also inspired followers among Chinese Marxists. See Meisner, *Li Ta-chao*, pp.21-6.

When a nation is conceived primarily as a political community there is little to prevent political criteria from serving to define membership of the nation, or indeed from determining its constituent categories such as citizen, race or social class without reference to politics. The application of selective criteria for membership of the state should not surprise us: in democratic theory, politically-empowered citizens owe an obligation to the state in return for the rights and protections which it affords. Indeed, the transition from absolute rule to liberal democracy in the states of Europe was accompanied by the selective application of property rights and gender qualifications in determining rights of citizenship. When membership of the nation, however, is a derivative of membership of the state, there is no nation left to which the disempowered might appeal. The nation is exclusively the body of those empowered by the state itself.

State, Nation and Class

'Class' entered nationalist discourse as an alternative to 'citizen' and to 'race' in conceiving of the nation as a political community. And it was employed, like citizen and race, as an icon of state sovereignty and national unity. Communists employed the idea of class much as liberals used the ideal of the citizen, or the Nationalists used race, to assert the essential unity of the Chinese people in the face of primordial attachments to lineage and community, and in light of the need to relate the nation to the world. This last point is worth emphasizing. Nationalists and Communists, in particular, derived their different conceptions of the nation from distinctive historical and ethical conceptions of the world order within which the nation-state happened to find itself — in the one case a 'struggle for survival' among races, and in the other a struggle for supremacy among international class formations. The Communists and Nationalists both turned their respective assessments of the world order back upon the nation in an effort to reconstitute the nation as a full and equal member of the world community; that is, as a state.

It is customary to go about analysing the relationship between Marxism and anti-colonial nationalism in one of two ways, the one rather more and the other rather less sympathetic to the Marxist project. Both take Lenin as their point of departure and neither shares the antipathy to nationalism found in the early Marxian canon. 'The great mass of proletarians are, by their very nature, free from national prejudices . . . ' commented Engels in 1845, after a visit to the Festival of Nations in London. For Engels, as for Marx himself, substituting a proletarian state for a bourgeois state meant unmasking the fallacy of the nation, in effect demolishing national consciousness: 'Only the proletarians can destroy nationality, only the awakening proletariat can bring about fraternalism between the different nations'.[34] The 'Theses on the National and Colonial Questions' produced under Lenin's direction in the 1920s identified a more positive role for national consciousness.

The first line of approach to which I refer remains sympathetic to Lenin's purpose: it traces anti-colonial sentiments back through the deliberations of Lenin and the Communist International (Comintern) to show the instrumental role of Marxist socialism in emancipating colonial and semi-colonial states. The second — much less sympathetic to Lenin — also focuses on Communist Party ideology, organization and tactics but sees Marxism-Leninism as supplying a powerful organizational framework and a potent ideological formula that together tip the balance in favour of Marxist-Leninist parties competing against more naive nationalist movements in the struggle for state power. The two approaches are related to the extent that they focus, for better or worse, on the instrumental aspects of Marxism-Leninism in anti-colonial movements. Both also assume the nation of the post-colonial state to be self-evident and unproblematic: the nation is the national people on whose behalf the revolutionaries fight for state unity and sovereignty, not least among themselves.

Certainly China's Marxist-Leninists never abandoned the idea of a distinctively Chinese nation when they set out to create their new state. To the contrary, where Engels attacked the bourgeois state on the ground that there was no common good or nation which the state could rightly claim to represent, Chinese Leninists attacked the 'bourgeois', 'feudal' and 'bureaucratic capitalist' states (specifically the early Republican, warlord and Nationalist ones) because each failed to represent the Chinese nation *adequately*. Their attacks indirectly affirmed the existence of a Chinese nation on whose behalf they proposed to carry out their revolution. But the nation needed to be reconfigured in order to merit and to attain its own salvation; hence the content of the nation was under negotiation at every point in the state-building process. In this respect Marxism-Leninism was little different from other procedures for identifying the nation in nationalism: like liberal theory and racial nationalism, it offered useful insights for state-builders intent on giving content to their nation. If China's Marxist-Leninists are to be counted nationalist, then, it is not just in Lenin's sense of national strategists pursuing international proletarian revolution but in the sense of state-builders searching for a nation which they might represent adequately in the form of the nation-state.

The moment of arrival of the 'class nation' came over the period of the May Fourth movement and Nationalist Revolution, from 1919 through the late 1920s, when the idea of class intersected with the idea of the nation in three distinct and mutually reinforcing ways. The first, heavily indebted to the

---

34   See Karl Marx and Frederick Engels, *Collected Works 1845-48* (Lawrence and Wishart, London, 1976), vol.6, p.6. Ronaldo Munck highlights this ambivalence in *The Difficult Dialogue: Marxism and Nationalism* (Zed Books, London, 1986), p.6.

anarchists' early experiments in class-analysis of the international system, conceived of China as a national community possessing all of the characteristics (and deserving all of the sympathy) of the classic proletariat in Marxian social analysis. The patriarch of the Chinese Communist Party, Li Dazhao, located the domain of class struggle in the contemporary era in the field of international relations. The unit of class analysis was the nation itself: nations suffering imperialist oppression were labelled members of the international 'proletariat', and the oppressor nations were thought to make up a transnational 'bourgeoisie'. In this case, the idea of class served to establish China's place in the world as a distinctive class nation, on the model of the class nationalism identified by Abdullah Laroui in his typology of colonial nationalisms, within an evolving international class struggle.

But the idea of the class nation did not stop here. Class was married more intimately with the ideal of the nation when national revolutionaries tried to account for the marked degree of regional differences and local attachments among the people of China. The prospect of a nationally uniform mode of production giving shape to comparable social classes from one end of the country to the other offered new hope for a nation which appeared beset by highly localized cultural and social differentiation. With the aid of Marxism, regional variation in levels of economic development could be shown to be tending toward *historical* uniformity: when the forces of history were moving the entire nation inexorably and uniformly from one mode of production ('feudal') to another ('capitalist'), regional variation could be shown to signify no more than regionally differential rates of development along a uniformly national historical pattern.

This particular conception of national unity was first set out in arguments mounted against champions of provincial autonomy, in a debate over federalism in 1922. Communist Party Secretary-General Chen Duxiu showed as keen a determination as Sun Yat-sen to rule out the possibility that sentimental attachments to lineage and locality should be given institutional expression at the political level. To preserve the integrity of the state, Chen and Sun asserted the unity of the nation. Both resorted to essentialist characterizations of the Chinese nation — Sun as race, Chen as a configuration of revolutionary classes — in an attempt to deny that there were significant categories of difference dividing the country into distinctive regions along cultural, social or ethnic boundaries. For example, while targeting warlords for forcibly dividing the country, Chen also challenged the legitimacy of all other emblems of cultural and socio-economic diversity which threatened to do the same. He mounted a range of arguments to explain why there would be little scope for introducing a federalist or regionally-differentiated political system in China even if there were no warlords at all. His case was built on an assumption of the convergence of the Chinese nation around *national* social classes.

Federalism, argued Chen Duxiu, was best suited to countries with regionally differentiated economies, languages, religions and cultures. This was not the case with China. China was one country housing a single 'Chinese people' (*zhonghua minzu*) within a uniform socio-economic system. As China's economy was subject to the universal laws of history, the nation's million-strong industrial proletariat supplied the historical fixative to bond their four hundred million compatriots into one. 'The economic situation of the people of China is uniformly and gradually moving from the stage of agriculture and handicraft industry to that of industrial production', pronounced Chen, in September 1922. 'There is little difference between north and south'.[35] The same social, or class, differences which divided the north also prevailed in the south; so, paradoxically, social division served to mark China's unity as a nation.

While Chen Duxiu could hardly deny that there were differences of custom, language and religious belief among the people of China, he was inclined to deny that there was a regional aspect to their variation. Cultural and religious distinctions were national in scope and hence offered little comfort to advocates of local self-government under a federal system:

> Although there is some slight difference in pronunciation in the native language, the written script and structure of the language are identical. And although there are religious distinctions among Buddhism, Daoism, Christianity and Islam, in no case do these correspond with places of dwelling.[36]

Chen could claim with confidence that there was little correspondence between religious belief and geography because Tibet, Xinjiang and Mongolia were not at issue among his partisan readers. His reference to the common Chinese script served a similar purpose in asserting the unity of the Han peoples despite immense regional variety in their spoken vernaculars and the recognized strength of their local attachments. In assuming that the people themselves were misled in their loyalties, Chen employed class in much the same way that Chiang Kai-shek was later to use the term 'race': as a signifier of the unity of the national people which the people themselves could not yet fully 'comprehend'.

Chen's comrade, Cai Hesen, went a step further in arguing that political differences between north and south, or between liberal and mass democrats, could also be reduced to differences between social classes. Hence 'class warfare' (*jieji zhanzheng*) would ultimately supply a force for unity sufficient to overcome regional political differences as well as cultural and economic ones:

> The domestic chaos and fighting of the last decade is not a struggle for territory between 'North' and the 'South', nor a struggle over 'Protecting the Constitution' or 'Breaking the Constitution', nor even a struggle between 'Unity' and 'Division'.

---

[35]   Chen Duxiu, 'Liansheng zizhi yu Zhongguo zhengxiang' [The Federal System and China's Political Situation], *Xiangdao zhoubao* [The Guide Weekly], vol.1 (13 September 1922), p.2.

[36]   Ibid., p.2.

It is a struggle between the old dominant feudal class and the newly arisen revolutionary class: a kind of class warfare.[37]

Cai Hesen's comments on the class character of political disputes anticipated the third point of entry of class into revolutionary nationalism. The idea of class helped to distinguish true and false members of the nation by helping to identify allies and enemies of the revolutionary state itself.

Revolutionary nationalists did not set out to *make* class enemies at the outset of their national revolution. The Nationalists were inhibited from doing so by their ideology, and the Communists proposed to refrain from doing so at least until the completion of national reunification. For all concerned, the Nationalist Revolution of the 1920s was to be an 'all class' affair.[38] This did not mean that the revolution lacked a political target or that it failed to make tangible political enemies. Sun Yat-sen identified enemies among the remnant functionaries of the Qing and supporters of warlord administrations. There were even enemies within the ranks of the revolutionary party itself. Some Nationalists objected to the blanket condemnation of warlords for fear that it would alienate the party's warlord allies, and others feared that the militant tone of anti-imperialist rhetoric was bound to make life difficult for them in the foreign concession at home or in colonial societies abroad.[39] Many Nationalists also felt uneasy about admitting Communists into their party and were embarrassed by their party's close association with the Soviet Union. On the Communist side, disputes erupted within the Communist Party over the details of its cooperation with the Nationalists and over the high-handed attitude of the Third Communist International (Comintern) and its advisers in China. And, in Moscow, the rationale and conduct of the alliance was a source of controversy within the Soviet leadership and among the major institutions which claimed a legitimate interest in the matter, including the Comintern,

[37]   Cai Hesen, 'Wuli tongyi yu liansheng zizhi: junfa zhuanzheng yu junfa geju' [Military Reunification and Federalism: Warlord Dictatorship and Warlord Separatism], *Xiangdao zhoubao*, no.2 (20 September 1922), p.14.

[38]   The Chinese Communist leader Chen Duxiu went so far as to suggest that an 'all class' revolution was the only kind of revolution possible in China at this time. Chen Duxiu, 'Zhongguo guomin geming yu shehui ge jieji' [China's National Revolution and its Various Social Classes], *Qianfeng* [The Vanguard], no.2 (1 December 1923). On the side of the Nationalists, needless to say, this was an axiom of the revolution. Sun Yat-sen believed that the 'entire country' would rise up and overwhelm the forces of militarism and imperialism and carry the Nationalists to power. See Sun Yat-sen, *Guofu quanji* [The Complete Works of the Father of the Country] (Dangshi weiyuanhui, Taipei, 1973), vol.2, p.598.

[39]   See my 'The Irony of the Chinese Revolution: The Nationalists and Chinese Society, 1923-1927', in John Fitzgerald (ed.), *The Nationalists and Chinese Society, 1923-1937: A Symposium* (Melbourne University History Monographs, Melbourne, 1989), pp.13-43.

Narkomindel and Profintern.[40] But political enemies, generally speaking, were not conceived in terms of social classes until the revolution got underway, for early misgivings and disputes among all parties to the revolution were arbitrated around a common agreement on the political goals of the revolution to 'overthrow warlords and imperialism'. These twin goals served as a common test for telling who were the friends and the enemies of state and nation alike.

Few made any connection between warlords and the social forces of 'feudalism' before the revolution got underway; warlords were enemies chiefly because they held guns and pointed them in the direction of the revolutionaries.[41] Even the Comintern counted class status an inadequate basis for distinguishing friends and enemies in the Chinese revolution. Its 'Directives on the Application of the 1920 Agrarian Theses' set an important precedent for flexible interpretation of agrarian feudalism by noting that whether or not the landlord class should be singled out for struggle in the national phase of revolution depended upon the position landlords adopted toward imperialism, rather than the nature of their relations with the struggling peasant masses.[42] Here the Comintern established the cardinal principle that political attitudes toward a national enemy offered a more reliable guage for identifying friends and enemies in national revolution than class status *per se*. Another criterion for identifying friends and enemies was Lenin's remark on

---

40   See S. T. Leong, *Sino-Soviet Diplomatic Relations, 1917-1926* (Australian National University Press, Canberra, 1976); Conrad Brandt, *Stalin's Failure in China, 1924-1927* (Norton & Co., New York, 1966); Robert C. North, *Moscow and Chinese Communists* (Stanford University Press, Stanford, 1963); Alan S. Whiting, *Soviet Policies in China, 1917-1924* (Stanford University Press, Stanford, 1953).

41   Chinese nationalists and Comintern agents drew extensively on the writings of Marx and Lenin when they wrote of feudalism but they ultimately arrived at an understanding of the role of warlords in nationalist politics which came closer to the writings of German nationalists — in particular to Max Weber's critique of Junkers in the modern German state — than to any in the Marxian canon. Marx attributed a social base to feudalism and Lenin targeted the social base of feudal lords in national liberation struggles, but it was Weber who first singled out the great feudal lords as political enemies of the nation-state. Weber believed that in the face of international competition the principle of the nation assumed priority over all other values and hence that political elites which failed to conform with the nation-building enterprise surrendered their moral authority to govern. When he set out this principle in his inaugural lecture at Frieburg in May 1895, Weber pronounced that the Junkers were unfit to govern because they employed Polish day-labourers in place of German ones. This he deemed a slight on the German labouring classes, sufficient at least to show that the Junkers lacked the kind of national consciousness Germany demanded of its leaders in an age of competing nation-states. If Junker authority lacked an ethical foundation it was because the Junkers refused to recognize and to comply with the national interest and not, as Marx or Lenin would say, because they were the corrupt vestiges of a dying social order.

42   See Jane Degras (ed.), *The Communist International, 1919-1943, Documents* (Frank Cass and Co. Ltd., London, 1971), vol.1, pp.394-8.

the ownership of large estates. In its 1922 'Theses on the Eastern Question' the Comintern identified the domestic enemy of national revolution as 'feudal' large landowners and confirmed Lenin's call for the expropriation of their properties. These twin criteria — political attitudes and ownership of 'estates' — were considered closely related in practice, because 'alien imperialism' makes the 'feudal' elite an 'instrument of its rule'.[43] The Comintern explicitly identified the feudal class in native Chinese society as the *'tuchuns'*, or warlords, which were equated with the Junkers of the old German states and elevated to the status of a social class accordingly. Warlords came to be counted feudal on a number of different counts — for dividing the polity into regional satrapies and opposing the development of the bourgeoisie and of 'bourgeois democracy' — but if they represented anything other than themselves it was thought to be the alien force of foreign capital in its highest stage of imperialism.[44] Their presumed role in representing the greater landlord class came some way down the list of warlord crimes. It was enough that they seemed to be dividing the national cake and surrendering it, on a plate, to foreigners.

In the event, the maxim that warlords and imperialism were enemies of the nation was sufficiently flexible to accommodate domestic 'feudal' social forces among the enemies of the nation as well. Indeed, any institution or group of people reluctant to take up the invitation to attack feudalism and imperialism, or perhaps bold enough to challenge the right of the revolutionaries to define the friends and enemies of the nation on their behalf, could with good reason be counted an ancilliary of feudal interests or a lackey of imperialism. As late as April 1924, Chen Duxiu distinguished radical from conservative factions within the Nationalist Party by the simple expedient of identifying party members' attitudes to the twin political goals of the revolution. Chen announced that the class origins of his enemies were quite immaterial.[45] But this simple act of faith no longer sufficed after 1925. With the collapse of the May Thirtieth Movement in Shanghai, and in the ongoing struggle for local power in the revolutionaries' southern base in Guangdong, friends and enemies of the revolution declared themselves by their collective positions on the contest for state power between the revolutionaries (representing the nation) and the liberals, chambers of commerce, local elites and warlords who resisted them.[46] By virtue of their opposition to the

---

[43]   Ibid., pp.382-93.

[44]   Michael Luk, *The Origins of Chinese Bolshevism: An Ideology in the Making, 1920-1928* (Oxford University Press, Hong Kong, 1990), p.147.

[45]   Chen Duxiu, 'Guomindang zuoyipai zhi zhen yiyi' [The True Significance of Left and Right Factions in the Nationalist Party], *Xiangdao zhoubao*, no.62 (23 April 1924), pp.3-4.

[46]   This argument is set out in greater detail in John Fitzgerald, 'The Misconceived Revolution: State and Society in China's Nationalist Revolution, 1923-1926', *Journal of Asian Studies*, vol.49, no.2 (May 1990), pp.323-43.

revolutionaries these groups effectively excluded themselves from membership of the nation. Class struggle then entered China's national revolution at the invitation of the party-state, under Nationalist Party auspices, not as an instrument of social revolution but as a technique for reconfiguring the nation in a form consonant with the unity which the revolutionary state sought for itself.

Marxism, Nationalism and the Class Nation

Can nationalists turn upon their own 'people' without surrendering their claim to be nationalist? In referring to nationalism in China, we generally refer to its meaning at a particular point in its own development when nationalist thought identified the state with the Chinese 'race'. This is certainly the meaning of the nation conveyed to the West in China's protracted civil war. When Chiang Kai-shek went looking for a stick with which to beat the Communists, it was the ferocity of their campaigns against 'their own people' which most clearly marked them as national enemies:

> It is only too clear now that Communists can never have any sense of loyalty to their own country: they are devoid of patriotism or national consciousness. In fact they have no love for their country but they will deliberately work against national interests. They feel no compunction even if . . . they should be called upon to *perpetrate genocide on their own people.*[47]

In the 1930s, by Nationalist reckoning, fighting Communists was more patriotic than fighting Japanese troops on China's soil because the Communists threatened far more than the territorial integrity of the country. They challenged the ego boundaries of the national self. The Nationalists thought of themselves as a movement for uniting a divided people, and believed that any attempt to exacerbate existing divisions within society or to turn one part against another was treasonous.[48] In the Communist Party of China, the Nationalists confronted not only a rival political movement but an alternative definition of the nation.

Neither definition could countenance the other. To the makers of Nationalist China any concession that yielded the fundamental integrity of the race (however fictional this idea) was not an alternative to national extinction but a *form* of national extinction. The rhetoric of the civil war which swept the Communists to power in the 1940s retained the essentialist style of thought characteristic of modern Chinese nationalism, although in this case elaborated around the idea of social class. On the twenty-eighth anniversary of the founding of the Communist Party in 1949, when Mao Zedong redefined the 'people' on behalf of the People's Republic of China, he raised once again the

---

[47]   Emphasis added. Adapted from Chiang Kai-shek, *Soviet Russia in China* (revised edition) (Farrar, Strauss and Cudahy, New York, 1968), pp.88-9.

[48]   Sun Yat-sen, *San Min Chu I*, pp.4-6.

central issue of China's national revolution. 'Who are the people?', he asked. 'At the present stage in China, they are the working class, the peasantry, the urban petty bourgeoisie and the national bourgeoisie'. These four classes were selected for inclusion on the national flag of the People's Republic in the form of four small stars orbiting the greater star of the People's state. The rest — 'the landlord class and the bureaucrat bourgeoisie, as well as the representatives of those social classes' — were excluded from the insignia of state and from the ranks of the 'people'.[49]

The composition of the 'people', as Mao implied, was to change once China had moved beyond its 'present stage'. And so it did. The landlord class and the 'petty' and 'national' bourgeoisie were eliminated as social classes over the first decade of Communist Party rule, after which class struggle no longer characterized relations among actual social classes. Instead, it characterized relations between the state and the survivors of earlier class struggles (the 'bad class elements', as they were known), and came to be identified with conflicts among competing 'class ideologies' within the structure of the state itself. Subsequent political conflicts at the highest levels of party and state entailed terrible suffering for the dispossessed scions of the landlord and petty-bourgeois classes, who were held to account for the errors of their 'representatives' among Mao's political enemies. Nevertheless, they no longer constituted a social class in the sense of a social formation. Bad class elements were kept alive beyond the collapse of their class formations chiefly to provide a 'real' social referent for Mao Zedong's political enemies to represent, and to be taunted and killed as political struggle intensified within the higher party and state apparatus. Bad class elements were hostage to the fortunes of arch unrepentant capitalist roaders.[50]

Having given content to the nation, the category of class (like that of the nation) became an essentially contested concept within a discourse of state power. It was then shown to be as unstable as the category of the nation. It was not *sufficient* to be born a peasant or a worker to warrant inclusion among the 'people', nor was landlord or bourgeois class background a sufficient principle of exclusion. The only reliable criterion for inclusion among the People was class 'attitude', expressed in the form of support for Mao Zedong himself. In appropriating the right to name the 'people', to represent it and to

[49]   Mao Zedong, 'On the People's Democratic Dictatorship', 30 June 1949, in *Selected Works of Mao Tse-tung* (Foreign Languages Press, Beijing, 1969), vol.4, pp.411-24, esp. 417-18.

[50]   The distinction between class struggle in the literal sense (against people of bad class background) and in the metaphorical sense (against people who followed the wrong political 'line') was tenuous at the best of times, but was nevertheless maintained in order to give 'line' struggle a significant social referent. In the Cultural Revolution this distinction became the axis of factional struggle within the Red Guard movement itself. See Jonathan Unger, *Education Under Mao: Class and Competition in Canton Schools, 1960-1980* (Columbia University Press, New York, 1982), pp.122-33.

speak on its behalf, Mao also reserved the right to identify each of its subsidiary categories. Class, like nation, came in the end to mean anything that its self-appointed representatives chose to make it.

Mao's approach to the category of social class was not quite as cavalier as it might appear. Indeed, it was the culmination of a tradition of state nationalism stretching back to the turn of the century in which state-builders reserved the right to identify who it was that made up the nation and who exercised that right in ways consistent with their claims to state sovereignty. Conservatives and reformers in the mid-nineteenth century, reformers and revolutionaries at the turn of the century, Nationalists and their Communist rivals in the early stages of China's national revolution all presumed that the nation had no name of its own, all assumed the right to give a name to their nation, and, in naming it, to represent it as a state. None conceded that there might already have been a nation in existence capable of representing itself. When the Communists drew their line beyond race and traditional high culture, and isolated class as the essential feature of the nation, they did not reach beyond the limits of nationalist thought itself. All they did was move the line a little further in the direction of the state.

The point at issue here is not the existence of social classes in early twentieth-century China, nor even the salience of class analysis in social revolution. It is, rather, the manner in which the idea of class took root in state-oriented nationalism. Class first entered the vocabulary of radical activists around the turn of the century along with all that was modern and cosmopolitan. Reference to a revolution of social classes was commonplace among anarchists who were not in the least concerned about the reunification of the state and who were only marginally interested in the attainment of national 'wealth and power'.[51] China's early champions of social revolution employed class analysis in the hope of identifying social forces which might eliminate the state entirely. It was the ethical community of the nation, not of social class, which required the clearest elaboration and closest justification in early revolutionary thought. Social classes were thought to exist in the natural order of things. The nation, on the other hand, appeared an irrational and artificial contrivance born of the international state system.[52] Nevertheless, the

---

[51]   Martin Bernal, *Chinese Socialism to 1907* (Cornell University Press, Ithaca, 1976); Peter Zarrow, *Anarchism and Chinese Political Culture* (Columbia University Press, New York, 1990); Dirlik and Chan, *Schools into Fields and Factories*. Note especially Dirlik's chapter on ethics in *Anarchism in the Chinese Revolution*.

[52]   Even Zhang Binglin, one of the foremost nationalist theoreticians of the turn of the century, considered the nation arbitrary and accidental: 'Now, in this multitudinous universe, the earth is but a small grain of rice in a vast granary, yet today [we] who live on it have divided it up into territories, we protect what is ours and call it a "nation". Then we established institutions, divided [ourselves] into various classes, and called it "government"'. Nations and states were 'determined by happenstance' and had no rationale other than their historical emergence as categories for organising the affairs of men. Cited in Zarrow, *Anarchism*, pp.51-2.

anarchists' pioneering conception of the world community as an aggregation of social classes made possible a radical reconfiguration of the nation itself as a class community when the time was ripe.

Among nationalists, on the other hand, it is easy to overestimate the appeal of Marxist socialism. There was in fact an immense reluctance to embrace the idea of class division and class struggle within nationalist thought. Divisive social revolution was thought to accompany some other kind of revolution than the national one planned for China. So the first Nationalist to embrace Marxist theory, Hu Hanmin, was happy to apply historical materialism to the development of Confucian ethics but saw little merit in extending his analysis to the social, economic and political life of the country because 'historical materialism' was predicated on social violence.[53] Like his leader in the Nationalist Party, Sun Yat-sen, Hu maintained that the Principle of People's Livelihood offered an adequate substitute for historical materialism in the Chinese revolution because attention to the livelihood of the common people would pre-empt the development of class struggle.[54]

Few national revolutionaries outside the Nationalist Party favoured the idea of class struggle either. The Nationalist Party's authority on Comintern thinking, Henk Sneevliet, had shown little inclination to exclude the Indonesian bourgeoisie from the nationalist program on an earlier assignment in the Dutch Indies, and Sneevliet does not appear to have raised the prospect of targeting the Chinese bourgeoisie in his discussions with Sun Yat-sen.[55] Sneevliet was of course a partial and partisan source on Comintern thinking about the place of class struggle in national revolutionary movements. The more brazen Indian Comintern delegate, M. N. Roy, advocated class struggle against the Indian bourgeoisie. But in Moscow Roy made little headway against Lenin, and even within the Indian nationalist movement his impact was limited.[56] Nor were many Chinese Communists persuaded at the outset that class struggle against China's traders, industrialists or landlords had a significant part to play in a war of national liberation. When Li Dazhao transferred the domain of class struggle to the arena of international relations, with China playing the part of the proletariat, he was fully conscious that his formulaic adaptation of the materialist conception of history minimized the prospect of class struggle in China's own revolution. In fact, this was the whole point of the exercise. There was little incentive for either Nationalist or Communist Party theorists to relinquish the modern ideal of the unified nation or to abandon the inherited Confucian ideal of social harmony until both ideals had been rendered untenable *within nationalist thought itself*. In this respect,

53   Joseph Levenson, *Confucian China and Its Modern Fate: A Trilogy* (University of California Press, Berkeley, 1968), vol.3, pp.28-30.

54   Sun Yat-sen, *San Min Chu I*, p.380 ff.

55   Tony Saich, *The Origins of the First United Front in China: The Role of Sneevliet (alias Maring)* (E. J. Brill, Leiden, 1991).

56   See Seth, 'Marxism and the Question of Nationalism'.

exaggerating the appeal of Marxism to nationalists only obscures the significance of what took place within nationalist thought over the twenty or thirty years leading to the establishment of the People's Republic.

Marxism-Leninism became a plausible option within nationalist thought only after class struggle ceased to present an obstacle to its acceptance. Hence the establishment of a rationale and a rhetorical framework for inserting class struggle into nationalism was the most significant development of China's national revolution. This took place, we have noted, in three phases. In the May Fourth movement, class struggle was analogous to the struggle among nations, and between wealthier and stronger states and the territories they sought to bring into their colonial empires. From 1922, class struggle against 'feudal' military forces was also conceived as a nation-building enterprise within China, promoting the historical evolution of a uniformly national mode of production. And from 1925 throughout the period of the civil war, the reluctance of certain powerful and well-organized groups in society to follow the directives of the revolutionaries singled them out for class struggle as well, again in the name of saving the nation. In this case, advocacy of class struggle against the bourgeoisie and the landlord classes served the further function of destroying the only social formations that held any prospect of staging effective local resistance to an expanding party-state.

The institution of the party-state was crucial to this development. The Communist and Nationalist Parties saw themselves as institutions for 'representing' the national people until they had come to a realization of their own unity (as race or as class) through political struggle and political education. Those who persisted in displaying indifference to imperialist influence or disregard for political partition under warlord rule, despite ample warning, betrayed in their behaviour that they belonged to the counter-revolutionary 'class'. The idea of class struggle then ceased to be an unpalatable option in nationalist thought and came to appear, instead, a palatable necessity.[57] If the people themselves were divided over the fundamental issue of who should rule them and how they should be ruled, then only some of them deserved to be included among the people of the nation. So Marxism made possible a radical re-imagining of the national self in terms of class: class offered a rational principle for exclusion from the nation of those social groups resisting the expansion of the revolutionary state.

Nevertheless, the appearance of class struggle in the revolution did not signal the Communist Party's departure from nationalism nor transform the revolution into a socialist enterprise. The dispute associated with class struggle took place within nationalist thought itself, testing the limits of an established consensus on the composition of the nation and forcing a massive rupture in

---

[57]   The slogans and posters advocating 'class struggle' in Guangzhou in the 1920s declared not that class struggle was glorious but that 'class struggle is inevitable'. See Edward Kenneth W. Rea (ed.), *Canton in Revolution: The Collected Papers of Earl Swisher, 1925-1928* (Westview Press, Boulder, 1977), p.32.

nationalist thought between a continuing commitment to Sun Yat-sen's vision of the nation as 'race' and an alternative vision of the nation defined by class. The question at issue, in Chatterjee's terms, was how to essentialize the national self. Ideological differences which divided the Nationalists and Communists in the Chinese national revolution are best characterized, then, not as a struggle between Marxism-Leninism and nationalism, but as a struggle between two phases of nationalism, or more particularly between two highly competitive state-building parties over the content of the nation and the form of the state that would act to represent it.

Conclusion

A schematic analysis of the kind offered here runs the risk of ignoring all that is accidental in history. Winners appear to gain a moral victory; losers not only lose power, but seem to lose the plot as well. Yet the Chinese nation need not have been defined along the statist lines oulined above, nor need the identity of the nation have been linked with class in quite this fashion. There was, we have noted, a strain of socialist thought in Chinese anarchism which was not preoccupied with questions of national sovereignty, wealth and power. So, too, there was a Chinese people long before nationalists began lamenting the failure of the people to cohere in quite the way they wanted. The nations of citizen, race and class may well have been inventions of the state designed to overcome differences dividing the people of China, but these differences have all along been mediated by a common agreement among individuals and communities that they happen to belong together, after a fashion.

The many people who live in China have a long history of their own, preserved not in records of state but in immense repositories of cultural memory that is captured in story and song, festival and ritual, street news and, today, on television and film. Richard Madsen has recently called for the application of a new kind of political sociology more sensitive to models of community consciousness outside of the statist framework — in contests over written histories, in commemorative ceremonies, opera and literature, and in the immense storehouse of collective memory, to serve as a corrective to the state orientation of much political scholarship.[58] The reasons for doing so are more than academic. The relationship between state and nation is under negotiation in China today to an extent that defies all precedent.

It is not just that official configurations of the nation are under challenge. True, the national flags of the People's Republic of China and of the Republic of China on Taiwan no longer signify the nation and the polities they represent. On Taiwan, the national flag and national anthem of the Republic

---

[58]   Richard Madsen, 'The Public Sphere, Civil Society and Moral Community: A Research Agenda for Contemporary China Studies', *Modern China*, vol.19, no.2 (April 1993), pp.183-98.

still make explicit reference to the Nationalist Party at a time when the state is moving toward a multi-party system. The flag, with its Nationalist Party insignia of a blue sky and white sun on the canon, and the anthem referring to the nation as 'our party' (*wu dang*), both recall the origins of the state in the single-party Nationalist state from which Taiwan is gradually moving away on a raft of political reforms that are leaving both party and flag behind. On the mainland, the flag of the People's Republic betrays its origins in the state-orchestrated class struggles of the Communist revolution. With four small stars representing the 'revolutionary' social classes of the nation, all orbiting the greater star of the Communist state at the centre of the canon, the flag of the People's Republic signifies not only the victory of the classes which comprise the nation but also, by their omission, the defeat of the counter-revolutionary classes which never quite made it onto the flag. As early as the Cultural Revolution, when the 'classes' starred on the flag were encouraged to wage star-wars among themselves, a generation of school children was taught to honour the flag without being told what it was they were saluting.[59] More recently, the commitment to the politics of class struggle which once guided the selection of stars is at odds with the ethic of getting-rich-quick which underpins the economic reform program of Deng Xiaoping. The big star is still in the ascendant, but the flag's selective assemblage of social classes heightens the asymmetry between state and nation by reminding those who salute the flag (and know what they are saluting) that the Party's ideological foundations no longer match the direction in which the country is heading.

More importantly, where the state should turn to find its nation and what shape the nation will assume on the flag depends to a greater degree than ever before on the compliance of the people of China in forfeiting the right to name themselves. Indeed, it is not simply the shape of the flag that is at issue today but the fundamental premise that the state reserves the right to define the nation and to specify its relationship to the state. In the history of Chinese nationalism the state (or state-builders) have assumed this right without question. To the extent that the line between state and nation has been blurred, and that love of country has been indistinguishable from love of the state, China's intellectuals have tended to go along with it all. As Fang Lizhi recalled in 1989,

> I remember in my younger days joining in on the criticism of our poor old teachers, who would always defend themselves by saying 'At least I'm patriotic; at least I love my country'. Our standard reply was 'But what country do you love? A communist country? or a Kuomintang country?' Of course what we were implying was that they weren't really patriotic at all. In this context, patriotism obviously

---

59   W. J. F. Jenner, *The Tyranny of History: The Roots of China's Crisis* (Penguin Press, Harmondsworth, 1992), p.66.

does not mean loving your native place, your rivers, your soil, your cities; it means loving the state.[60]

Fang Lizhi's ironic self-parody highlights a revolutionary development in contemporary China. Patriotic nationalism has taken root outside the state itself. In the political reform movements which followed immediately on the Cultural Revolution, reform was understood to mean restoring the ideological faith of a jaded community, or restoring the sheen of a tarnished party. More recently, however, this restorationist tendency has yielded to a wider recognition of the distinction between the Communist Party and the state, on the one hand, and between the state and the nation on the other.[61] Distinctions of this kind make room for a conception of a nation and for a form of state quite different from any which have come before in China. This revolutionary development does not, paradoxically, require a political revolution: the revolutionary discourse of the 'nationless state' has little traction in a nation which is sufficiently confident to name itself, and in a state which does not presume to tell the people of China who they are.

---

[60]   Fang Lizhi, 'On Patriotism and Global Citizenship', speech of 25 February 1989, Beijing; transcribed by G. K. Sun, translated by James H. Williams, in George Hicks (ed.), *The Broken Mirror: China after Tiananmen* (Longman, Harlow, Essex, 1990), pp.xxi-xxv.

[61]   Merle Goldman, Perry Link and Su Wei, 'China's Intellectuals in the Deng Era: Loss of Identity with the State', in Lowell Dittmer and Samuel S. Kim (eds), *China's Quest for National Identity* (Cornell University Press, Ithaca, 1993), pp.125-53.

FOUR

How China's Nationalism was Shanghaied[*]

Lucian W. Pye

What kind of a nation-state are the Chinese people and their leaders shaping for themselves as they enter the second century of the 'Chinese revolution'? The quest for national greatness and modernization that began with the early reformers as a quest for 'wealth and power' continues. The relationship of nationalism and modernization is unquestionably a fundamental problem in the history of modern China. Indeed, one can ask whether there is any theme about China that is more hackneyed than 'nationalism and modernization?' What can possibly be said that is new on the subject?

What is new is the urgency of the question because we are now seeing, as a part of the worldwide crisis of communism, the unrelenting erosion of Marxism-Leninism-Mao Zedong Thought as the basis of state legitimacy in China. The expectation is that nationalism will have to fill the void created by the 'crisis of confidence' and by the collapse of the myth of socialism as magic. If the future of China lies with nationalism, we had better get a clear understanding of precisely what are its characteristics in China. What are likely to be the distinctive features of Chinese nationalism in a post-Marxist-Leninist era? More importantly, how will the configurations of Chinese nationalism affect the prospects for the modernization of Chinese society and politics?

It is my intention to argue, firstly, that the relationship between nationalism and modernization has taken a form in China that is different from what has occurred anywhere else. I want to argue, secondly, that in spite of the greatness of Chinese history, in spite of the manifest durability of everyday

---

[*] An earlier version of this chapter was delivered as a Wei Lun Lecture at the Chinese University of Hong Kong. That earlier version has appeared, in translation, in the Chinese-language magazine *Ershiyi shiji* [21st Century] (Hong Kong), no.9 (February 1992), pp.13-26.

Chinese culture — that is, in spite of the weight of many of the standard building blocks of nationalism — the historical pattern of China's modernization has left China with a relatively inchoate and incoherent form of nationalism. Stated another way, the primordial building blocks of ethnicity and cultural habits have in some respects preempted the field and obscured the fact that, for fundamental reasons, nationalism in China has remained nascent and amorphous. Thus, paradoxically, although China produced one of the world's greatest civilizations and still has a powerful and tenacious culture, it now has in modern times a relatively contentless form of nationalism. Yet, even more paradoxically, the Chinese political class, in spite of such a formless nationalism, has been able to exploit the mystique of patriotism to neutralize politically the very Chinese who have been the most successful in modernizing.

Two Elusive Subjects

Before proceeding with the Chinese case it is necessary to clarify and define the two very elusive concepts of nationalism and modernization. When we speak of nationalism and modernization it might seem that we are dealing with straightforward and commonsense topics, but in fact these are two very tricky subjects which are not easily pinned down and analysed. The problem with nationalism is that it properly involves only those sentiments associated with the idea of the nation-state, but people popularly confuse it with a variety of other sentiments associated with basic forms of group identity. 'Modernization' is also popularly a confusion of ideas ranging from Westernization and economic development to middle-class practices. As a result it is often overlooked that the essence of modernization is a blending of parochial cultural values and the universal norms associated with the world culture.

Nationalism has become a very fuzzy concept because we have tended to lump together under its label all manner of identities and primordial sentiments. Nationalism should not be confused with tribalism, ethnicity, or shared cultural, religious and linguistic identities. Given that nationalism involves only those sentiments and attitudes basic to orientations toward the nation-state, frequently these other primordial identities work against the creation of a unifying sense of nationalism. Even when a country is relatively homogeneous in terms of culture and religion, the spirit of ethnic identity may not be directed toward the state. In other situations such primordial sentiments can indeed contribute to sharpening the feelings about 'we-ness' and 'they-ness' that are also basic to nationalism. But there is something additional and distinctive in the idea of nationalism because it must include the distinctive set of ideals, myths, symbols and values that can serve as the inspiration for a nation-state. The primary identities of race, culture and ethnicity can exist before there is the nation-state, and they can fuel the passions of nationalism after the nation-state is founded, but nationalism must have an additional dimension that is associated with the uniqueness of the particular nation-state. Nationalism provides not just the basis of loyalty of a people to their nation-state but also defines the role of leaders, and in so doing sets limits on their conduct.

Students of nationalism correctly insist that nationalism appeared only with the emergence of the nation-state in Europe, and that it has spread to the rest of the world only with the creation of modern nation-states. The age of nationalism came only with the formation of the modern nation-state system. The new era of nationalism was formed by people's reactions to their own state and to the state system as a whole. Nationalism is therefore a modern sentiment. Hence, the traditional Chinese 'Middle Kingdom Complex' or the concept of Han chauvinism should not be treated as the same thing as Chinese nationalism. The contemporary sentiments and imagery of nationalism can, however, have their tap-roots in past identities, for history is, of course, a prime source for the ideals that are basic to nationalism. Indeed, how people share their collective memories forms much of the content of their nationalistic identity, and with a loss of those memories there may come a void in their collective feelings. Nationalism embraces the ideals of a society and a people's sense of how they are distinctive and precious in contrast to other peoples. In the words of John Stuart Mill: 'The strongest cause for the feeling of nationality . . . is identity of political antecedents; the possession of a national history, and consequent community of recollections; collective pride and humiliation, pleasure and regret, connected with the same incidents in the past'.[1]

Modern social science has contributed to the confusion about the distinction between nationalism and other forms of collective bonding. In the earlier works of such scholars as Hans Kohn, Carleton Hayes, E. H. Carr, Robert MacIver and Rupert Emerson there was generally a conscientious attempt to distinguish between those sentiments attached to the nation-state and other feelings of group identity. Indeed, a central issue in much of the debates as to whether a particular colony was 'ready for independence' was the question of whether the ethnic, religious and other identity divisions among the people had been superseded by adequately strong sentiments of identification with what would be the new nation-state. However, as scholars sought to uncover the foundations of the spirit of nationalism, they tended to blur the distinctions. Thus, Karl Deutsch identified nationalism with basic patterns of social communications which he found to be critical for forming a sense of community.[2] Harold Isaacs carried the analysis even further by

---

[1]   John Stuart Mill, *Representative Government* (1861), quoted in Karl Deutsch, *Nationalism and Social Communications* (MIT Press and John Wiley, New York, 1953), p.5.

[2]   Deutsch, *Nationalism and Social Communications*.

identifying all the major elements that can shape group identity — such as skin colour, language and religion — and associated them with nationalism.[3]

Yet, if we are to understand better the political role of nationalism it is now apparent that we need to separate such primordial sentiments from those that are focused on the nation-state. We can see that this is the case when we look at what has happened in many of the newly emerging nations of the Third World, where such tribal sentiments have not contributed to the creation of enduring bonds of nationalism. In many of the new states, ethnic and religious identities not only failed to contribute to the formation of a new spirit of national identity but actually worked against the building of nationhood. As a result, the assumptions of the 1950s that strong racial and other primordial sentiments could become the stuff of strong nationalism proved to be incorrect. The story of nation-building is that primordial sentiments are not enough; there must be a distinct set of ideals, aspirations, heroes, and symbols that are associated with the political system as a part of the larger nation-state system.

Moreover, the identification of nationalism cannot be limited to merely some partisan political party or faction. Nationalism is more than loyalty to a party or particular leader. Naturally, politicians will try to identify themselves with nationalistic sentiments, and certainly some leaders and parties are ideologically more committed than others to strengthening the ideals of nationalism. However, if a group of leaders tries to claim that patriotism is associated only with supporting their partisan positions, and that everyone else is unpatriotic, their behaviour can only be seen as an example of politics and not a manifestation of true nationalism.

So when we look for the substance of Chinese nationalism we have to identify those sentiments that are different from either the Chinese sense of ethnic and cultural identity, or the attitudes toward current policies and leaders. Above all, it is important to distinguish Chinese nationalism from all the powerful sentiments associated with Chinese cultural and ethnic identity. Chinese cultural and ethnic realities are, of course, critical factors in shaping Chinese political behaviour, but to understand the likely direction of Chinese historical development we also need to have a clear sense of the more specific ideals, myths, heroes and symbols that can inspire Chinese nationalism as the Chinese seek the goals of modernization. The extraction of a coherent and inspiring form of nationalism from the all-embracing concept of Chinese ethnicity has not been easy. Sun Yat-sen sought to articulate an early version of Chinese nationalism, but The Three Principles (*Sanmin zhuyi*) soon became merely the orthodoxy of a partisan political party. Mao Zedong could boast that under him China had 'stood up', but aside from his partisan version of Marxism-Leninism he deflated Chinese nationalism when he said the Chinese people were a 'blank sheet of paper'.

---

[3]   Harold Isaacs, *The Idols of the Tribe* (Harvard University Press, Cambridge, 1989; originally published by Harper & Row, New York, 1975).

Nationalism must also respond to the times, which means that when there is rapid social or revolutionary change the character of nationalism in the particular society can become quite unpredictable. Revolution can solidify nationalism, as in the case of France; but revolutionary changes can also produce a confused and disillusioned people with little feeling of nationalism, as in some of the corrupted new nations of post-colonial Africa and Asia. This is why the relationship of nationalism to the profound changes associated with modernization is so fundamental to the course of history.

Modernization is an equally elusive subject which, like nationalism, emerged out of Europe during the process of creating the nation-state system, and has spread to the rest of the world as societies have become engaged in the nation-building processes. Initially, it was common to confuse modernization with Westernization, but increasingly we have come to see modernization as being associated with international standards, universalistic knowledge such as science and technology, and the values and practices appropriate for advanced contemporary societies. Modernization, like nationalism, is fundamentally a state of mind. It calls for a heightened level of consciousness, a capacity for empathy, and a break from the rigidities of traditional orthodoxies.

The relationship between nationalism and modernization is obviously complex. They can reinforce each other or they can be antagonistic. In both nationalism and modernization, there are also tensions between parochial and particularistic considerations, on the one hand, and cosmopolitan and universalistic standards, on the other. The building blocks of nationalism must emerge out of the historical traditions and legacies of a society, but nationalism has significance only in the context of relations with other nation-states, and thus it is also responsive to cosmopolitan standards. Modernization similarly reflects cosmopolitan values and universalistic norms, but it also has to resonate with the parochial traditions of the particular society if it is to take root and become a significant force. Thus, nationalism and modernization contain within themselves tensions between the parochial cultures of a society and the universialistic norms of the cosmopolitan world. In this way, nationalism and modernization are twin driving forces which shape the historic processes of nation-building and political development. They can also work against each other to paralyse progress.

The Chinese Difference

In the 1950s and 1960s it was commonplace for scholars to treat nationalism and modernization as the most important dual forces in the emerging states of the post-colonial world. The study of political development soon expanded to include most of the Third World of Asia, Africa, and Latin America. It is significant, however, that the study of China was generally not included in this great intellectual endeavour. There were various reasons why this was the case. China at the time was vigorously engaged in pursuing its quest for a Marxist-Leninist utopia, and most American scholars interested in the developing world wanted to get away from Cold War issues. Moreover, China specialists were happy to accentuate the distinctiveness, indeed the uniqueness, of China, and thus they preferred not to put the study of China into a comparative context. Students of comparative communism also found Maoism to be distinctive, if not peculiar, and hence China was not treated as a part of their central concerns. For all these reasons China was not included in comparative studies at a time when nationalism and modernization were popular subjects in political science.

Now as we examine in greater detail the themes of nationalism and modernization with respect to China it becomes apparent that perhaps there were deeper and more fundamental reasons why China did not fit the general pattern and thus why it required special treatment. Elsewhere in the post-colonial world, nationalism and modernization were reinforcing forces, but in China they have been essentially antagonistic forces. Elsewhere the articulators of nationalism were the most modernized people in the country. Westernized intellectuals were the group who gave voice to the new ideals of independence and nationalism. The anti-colonial leaders of South and Southeast Asia and of Africa were people like Gandhi, Nehru, Nkrumah and Sukarno, who were at home in both the modern world and their respective traditional cultures. They had acquired out of their own life experiences a vivid sense of the challenge of combining modern and traditional practices.

In contrast, in China, political power — and hence the advantaged position for shaping nationalism — was never firmly in the hands of the best educated or the most modernized people. Those who have held supreme political power in mainland China have reflected mainly the cultures of interior China, and few have experienced deep immersion in the modern world or even spoken a foreign language. Whereas, elsewhere, the most modernized people were accepted as appropriate spokespersons for the nationalistic ideals of the society, in China they generally were suspected as being less than fully 'Chinese'. Thus from the Boxer rebellion to the latest 'anti-spiritual pollution' campaign, the Chinese political class has routinely treated modern, Western-educated Chinese as being tainted, flawed people, unworthy of being leaders of Chinese nationalism. It is true that Sun Yat-sen was Western trained and members of the Soong family were politically influential in the 1940s, but these and a few others were the odd exceptions to the general rule that China's political class contained few modernized people — especially when compared to the nationalist leaderships in the former colonial countries.

The story becomes even more complex because of the distinctive Chinese ways of thinking about the relationship between China's cultural legacy and the goals of modernization. Unlike in other countries, many Chinese intellectuals have at times adopted a totally hostile view toward their own great traditional culture, calling for the complete rejection of the past and a boundless adoption of Western culture. From the May Fourth Movement of three-quarters of a century ago through the Maoist years to the television program 'River Elegy' (*He shang*), there have been repeated attacks on

China's cultural heritage. The motives, of course, varied and the visions of what the new 'modern' culture should entail also have differed. There have been times, too, when other leaders, and particularly some intellectuals, have gone to the opposite extreme and tried to idealize Chinese traditions. But what was idealized was not the realities of the living Chinese mass culture; it was abstractions of a romanticized past. Thus, between the two extremes of either nihilistically denouncing Chinese civilization or romanticizing it, most Chinese intellectuals and political leaders have consistently failed to do what their counterparts in the rest of the developing world have tried to do, which was to create a new sense of nationalism that would combine elements of tradition with appropriate features of the modern world culture.

The Chinese difference stems in large part, I believe, from the fact that China's response to the West was quite distinctive and fundamentally different from those of most African and Asian countries which experienced European colonial rule. The parting in the road became clear in the developments after 1949. In fact, Western scholars such as Joseph Levinson and Mary Wright, who were writing mainly against the backdrop of pre-1949 China, described the problem of Chinese nationalism in terms very much like those commonly used later relating to the issues of tradition, modernization and nationalism in the post-colonial countries. However, the differences between China and the rest of the developing world cannot be seen as solely the consequences of China's commitment to Leninism. They had their seeds in the distinctive circumstances of China's initial exposure to the forces of the modern world of nation-states. China's initial contacts with the West set in motion a distinctive history because it led to the unique treaty port system. This system was remarkably effective in helping to modernize significant segments of Chinese society but it also sharpened the distinctions between coastal China (including Hankow on the Yangtze) and interior China, thereby intensifying the tensions between nationalism and modernization. The differences between the treaty port system and the various forms of colonial rule elsewhere thus had a lasting effect in making the Chinese experience with modernization distinct.

Treaty Ports and Colonies: A Fundamental Difference

The system for managing trade and intercultural relations which evolved out of the treaty ports along coastal China was indeed quite different from what took place elsewhere under direct and even indirect colonial rule. The differences have been obscured largely because Chinese spokespeople of all ideological persuasions have insisted ever since the 1920s that China suffered from imperialism in the same way as did all the other colonial countries of Asia and Africa. Yet there was in fact a tremendous difference. Elsewhere, colonial rule involved complex human interactions as modernizing natives engaged in intense and direct personal relationships with representatives of the colonizing country. Indians, for example, knew what Englishmen were like and therefore colonialism was not an abstraction. The relationship was a psychologically complex love-hate affair. The Chinese, however, generally had little direct contact with the 'imperialists', and therefore for them the threat of foreign penetration and the evils of the 'unequal treaties' were abstractions. The psychology was thus totally different.

There is no reason to doubt the genuineness of Chinese feelings of humiliation; indeed, the Chinese may have had more grievances than people who are fully colonialized. Yet, the objective fact remains that China did have a distinct history with respect to the challenge of becoming a modern nation-state. While it is true that there were variations in the forms of the direct and indirect colonial rule from country to country, the treaty system which emerged out of the cultural and power clashes between China and the West was still unique. (Japan and Turkey did experience the constraints of extra-territoriality, but only for a brief period, and hence they were in no way comparable to the Chinese experience.)

John K. Fairbank in his pioneering work detailed the early story of the creation of the treaty port system. He traced what he called 'the compromise between China and the West', which produced, in his coined word, a 'synarchy', in which there was 'a joint Chinese and Western administration of the modern centers of Chinese life and trade in the treaty ports'.[4] Unfortunately, other scholars did not follow the path Fairbank charted when he suggested that China's experiences were unique. Instead the general tendency has been either to try to fit the subsequent history of Chinese developments into the Procrustean beds of various theories of imperialism or to dismiss the significance of the Western impact entirely and to emphasize domestic developments as autonomous forces in China's modernization attempts.

The fundamental and lasting effect of the treaty port system was that it provided vivid and all-too-concrete evidence of the weaknesses of Chinese political rule and the apparent merits of foreign rule. The huge mass population of interior China were cursed with the incompetence, inefficiency and corruption of government by warlords, while in the enclaves there was an environment where Chinese could prosper and realize the spirit of modern life. The Chinese who went to the enclaves had undeniably voted with their feet in favour of foreign rule over Chinese rule. Interior China was thus seen as the real China, but it was a flawed and, in modern terms, a disgraced China. For the Chinese in the enclaves there was an inescapable sense of guilt as they became more nationalistically conscious. For the Chinese of the interior there was shame and humiliation as they became more conscious of modernization.

This was quite different from the colonial world in which there were no options between foreign and native rule and where the contrast was between the realities of colonial rule and the utopian ideal of independence. Nationalist leaders there could articulate ideals that would combine the best of their

---

[4] John K. Fairbank, *Trade and Diplomacy on the China Coast* (Harvard University Press, Cambridge, 1953; paperback edition Stanford University Press, 1969), p.462.

historical traditions with the best that the West had to offer. The awakening of political consciousness was thus an act of linking nationalism and modernization. Colonial rule, especially in its terminal phase, was designed so that power would flow naturally to those with modern knowledge and skills. From India to Indonesia, from Burma to the Philippines, and throughout Africa, people, by becoming in their own lives more modern, were also becoming the acknowledged champions of nationalism. There were often competing career paths between the political leaders in the nationalist movements and the modern-trained administrators — in India, for example, between the Westernized leaders of the Congress Party and the Indian Civil Service — but the two channels were essentially complementary in rendering nationalism compatible with modernization.

The spirit of nationalism that grew out of the anti-colonial movements was extremely idealistic, so that after a few years of independence there were profound reactions of disillusionment and cynicism in country after country in the Third World. It is also true that many of the modernized spokespeople for the new nationalisms of the emerging nations failed to successfully integrate the symbols and ideals of their traditional cultures and their new national aspirations, so that when their countries ran into difficulties the new spirit of nationalism collapsed and ethnic tribalism came to dominate politics. This phenomenon serves, however, to reinforce the major point that it is necessary to recognize the distinction between real nationalism and primordial sentiments.

In China it was the environment of the treaty ports which produced the most successful communities of modernizing Chinese, but since they consisted of people who had chosen foreign rule over Chinese rule they were not accepted as articulators of Chinese nationalism. The roots of the tension about nationalism in China can thus be largely traced back to the treaty port system, which helped create the division between the enclave cultures of coastal China, which gave dynamism to the country's modernization, and an interior China, with its claim of being the authentic China. This profound division has had enormous consequences in dictating what has been legitimate in the articulation of Chinese nationalism. The divide has fuelled decades of suspicion that modern, cosmopolitan ways are a threat to China's national spirit. It helped create the belief that intelligent Westernized Chinese were somehow less patriotic, less worthy representatives of their country than the more parochial people of interior China. All of this was especially unfortunate because it rested upon a serious misunderstanding about the realities of Chinese life in the enclaves.

The Maligned Treaty-Port Chinese

For a number of reasons, a huge body of myths and half-truths has grown up about the social, intellectual, economic and cultural nature of the treaty ports, which has conspired to minimize the remarkable achievements of the treaty-port Chinese and to exaggerate the importance of the foreigners' role in what was accomplished in the enclaves. In the understandable efforts of Chinese to express their frustrations about their sense of humiliation, a picture was created of the treaty ports as sordid, immoral cities — squalid places that needed, as the conquering Communists certainly believed, to be totally cleaned out and brought into line with the standards of life in interior China. Western scholars have contributed to this maligning of the treaty-port culture. Some have idealized uncontaminated Chinese culture and heaped scorn on the spread of Western practices and values. Others have suggested that something 'went wrong' because the treaty ports failed to modernize all of China — something some people thought interior China under Mao was going to be able to do.

The conventional picture that has emerged out of this image-making has, ironically, created caricatures which shamefully deprecated the worth of Chinese and grossly magnified the influence of Westerners. The Chinese in the treaty ports were depicted as either starving beggars or foppish playboys, denizens of unlimited brothels and night clubs. If the number of prostitutes conventionally quoted for the city was correct, it would have implausibly meant that one-tenth of the women of Shanghai were whores. It is true that Shanghai did have a well-established criminal underworld, including the notorious Green Gang, whose influence extended into the realm of Chinese politics. This was in part because, as Frederic Wakeman has noted, 'What made Shanghai special, and more like Chicago than Calcutta, was the Chinese equivalent of boot-legging during Prohibition: refining and selling narcotics during a period when the national government, with the co-operation of the League of Nations, was ostensibly trying to suppress opium addiction'.[5]

The foreigners supposedly lorded it over all Chinese and presumably had no social contacts with the natives. One might get the impression from the myths that there were no Chinese living in the concessions. Fred C. Shapiro, writing in *The New Yorker* and reacting against the efforts of the current policies of the People's Republic to try to segregate foreigners and Chinese in government-run stores and hotels, repeats the false propaganda of the Communists that '. . . the only Chinese admitted into their precincts [that is, the concessions] were laborers, clerks, and servants'.[6] This would suggest that the tens, indeed hundreds of thousands of middle and upper-class Chinese simply did not exist. The myth of 'foreigners only' would deny as insignificant the largest concentrations of Chinese professional people in the country — including a multitude of journalists, writers, lawyers, academics and doctors, to say nothing of merchants and bankers. The picture of enclaves of foreigners misses the fundamental fact that Shanghai and all the lesser treaty cities running from Tianjin to Canton were essentially Chinese cities. I

---

[5]   Frederic Wakeman, Jr., 'Policing Modern Shanghai', *The China Quarterly*, no.115 (September 1988), p.416.

[6]   Fred C. Shapiro, 'Report from China', *The New Yorker*, 12 October 1990, p.80.

have yet to find a single foreigner who attended the Shanghai American School in the 1930s who did not grow up in the French Concession or the International Settlement surrounded by middle-class Chinese families. In the Tianjin British Concession it was almost impossible not to have Chinese neighbours. The myth of the treaty ports as purely foreign settlements as late as the 1920s and 1930s was inspired by political propaganda. Indeed, the leftist picture of treaty-port society was largely drafted out of the doctrines of Leninist imperialism in which international capitalism dominated the 'colonies and semi-colonies', and the national bourgeoisie were ineffectual actors. Today when Marxist-Leninist theories are widely discredited around the world, it is time to look at Chinese developments through lenses other than those provided by that paradigm. The failure of Leninism calls for a re-evaluation of the stereotypes produced by Leninist theories.

As a result of these myths and half-truths most people have forgotten, or were never aware, that between the two world wars Shanghai was the most sophisticated and the most cosmopolitan city in all of Asia. Shanghai's pre-eminence was based on much more than just its dominant role in international finance and trade. In the artistic and cultural realms Shanghai stood out above all other Asian cities. Tokyo at the time was in the grip of its single-minded military rulers; Manila was more like country club America; Batavia, Hanoi, Singapore and Rangoon were all sleepy colonial administrative centres; only Calcutta had much intellectual life, but it fell far short of what was taking place in Shanghai. Large audiences of Chinese attracted to Asia the leading concert performers of Europe and America, who then might or might not go on to other Asian cities. Hollywood films went first to the Odeon in Shanghai before being sent on to Tokyo and to the other leading Asian cities. The Shanghai Conservatory founded in 1928 began training international-class musicians in the 1930s. In one year the Commercial Press published more titles than did the entire American publishing industry. (There is no way of telling how many of the books were pirated.) Shanghai had more newspapers than any other Asian city. There were also numerous sophisticated journals and magazines including, for example, the *Dongfang zazhi* [The Far Eastern Miscellany], which was an interesting combination of the *Atlantic Monthly* and *Time* magazine. Shanghai was second to none in the size of its community of writers and artists and intellectuals.

It is therefore wrong to think of the treaty ports as the product of foreign efforts. Shanghai's remarkable accomplishments, like Hong Kong's equally impressive achievements in the post-World War II period, came almost entirely from its hard-working, creative, talented middle-class Chinese. As Marie-Claire Bergère has been arguing for years, it was in Shanghai that China started its 'apprenticeship in modernity' and created between 1900 and 1930 a new 'civilization of the coast' composed of a steadily growing middle class.[7] During the interwar period, an 'enterprising cosmopolitan urban society blossomed in Shanghai; it was a new Chinese society. For Shanghai very obviously was Chinese'. Much of the dynamism did come from commerce and other economic activities, which produced a new 'generation of businessmen and industrialists that included such men as H. Y. Moh, C. C. Nieh, the Chien brothers and the bankers K. P. Chen and Chiang Kia-Ngau'. Whereas, as Bergère points out, in interior China 'anarchy remained the only alternative to orthodoxy', in Shanghai 'the bridgehead of world civilization was also an outpost of unorthodox China for whom modernization was only the most recent heresy'.[8]

The foreign population of Shanghai was never as large as the myth made it. It was only after the successes of the treaty-port Chinese in creating their modernizing societies that the foreign populations grew. In 1865 there were 55,465 Chinese and only 460 foreigners living in the French Concession.[9] The foreign population of Shanghai reached a high point of less than 60,000 in the 1930s, but this was because the city became an asylum for refugees, first for about 15,000 White Russians and then some 5,000 German and Austrian Jews fleeing Hitler. Another 20,000 residents were Japanese. There were, however, less than 9,000 British, some 4,000 Americans and 2,500 French — a total of less than 15,500 of the nationals who were thought to dominate Shanghai.[10] Living with these foreigners in the International Settlement and the French Concession were nearly one and a half million Chinese, and in the surrounding urban area another four million Chinese. The Hong Kong of today has a higher proportion of foreigners and foreign capital investment to Chinese than Shanghai had in the 1920s and 1930s, and anyone who knows Hong Kong knows that it is a product of Chinese genius.

Although it is true that the various treaty-port concessions were administered at the top by foreigners, the actual management of most of the day-to-day affairs of government was in Chinese hands. As late as 1875 there were only 23 French in the administration of the French Concession. By the 1930s Shanghai had less than 500 British administrators and police officials, who presided over a civil service that was essentially Chinese, and only some 100 to 150 French worked in the administration of their concession. In all of

---

7   See such works of hers as ' "The Other China": Shanghai from 1919 to 1949', in Christopher Howe (ed.), *Shanghai: Revolution and Development in an Asian Metropolis* (Cambridge University Press, Cambridge, 1981). The quotations are from Gregor Benton's review of *La Chine au XXe Siecle*, edited by Marie-Claire Bergère, Lucien Bianco and Jurgen Domes, *The China Quarterly*, no.122 (June 1990), p.318.

8   Bergère, '"The Other China"', pp.9, 13, 14.

9   Betty Peh-ti Wei, *Shanghai: Crucible of Modern China* (Oxford University Press, Hong Kong, 1987), pp.67-8.

10   Rhoads Murphey, *Shanghai: Key to Modern China* (Harvard University Press, Cambridge, 1953), p.23.

the other treaty ports, Chinese personnel were critical for the smooth and orderly running of affairs.

The Chinese population of Shanghai constituted a genuine society that was forging a distinctive lifestyle that was both modern and Chinese. The large middle class was composed of families that were rearing children who could successfully operate in the modern world while also appreciating Chinese traditions. There thus emerged a distinctive and powerful Shanghai culture. It was this culture, as Lynn Pan has pointed out, which produced such outstanding people as An Wang and I. M. Pei (and Yo-yo Ma, born abroad to a Shanghaiese family).[11] The propaganda attacks against Shanghai have sought to depict as decadent a pattern of social life that revolved around regular tea dances, racetrack meetings, and movies and concerts. But these were the pleasures of a people who were engaged in the historically important task of creating a modern, dynamic community of Chinese who could with dignity be a part of the modern world. It is probably safe to say that there never has been another place in which more Chinese lived a middle-class lifestyle in single-family houses than in the French Concession during that period.

The Shanghai schools took the lead in the transition from the traditional Chinese *belles lettres* emphasis to applied modern knowledge. Middle-school graduates were trained in mathematics up through calculus. Shanghai and the treaty ports in general produced a grossly disproportionate number of China's engineers and diplomats. Even today a high proportion of the technocrats throughout China have a Shanghai background.

The political and psychological significance of the presence of Western power cannot be denied. There was the US Asiatic Fleet with its Yangtze Patrol, and there were the legation guards in Beijing. Nevertheless, while in no way dismissing the Western imperial impact or whitewashing the actions of Western governments, the fact remains that in coastal China there did develop a significant community of modern Chinese who were totally at home in international ways — and who accomplished much for which the Chinese should take pride. I write this in full recognition that the standard view has been to dismiss the treaty-port Chinese as historically insignificant people — in R. H. Tawney's phrase, 'a fringe stitched along the hem of an ancient garment'.[12] The conventional view (vigorously stated by, for example, Rhoads Murphey) was that the treaty ports were 'failures', that interior China 'successfully' warded off the West, and that Mao Zedong proved that peasant China was the real future of the country.[13] It is conventional from this point of

---

[11] Lynn Pan, *Sons of the Yellow Emperor* (Little Brown, Boston, 1990), pp.281-2.

[12] R. H. Tawney, *Land and Labor in China* (London, 1932), p.13, quoted in Rhoads Murphey, *The Outsiders: The Western Experience in India and China* (University of Michigan Press, Ann Arbor, 1977), p.1.

[13] Rhoads Murphey, *The Treaty Ports and China's Modernization: What Went Wrong?* (University of Michigan Centre for Chinese Studies, Ann Arbor, 1970).

view to say that the crisis of twentieth-century China entailed a need to ward off foreign encroachment and the threat of imperialism. Yet to the extent that this was a key problem, it could be argued that the rising middle class of the treaty ports in fact comprised China's most successful defenders against 'imperialism'. These communities of talented people demonstrated that Chinese could take on 'international capitalism' and excel in modern activities to the point of blunting any threat. What they were doing in the prewar era was exactly what Chinese have accomplished in the postwar years in Taiwan, Singapore and Hong Kong.

Some modern Chinese writers are beginning to appreciate the remarkable accomplishments of the treaty-port Chinese. For example, Lynn Pan, in her interesting study of the Overseas Chinese, notes that 'Treaty-port Chinese were those who succeeded in becoming truly bicultural, behaving in a Western mode without a debasement of their own', and that 'The treaty-port Chinese were better able to do that difficult thing, snap the tough thread of Chinese history and achieve the happy balance which has always eluded their cousins in China: the balance between modernity and Chineseness, between moving with the times and remaining themselves'.[14]

The accomplishments of the Shanghaiese involved far more than just creating a new lifestyle. They built the foundations for many very substantial industrial enterprises which have been remarkably enduring. During the Nationalist period, for a decade from 1927 until the Japanese occupation in 1937, the Nanking government constantly put the squeeze on the Shanghai capitalists.[15] After the establishment of the People's Republic the phenomenon of Shanghai as an economic powerhouse but a political weakling continued. In spite of the flood of refugee capitalists who left Shanghai to help energize Hong Kong's economic miracle, the Shanghai economy they had created continued to serve as the motor force of the PRC economy. For more than forty years Shanghai has been the main source for technical, administrative, and diplomatic talent for the People's Republic. Even though Shanghai has had to dispatch to the rest of China more than two million of its most skilled people, it has remained the work-horse of the Chinese economy, providing during the first decades of the PRC nearly one-half of the funds of the national

---

14   Pan, *Sons of the Yellow Emperor*, pp.373-4.

15   There has been a long debate among historians about the relationship between the Kuomintang government and the Shanghai capitalists. The left has generally perceived an alliance between the two. Others have seen a much more complex relationship in which the autonomous state squeezed the capitalists for its own interests. Thus Parks M. Coble, Jr. writes that, '. . . relations between the two groups were characterized by government efforts to emasculate politically the urban capitalists and to milk the modern sector of the economy. Concern with revenue, not the welfare of the capitalists or the possibility of economic development, dominated Nanking's policies . . . The capitalists were stymied as a political force and, by 1937, had become an adjunct of the government.' *The Shanghai Capitalists and the Nanking Government, 1927-1937* (Harvard University Council on East Asian Studies, Cambridge, 1986), p.3.

government. As late as 1985 Shanghai was still being exploited, to the extent that it had to contribute between 85 and 86 per cent of its revenue to the central government.[16] During these forty years Shanghai received almost no replenishments of capital, but it has been strong enough to keep on helping the rest of China. It was not until 1994 that the leadership in Beijing began helping Shanghai once again to become a leader in its competition with Guangdong by putting resources into the 'New Pudong' project.

In retrospect it is surprising that it could once have been said that what took place in Shanghai was the exploitation of China. If that was exploitation, it is a pity that there was not more of it throughout China. From today's perspective, it is astonishing that the talented, successful Chinese of coastal China were made to feel that they were somehow flawed people, no longer real Chinese. Worse still, they were made to feel that they could prove their *bona fides* as loyal Chinese only by deferring to a political class that had its roots in parochial, interior China. Successful entrepreneurs and industrialists generally developed an apolitical mentality, as they concentrated their attention on their private enterprises and minimized their involvement in the nation's business. As a result, the social and economic achievements of these treaty-port Chinese were circumscribed, and China did not develop even the beginnings of a true civil society. For all of their accomplishments, these modernized Chinese could not produce a nascent establishment which could represent society's interests and serve as a disciplining check on China's parochial political leaders.

At best, as Mark Elvin has shown, these middle-class Chinese did often perform at the local level as an establishment in support of governmental services. In quiet, inconspicuous ways they could at times act to improve local urban governments, but in terms of national politics and the task of creating a sense of nationhood, they were essentially impotent.

The Treachery of the Intellectuals

Thus, for all their successes as modernizers, the treaty-port Chinese could not create the bases for a more pluralistic civil society for the country as a whole. Nor could they contribute much to the defining of a new sense of modern Chinese nationalism. One important reason was that the intellectuals, who had also sought out the security of the treaty ports, chose to contribute to the myths about the decadence of the treaty-port Chinese. Many of these modernizing intellectuals, mainly the writers, had adopted quasi-Leninist views about the treaty ports being the evil work of international capitalism.

Indeed, it was profoundly significant for the modernization of China that most of these writers expressed strong antipathies to both traditional Chinese culture and the lifestyle of the most modernized Chinese of the enclaves. They themselves easily became certified as modern thinkers and radicals simply by

---

[16]   Wei, *Shanghai: Crucible of Modern China*, p.266.

attacking features of the traditional family system, including arranged marriages, concubinage, and the patriarchal authority of the father. At the same time, they caricatured the middle-class society of coastal China. Almost all of these writers lived in Shanghai or other foreign concessions. They had thus voted with their feet in favour of foreign rule. As a result, they seemingly shared some deep psychological feelings of guilt and shame over abandoning Chinese culture. Hence the issues of modernization were particularly troublesome for them. By their actions they were saying that so-called 'imperialism' was preferable to living under a Chinese government. To reduce their feelings of guilt they had to attack all they saw as being associated with 'imperialism' and praise what they wanted to believe was the revolutionary spirit of mistreated workers and peasants. Typical of the populism of the intellectuals was the advice of Li Dazhao, a founder of the Communist Party, to his students to 'leave the "corrupting life" of the cities and universities and "go to the villages . . ." and the "wholly human life" of the countryside'.[17]

By this simple-minded formula of denouncing two abstractions, 'imperialism' and 'feudal practices', leftist Chinese writers were able to avoid engaging in honest introspection so as to confront the hard psychological issues of cultural change. It is quite clear in the short stories that Harold Isaacs collected in *Straw Sandals* that the most famous of the left-wing authors had little sympathy for the culture being created by the successful Chinese of enclave China, even though they themselves knew that world better than the peasant world of interior China which they generally idealized. In reading many of their short stories today, one is struck with how the characters are little more than stereotypes of the Marxist-Leninist categories of good and bad people. There are the all-powerful but heartless foreigners representing imperialism, the pathetic Chinese lackies of the foreigners who are enamoured of all things Western, and, of course, the exploited but virtuous workers and peasants. Ba Jin, in one of his short stories, portrays a Chinese who was envious even of the life of a foreigner's dog.[18] Even Lu Xun, who found all manner of flaws in his fellow Chinese, was moved to write about how a lowly rickshaw puller showed more human compassion and generosity of spirit than he, Lu Xun, had shown in an accident in which a rickshaw hit an old woman.[19] Content with their superficial politicized fiction, no Chinese writer, except arguably Lu Xun, came close to matching the rich human understanding and the complex subjective worlds that were explored by Indian, Japanese and even Malay and Indonesian writers.

---

[17]   Maurice Meisner, 'Leninism and Maoism: Some Populist Perspectives on Marxism-Leninism in China', *The China Quarterly*, no.45 (1971), p.17; quoted in Murphey, *The Outsiders*, p.229.

[18]   Nathan K. Mao, *Pa Chin* (Twayne Publishers, Boston, 1987), pp.67-9.

[19]   'A Small Incident', *The Complete Stories of Lu Xun*, translated by Yang Xianyi and Gladys Yang (Indiana University Press, Bloomington, 1981), pp.36-8.

The propaganda theme of the political left that the treaty-port Chinese were decadent, spiritually polluted people was also graphically depicted in numerous Chinese films of the 1930s. Paul Pickowicz has reviewed some of the most popular of those films and shown how they consistently attacked the moral character of the most modernized Chinese.[20] *Peach Blossom Weeps Tears of Blood* was a simple morality play about a rich city boy falling in love with a poor but virtuous peasant girl; he takes her to the city with promises of marriage, gets her pregnant, but then his family blocks the marriage and so her father has to take her home, where she dies in childbirth. Pickowicz notes that:

> The helpless young woman is China. Her innocent and childlike beauty is natural . . . The slick young man recognizes her Chinese virtues and the uniqueness of her beauty. 'A city girl's beauty', he observes, 'depends on powder and rouge'. Yet, when he takes her to the city, she begins to wear fashionable clothes and to use makeup. When they first meet in the wholesome village environment, he declares, 'How chaste and beautiful! You can never find such in the city!' But, in the end, he seduces and corrupts the virgin.[21]

In *A Dream in Pink*, a writer becomes the example of the moral decline of Shanghai life. His wife is a pure and virtuous rural girl, a loyal and obedient wife, and a devoted mother. The writer, however, seeks out 'life in Shanghai's glittering entertainment quarters', meets a glamorous night-club girl who 'uses make up, smokes cigarettes, drinks alcohol, dances to Western music, and wears new-style clothing that exposes her breasts'. The writer falls for her and divorces his wife, who is 'quite literally left with nothing, on a cold, snowy street'.[22] But then the night-club girl gets bored and returns to her night life and to new lovers. In the end the writer is saved by his former wife's 'offer to forgive and forget'.

In *The Queen of Sports*, a girl from a rural family is sent to a special school for female athletes where she is quickly spoiled by success as a runner. 'She becomes arrogant, neglects her studies, applies makeup, wears fancy clothes, and begins to fraternize with slick, Westernized college lads who seem to spend all of their time smoking, drinking, dancing, and fornicating'. However, 'After seeing a classmate die following a gruelling race, she decides that the pursuit of individual [namely bourgeois] glory is wrong, gives up her title as "Queen of Sport" and resolves to serve others as an ordinary teacher of physical education'.[23]

A Bible for Daughters, with the scenario written by veteran Communist Party members, shows the tenth reunion of a class of women who have succumbed to the corrupt and debauched ways of Shanghai. Each in their own

---

20   Paul G. Pickowicz, 'The Theme of Spiritual Pollution in Chinese Films of the 1930s', *Modern China*, vol.17, no.1 (January 1991), pp.38-75.

21   Ibid., p.43.

22   Ibid., p.46.

23   Ibid., p.50.

way has lost the virtues of interior China, including one who was a feminist and leader of the women's movement but is now a loose modern woman with a string of lovers.

Other films, such as *Filial Piety, Little Angel, The Pioneers* and *Children of Troubled Times*, carried on the theme of the evils of the treaty-port people who were ruined by Western spiritual pollution. Rural, interior China in contrast was always shown as upholding purity and virtue. The puritanism of the Mao era and the morality of a Lei Feng were well established by the leftists, largely Communists, of the Chinese film industry long before the People's Republic imposed such simple-minded, black and white morality on all of China. Although in all industrializing countries there have been the conventions of praising the 'old values' of the rural society and seeing the city as a source of sin, the Chinese in the 1930s carried the theme to absurd lengths — because of the problem of the treaty ports being the focus of modernization. How troublesome the problem was can be seen from the fact that although the tradition of Chinese morality was always moderation and the Confucian golden mean, on this issue there was extremism. In attacking the modern lifestyle of the treaty ports there were no limits on exaggeration.

By dismissing the achievements of the treaty-port Chinese, the left-wing writers and film makers had no autonomous positions of their own from which to help shape the spirit of Chinese nationalism. Instead, their ideological commitments made them easy servants of a Leninist party. After the Japanese invasion, the majority, who identified with the Communists, were already psychologically prepared to accept the dictates of Mao Zedong's Yanan Forum speech in which he made it unambiguously clear that intellectuals were to obey the Party line and not seek individual creativity. Liu Binyan has described how his first experience on joining the Party was to learn that the 'original sin' was individualism as embodied in 'bourgeois ideologies', and hence one must oppose all that enclave China represented.[24]

There is no need to dwell on the sad story of how Chinese intellectuals lost their voice in post-1949 China. From the Anti-Rightist Campaign of 1957 through the Cultural Revolution and down to the contemporary attacks on 'spiritual pollution', Chinese intellectuals have had to defer to a version of Chinese nationalism that was hostile to coastal China and its values.

Chinese Values and Foreign Knowledge

The sad fate of the left-wing writers does not, of course, encompass the whole story of China's intellectuals, for there have also been those who gained foreign technical knowledge and modern scientific skills. Indeed, from the time of the 1898 reform effort through the May Fourth Movement and down to the Four Modernizations of the post-Mao period, a constant theme has been the importance of science and technology for creating China's wealth and

---

[24]   Liu Binyan, *A Higher Kind of Loyalty* (Pantheon Books, New York, 1990), ch. 2.

power. It is a theme which might have united nationalism and modernization, as happened in the former colonial countries. It is true, as in other spheres of life, that Chinese as individuals have demonstrated remarkable abilities to excel in modern science and technology. However, the political leaders, as guardians of Chinese nationalism, have had an easy time checking the influence of such modern-trained technocrats.

The formula for depoliticizing those with specialized knowledge goes back to the early Chinese formulation of a division between Chinese values, which were at the core, and Western technology, which was only useful, merely utilitarian. This division between what the Chinese reformers call *ti* and *yong* set the stage for checking the political power of technically trained people. The rationale of the formulation was that those who specialize in useful knowledge should yield authority to those who claimed to speak for essential Chinese values. Thus, young Chinese might be encouraged to seek out Western knowledge in the scientific and technical fields, but they were also made to understand that they would have to remain subordinate to the articulators of Chinese values. The tension between nationalism and modernization thus became institutionalized.

At the same time, a cap was placed on any dynamic processes for providing form and content to a modernized version of Chinese nationalism. The *ti-yong* formula which identified Chinese values as being of the essence, and hence to be protected against any form of contamination, was also a formula for making what was seen as 'Chinese' into a rigid orthodoxy. Instead of encouraging a dynamic process in which Chinese values could be creatively adapted to modern times, the formula worked to ossify 'Chinese' values.

It is of course one of the great ironies of modern Chinese history that Mao Zedong and the Chinese Communist Party leadership were able to turn the formulation inside out, while keeping its anti-modernist bias. The Confucian ethical values, which the early reformers had identified as being of the Chinese 'essence', were replaced by the foreign import, Marxism-Leninism, which could be strengthened by science and technology, but it was not to be polluted by other foreign or modern values. Mao opened the door to a selective but essentially hostile treatment of Chinese traditional culture. He attacked most of China's traditional culture as being 'feudal legacies', but he acknowledged that some elements of it might be preserved: 'To study the development of this old culture, to reject its feudal dross and assimilate its democratic essence is a necessary condition for developing our new national culture . . . '.[25] But he never specified what should be preserved of the old, aside from praising peasant life. Rather, he stressed that the new culture would be 'opposed . . . to all feudal and superstitious ideas.'[26] Most cadres got the point that it was safest to denounce all aspects of tradition in the light of

[25]   Mao Zedong, 'On New Democracy', *Selected Works of Mao Zedong* (Foreign Language Press, Beijing, 1965), vol.ii, p.381.

[26]   Ibid.

Mao's attack on specific examples of that culture, such as his angry statement about the film *The Life of Wu Hsun*:

> In the view of many writers, history proceeds not by the new superseding the old, but by preserving the old from extinction through all kinds of exertion, not by waging class struggle to overthrow the reactionary feudal rulers who ought to be overthrown, but by negating the class struggle of the oppressed and submitting to these rulers in the manner of Wu Hsun.[27]

The new *ti-yong* formula thus replaced the old version, in which Confucian values were of the 'essence' with Marxism-Leninism-Mao Zedong Thought. The result was still a rigid orthodoxy as the core. Worse still, the core had become only the partisan position of a party and hence there was not even a pretence that it could be the basis of a nationalism that was more than just the slogans of a partisan movement. Thus, over time the *ti-yong* formula has turned out to be a serious liability in China's search for a modernizing nationalism. The idea that it should be possible to separate sharply 'essential' Chinese values from 'utilitarian' modern knowledge has worked against the necessary integrating of the parochial and the cosmopolitan that is absolutely basic to any form of effective modern nationalism. By setting aside certain values as essential and 'Chinese', which must be preserved in uncontaminated form, the spokespersons for the formula have sought to ossify into a static orthodoxy the essential spirit of Chinese cultural identity, and thereby strip it of the dynamic and creative vitality of a living nationalism. A clever intellectual formula turned out to be a spiritually dampening approach.

Forty years of sustained attacks on traditional Chinese culture and the equally vigorous efforts to limit the spread of unacceptable modern ideas, all in the name of Chinese nationalism, has left Chinese nationalism without a substantive core which can be readily articulated. The way Chinese live and bring up their children of course endures, but what is missing in the expression of any substantial form of nationalism are the collective ideals and shared inspirations that can be coherently expressed in meaningful symbols and myths. The ethnic basis of nationalism, a sense of a physical 'we-ness' as against the foreign 'they-ness', remains intact, but there is a void as to the cultural ideals that can provide the substantive content for Chinese nationalism.

All manner of manifestations of ethnic identity, usually referred to as Han chauvinism, continue to endure. It is, for example, easy for Chinese to become passionate about the successes of their sports teams in international competition and to take collective pride in honouring them. Such sentiments, however, cannot provide the basis for a politically effective nationalism that can mobilize public opinion for collective tasks, and, equally important, they fail to place limits and constraints on the actions of the leaders.

---

[27]   Mao Zedong, 'Pay Serious Attention to the Discussion of the Film *The Life of Wu Hsun*', *Selected Works of Mao Zedong* (Foreign Language Press, Beijing, 1977), vol.v, p.57.

For nationalism to develop beyond being merely an expression of ethnic or racial identity, it has to take on a substantive content that can inspire the public while also establishing rules and norms for the behaviour of the leadership. When the content of contemporary Chinese nationalism is compared with other nationalisms, it appears to be exceedingly thin. There is little to compare with the substance of American nationalism with its mystique about the Declaration of Independence, the Constitution, the Bill of Rights, the Pledge of Allegiance, and the whole body of values (many even contradictory ones) that Samuel P. Huntington has called the American Creed — all of which makes it possible to think of some behaviour as being 'un-American'. Similarly, there seems to be no counterpart to the British feelings about the monarchy and parliament and all the norms which made it possible for colonial peoples, such as the Indians, to accuse their British masters of not behaving according to British ideals. It is impossible to imagine a Tibetan expecting to influence the conduct of a Chinese official by saying he was not acting according to Han ideals.

Deng Xiaoping spoke of the goal of 'Building Socialism With Chinese Characteristics', but he had trouble identifying those characteristics, which is further evidence of the problem of a lack of content in Chinese nationalism. The Party Central Committee journal *Qiushi* published a significant editorial providing the official view about the content of Chinese patriotism in the wake of Tiananmen, which stated that:

> Patriotism is history-specific, having different contents under different historical circumstances. Today, if we want to be patriotic, we should love the socialist New China under the leadership of the Communist Party. As was pointed out by Comrade Deng Xiaoping in one of his speeches in 1981, 'Some people say that not loving socialism is not the same thing as not loving our motherland. Is motherland an abstract concept? If you do not love the socialist New China led by the Communist Party, what else can you love? With regard to patriotic compatriots in Hong Kong, Macao, Taiwan, and other overseas areas, we should not expect them all to approve of socialism. But the least they can do is not oppose the socialist New China. Otherwise, how can they call themselves patriotic? When it comes to every citizen and every youth inside the People's Republic of China, we naturally have higher expectations.'[28]

This authoritative statement by Deng Xiaoping makes it absolutely clear that modernized Chinese cannot legitimately criticize Chinese government policies without being accused of being unpatriotic.

Ming Lizhi, a member of the Propaganda Department of the Central Committee, went further in the same issue of *Qiushi* in insisting on the 'unification of patriotism and socialism' when he wrote, 'In his National Day speech of 1989, Comrade Jiang Zemin pointed out in summarizing the basic

---

28   'Give Full Play to the Patriotism of the Youths of the May Fourth Movement', *Qiushi*, no.9 (1990), pp.8-9.

experiences of the past forty years of the new China: "In China today, patriotism and socialism are unified in essence." '[29] Ming went on to say:

> Patriotism is the premise of China's socialism and socialism is the inevitable conclusion of genuine patriotism. Li Dazhao, Mao Zedong, Zhou Enlai, Liu Shaoqi, Zhu De, Qu Qiubai, Dong Biwu, Wu Yuzhang, and some others of the first generation of the proletarian revolutionaries all underwent an historical transformation from being patriots to being steadfast socialists. They provided concrete and vivid examples of the unification of patriotism and socialism in China.[30]

Chinese scholars who support the proposal that 'Building Socialism With Chinese Characteristics' calls for a 'form of socialism that fits Chinese conditions' have defined such conditions as 'a backward economy, a poor infrastructure, overpopulation, limited arable land, a long history of feudalism, and a continued threat of imperialism which includes now the danger of bourgeois liberalization and a tendency to worship the West' — all of which are then said to call for a kind of socialism that '. . . promotes productivity as the main task, strengthens a socialist planned commodity economy, sticks to public ownership as the leading force but promotes alternative forms of ownership, and the other features of current official policies'.[31] Such a list provides little substance for defining Chinese nationalism. In no country should nationalism be reduced to merely the sum of current policy preferences. The ideals of nationalism with all of its myths and symbols should have their own domain, well above the arena of contemporary policy programs.

The Search for a New Identity

For much of the twentieth century, variations of the *ti-yong* formulation were assumed to provide a basis for defining the essence of Chinese nationalism and for identifying the features of modernization to be welcomed. But now there is a growing crisis. The formula at one time appeared to provide an objective, straightforward way for achieving both national development and modernization in a manner that could spare the Chinese the psychological turmoil common among people in other transitional societies. Paradoxically in China, which has been distinctive in witnessing a fundamental clash between nationalism and modernization, there has until now been relatively little subjective or psychological stress over modernization. Elsewhere in the former colonial world, where there has been objective harmony between the twin goals of nationalism and modernization, there has been more emotional

---

29 Ming Lizhi, 'Insist on the Unification of Patriotism and Socialism', *Qiushi*, no.9 (1990), p.15.

30 Ibid., p.17.

31 *Zhongguo tese de shehui zhuyi* [A Study of Socialism with Chinese Characteristics] (Zhejiang People's Publishing House, China, 1987), pp.14-21.

turmoil and psychological stress as people feel torn between two cultures, and with the intellectuals in particular claiming to be essentially rootless. The Chinese escaped such psychological stress because until the last few years the reminders of the awesome greatness of Chinese civilization were so omnipresent that most Chinese, whether coastal or interior, felt little need to articulate their sense of self-identity. Elsewhere in Asia and Africa, at each step of the way, thinking people felt compelled to define who they were as they went through profound processes of social change.

As the Deng-era reforms began to run into trouble in the late 1980s, there was, quite understandably, rising concern about a 'spiritual crisis', which had already been fuelled by the doubts flowing from the Cultural Revolution. The widespread reactions to the 'River Elegy' television series and the need of part of the leadership to denounce it as boosting nationalistic nihilism, suggest that many Chinese had arrived at a time of soul searching about their national identity and the meaning of modernization. The tightening of controls after Tiananmen did not stop this questioning about Chinese national identity. More articles have been published recently which reflect positive views about the relevance of traditional Chinese cultural values than at any time in the last forty years. In an article entitled 'On Using Traditional Culture as a Wellspring to Build a Socialist New Culture', Zhang Xinhua of the Shanghai Academy of Social Science argues that while much of Confucian thought was 'feudalistic' because it helped to serve the 'advantages of the feudal rulers', it also had 'its positive aspects [which] still contain much value for building culture, that should be regarded as an important resource for building a socialist new culture'.[32] Most of the positive features of Confucianism turn out, however, to be essentially versions of modern values. Yet there are signs of greater appreciation of the value of the cultural legacy which the Party has so relentlessly attacked for so long. The same Zhang Xinhua also writes:

> A decline of traditional culture often follows any social disorders and the destruction of an old dynasty. Culture is the spiritual pillar of the political structure, the economic system, and social relations; it is the wellspring of social cohesion. The loss of a people's cultural legacy can evoke the destruction of a traditional social structure and a deterioration or loss of national cohesion, leading to social turbulence and confusion. And once traditional culture and social structure undergo turbulence and destruction, a very long time will pass before another stable order can come about. And a new order must be accompanied by the continuity, rebuilding, and flourishing of the traditional culture under new conditions.[33]

There are thus signs among thinking Chinese of a new awareness of the need to try to articulate a more vivid sense of the collective identity of the Chinese people. Because of historical and racial considerations, they have no problem identifying those who belong to the collective 'we' and those who are

---

32   *Shehui kexue* [Social Science], no.3 (15 March 1990), pp.31-47, translated in JTRS-CAR-90-049, 11 July 1990, pp.103-6.

33   Ibid., p.104.

the 'they'. However, beyond this first step in establishing the boundaries of a national identity, the difficulties begin to arise because the historical legacies of Chinese culture have been so harshly attacked for so long. Moreover, those who have been the most successful in creating a modern culture have been equally attacked for being unpatriotic. Now that the ideology which interior China has used to defame coastal China has lost its international respectability and now that Marxism is no longer seen as being at the forefront of history, the Party hagiographers of Chinese nationalism are not sure where to turn to find the essence of a new sense of Chinese nationalism.

The problem is serious because the Chinese state now needs the power of an inspiring form of nationalism as it continues its struggle to modernize. The leadership seems ready to shift from the goal of 'Building Socialism With Chinese Characteristics' to that of 'building China with socialist characteristics', as Roderick MacFarquhar has put it. But the building blocks for a coherent nationalism are missing because the collective symbols and ideals of the culture have been so severely damaged. The rejection of the melding of Chinese nationalism and modernization, which was taking place in prewar coastal China, in favour of the less authentic nationalism based on Leninism has left China without a satisfying sense of either modernization or national pride.

Conclusion: Greatness Gets in the Way of Nationalism

The relationship between the two elusive concepts of nationalism and modernization is peculiarly complex as regards China. It is not easy to separate out what might constitute the essence of Chinese nationalism from the sentiments associated with Chinese ethnicity. It is self-evident that the Chinese people share the same blood, the same physical characteristics, the same ancestry and culture and the same written language, but this alone does not constitute a modern sense of nationalism. In a way these basic ethnic factors seem to be almost too overpowering, too all-embracing, to leave much scope for the formation of a distinct sense of modern nationalism, particularly because at every turn the emergence of the modern spirit has been dismissed as inappropriate to true 'Chineseness' in the eyes of the political leaders who have politically exploited Chinese ethnicity. The massive force of primordial sentiments tends to overwhelm all other possibilities of group identity, and little room is left for sentiments attached to China as a modernizing nation-state.

Put bluntly, the fundamental problem in China's modernization is that China is really a civilization pretending to be a nation-state. The greatness of that civilization is manifest in every aspect of traditional Chinese culture. The enduring strength of the civilization is what has kept China united as a single entity over the centuries. China today is what Europe would have been if the unity of the Roman Empire had lasted until now and there had not been the emergence of the separate entities of England, France, Germany, and the like.

But, of course, it was precisely the breaking up of Europe into separate nation-states that not only gave birth to the distinct phenomenon of nationalism but also produced the phenomenon we call modernization.

As indicated at the outset, nationalism, like modernization seen from a slightly different perspective, has to blend what is distinctive in a nation's culture with what is internationally or universally appreciated. For nationalism is not only the expression of a people's basic inner identity but is also shaped by interactions with other nations as both friend and foe. Unfortunately, those who have for much of this century articulated China's national interests have tended both to despise Chinese folk culture and to see mainly enemies in the outside world. Even before the May Fourth Movement and even more so after the establishment of the People's Republic, Chinese politicians and intellectuals have scorned the living culture of the Chinese masses while praising the 'people' in the abstract. All the aspects of the people's folk culture which should be the elements of a new Chinese nationalism have been denounced as superstition and 'feudal legacies'. All the themes, values, ideals and symbols that are basic to the daily lives and to the yearly cycles of celebrations of the Chinese people have been dismissed or totally ignored by those who claim to be articulating Chinese nationalism.

China's national leaders have in a perverse fashion entangled themselves in a pair of contradictions between their symbolisms and reality: they have idealized 'peasants' in the abstract but scorned their folk culture in practice, while simultaneously proclaiming the goal of modernization but attacking the successfully modernized Chinese. Some people might have thought that the prime responsibility of those who would formulate a dynamic sense of a new Chinese nationalism would have been to integrate and to give emotional content to precisely the two elements of Chinese life that they have dismissed. The task of nationalist politicians elsewhere has indeed been to try to make popular traditions meaningful in the context of modern social standards. Instead, Chinese political leaders have sought to combine two abstractions, their version of 'the masses' and their notion of socialism as being the 'wave of the future', while ignoring both the realities of Chinese popular culture and Chinese successes in modernization.

Why have the Chinese leaders turned their backs on this potential focus for a strong and vital sense of nationalism and instead worked to produce a shallow version of nationalism? As we have seen, the way in which the impact of the modern world came to China in the unique treaty-port system certainly contributed mightily to this development. The difficulty was compounded, however, because the political leaders of interior China needed to find a new basis of legitimacy for their rule to replace the collapsing Confucian system. The alternative they faced was either to encourage the development of competitive politics or to reserve for themselves the right to define a new moral order to replace the Confucian moral order. The first alternative might have resulted in the intermingling of ideas, ideals and concrete interests that could have produced a sense of nationalism that would have had constraining effects on subsequent partisan politics, much as a constitution does in successfully modernizing societies. The political leadership in China from the Republican era to the present could see that until such a strong and disciplining version of nationalism was established, there would be no basis for establishing binding rules for political competition and therefore they feared confusion and disorder. Thus at every turn they have opted for the second alternative, trying to make their partisan political views the basis of the new moral order and to force everyone to accept their views of Chinese nationalism. Fundamentally, each Chinese regime since the fall of the Qing dynasty has sought to re-establish the legitimacy of the Chinese state by formulating a new moral order to replace the Confucian order. In doing so, they have in effect tried to establish an essentially traditional political system rather than advance toward a modern one.

In the traditional Confucian system, government was run by morally superior people who had the responsibility to uphold a social order based on ethical principles. Most traditional societies similarly saw political authority as the defender of a religious-moral order. The process of modernization, however, has usually involved a transition from legitimacy based on a moral order to a political order based on law and responsive to the interactions of political processes, composed of competing interests. Unfortunately, the evolution of China did not include such a transition. Instead there was an attempt to re-establish a moral order, this time based on Marxism-Leninism-Mao Zedong Thought. Again, China was to be ruled by people who claimed to be morally superior people, and any challenge to the orthodoxy of their announced moral order was a direct threat to their legitimacy.[34]

The transition to a system based on the open interplay of political forces has been particularly difficult because Chinese civilization had, as one of its cardinal principles of social behaviour, the absolute rule that people should not assert their own self-interests. Selfishness was seen as an ultimate sin. The result has been that even as Chinese society became more diversified there has been no emergence of pluralistic interests. The successful residents of the treaty ports could not make open demands on the Chinese national government and therefore they never became a significant force in asserting society's modern interests. Whereas elsewhere modernization has given the forces of society a strong basis for checking and influencing the state, in China the state continues to dominate society.

This pattern has had profound consequences for China's political development, and especially for the character of Chinese nationalism. In most modern societies nationalism is a product of the awakened collective consciousness that arises out of the clash of group identities and the balance of forces among competing interests. The effort to define the collective interest, and to relate one's particular interest to it, may evoke the collective memory

---

[34] I have developed this argument in greater detail in 'China: Erratic State, Frustrated Society', *Foreign Affairs*, vol.69, no.4 (Fall 1990), pp.56-74.

and appeal to shared symbols and imagery. In the case of China, however, nationalism has not been forged out of the dynamic of competitive politics; rather, it has been based on the ideals associated with an imposed moral order. This has meant that Chinese nationalism has been almost indistin-guishable from the partisan interests of the rulers. Hence the tendency to see any criticism of current policies as an unpatriotic act.

The story of Chinese nationalism and modernization is thus a sweet-sour one. On the one hand stands the irrefutable evidence that Chinese as individuals can be outstanding successes in the modern world. Culturally and intellectually they have proved, both in the treaty ports and in their overseas communities, that they have no problem with modern careers and professions. On the other hand is the bitter fact that political authority in China has been a constant impediment to the development of a form of Chinese nationalism that can reflect the abilities and the successes of the modernized Chinese as individuals. The Chinese state continues to restrict the development of a civil society, and without such a society China cannot develop the political and social processes which could create the vibrant form of nationalism that is required to modernize a great civilization. Instead, the Chinese state, in trying to uphold a rigid, inflexible orthodoxy as a moral order, has relentlessly attacked both the modernized Chinese and the traditional symbols and ideals of the collective memory of the Chinese people. At the very time when the Chinese state needs the unifying forces of nationalism, there is very little there that can spiritually mobilize the Chinese people.

There is hope, however, that the goal of modernization still remains an agreed-upon objective at all levels of Chinese society. To attain this, eventually it will be necessary to discard the attempt to impose upon the country the orthodoxy of a moral order. The need for a more pluralistic politics will grow stronger. We therefore end with a paradox: Only if the Chinese state can discard its objective of seeking consensus and conformity and allow the disorderliness that comes with competition among the diffuse interests of society will China gain the unifying collective power of a dynamic nationalism. There is also another possibility, and this is that the Age of Nationalism may be passing into history as the homeland of nationalism, Western Europe, progressively lessens national divisions. If this is the way of the future, then perhaps China, with its relatively contentless nationalism, may be a leader and not just trailing behind. The Chinese, however, still seem to be frustrated as they continue on their search for wealth and power, modernization and nation-building. For them, the problem of a more coherent nationalism persists.

FIVE

Openness and Nationalism: Outside the Chinese Revolution

Wang Gungwu

The many slogans that emerged during the Tiananmen demonstrations of 1989 show all too clearly that many articulate Chinese do not see the 1949 Revolution as the culmination of the Chinese Revolution: that is, as the true revolution that followed thirty-eight years after the abortive one in 1911.

The Chinese Communist Party had, off and on, played down the 1911 Revolution as nothing more than a bourgeois nationalist movement that failed to lead to a genuine revolution. Instead, it had preferred to associate itself with the May Fourth movement of 1919 and linked the Party's origins (it was founded soon afterwards) with the movement's initial successes. In contrast, the Nationalist or KMT historians have ignored the 1919 movement and affirmed the 1911 Revolution as the actual beginning of revolution in China. They have always maintained that their party carried the flag for the 1911 Revolution and that this led to the foundation of the Nanjing regime in 1928.

There have been other views, but the two main interpretations are about whether there had been only one revolution — that is, with part one in 1911 and part two either in 1928 or in 1949 — or whether the 1911 Revolution was never a revolution and, therefore, that the only real revolution was the one in 1949.

The Two-Part Revolution

I do not subscribe to the notion that the 1949 Revolution was the only real revolution; I support instead the view that 1911 was part one and 1949 was part two, and that the 1949 Revolution was a most dramatic culmination of the process that had begun in the late 1890s with Sun Yat-sen and his supporters, as a process of restoring China to greatness through radical change, even revolution. The events of 1989 reaffirming the May Fourth movement remind us of a deeper underlying continuity, if only because its slogans have proven to be remarkably appropriate and because so much that had been hoped for at the beginning of this century remains still unaccomplished.

Thus the nationalistic question as to whether greater revolution, change or modernization was achieved outside the Marxist-Leninist-Maoist framework of the 1949 Revolution than inside may be clearer if it is placed in the context of a two-part revolution. That is to say, we should ask what was achieved under the one revolution that started in 1911 and is still going on today; and then compare that with what has been achieved on the mainland since 1949. This is a vast subject. All that can be attempted here is to explore the boundaries of the question.

The Communist leaders of the 1949 Revolution had set high standards of revolution for themselves — standards on a par with the Soviet Union, in their view the most revolutionary society at the time. They even thought themselves capable of by-passing the USSR to create the first communist society. In comparison, what happened in the name of the 1911 Revolution always looked modest, although, in the long run, perhaps no less revolutionary. The question might be worded in another way. Now that we can see that the impossibly high (even romantic) aims of the 1949 Revolution under Mao Zedong have not been attained, could we ask if a smaller revolution, cumulatively a series of little modernizations outside the 1949 Revolution, had not occurred? In particular, we might note the changes that have progressively transformed Chinese communities outside mainland China.

Let me briefly outline the main points which support the view that there has only been one Chinese revolution. In broad terms, the 1911 Revolution was inspired by the American and French revolutions, but from the start lacked the universal elements of both. Sun Yat-sen wanted to overthrow the *ancien regime* and the monarchy, and argued for a republican democracy. To do this by violent means certainly made it a revolution. But there was one major element which made it merely a Chinese revolution, and not part of a world revolution. Sun Yat-sen had to overthrow the Manchus, the non-Han minority who had conquered the Han majority more than 260 years earlier. Indeed, almost all of his supporters were initially more concerned with this factor than with any other. His Triad secret society colleagues thought no further. His literati or intellectual followers helped him raise this goal into a more sophisticated appeal for a modern Chinese nationalism. Only very few understood Sun Yat-sen's wish to establish a republic, an ultimately democratic republic. And although he did have his way, and the republic miraculously survived the machinations of President Yuan Shikai and the warlords who thought of restoring the monarchy, the 1911 Revolution was essentially a nationalist revolution to restore the rule of the Han majority and make China strong and prosperous again. And because the warlord era was chaotic, a precondition of such revolutionary success was for China to be reunified once again.

By the standards of world revolution (whether American or French), much of this would not be rated as revolutionary goals. Only the goal of a democratic republic would qualify, and a modern nationalism that transformed imperial subjects 'scattered like loose sand' (in Sun Yat-sen's words) into a politically conscious citizenry was certainly a necessary step toward the success of such a republic. In short, at the start it was a Chinese revolution and not one defined as revolution for the betterment of the human condition.

Nevertheless, modest though it was, it marked the beginnings of a revolution for China. It did achieve a republic and there was no turning back; after 1918, no further attempt was made at monarchical restoration. But up to 1919, this was a most imperfect republic, far from democratic, not even nationalist, and it did not unite China, least of all make China strong and prosperous. Hence the importance of the May Fourth movement. The Beijing students behind this movement in 1919 began by highlighting new standards of modern nationalism, focusing on anti-imperialism even more strongly than Sun Yat-sen. What was more, they were inspired by a new generation of intellectuals who elaborated on Sun Yat-sen's ideals and articulated them better than he had ever done. Sun Yat-sen had been trained in medicine and believed that China's future depended on advances in science and technology. He also believed in government by the people but stopped short of the universal ideals of 'liberty, equality and fraternity'. Indeed, he had a fatal misunderstanding about China that could be traced to his superficial knowledge of Chinese history. He believed that Chinese society was already free and, indeed, had too much freedom. What China needed instead, he thought, was discipline and a strong government that would curb the dangers of fragmentation and disunity.

During the May Fourth movement, two men, both professors, were outstanding in trying to give new direction to the Chinese revolution, and in trying to make it more revolutionary and less bogged down in mere national revival. The first was Chen Duxiu (educated in Japan), whose most famous statement was a manifesto for 'Science and Democracy'. The second was Hu Shi, educated in the United States, who launched a *baihua* (common language) movement essential for modern nationalism and for both scientific thinking and the democratic spirit. His most outstanding message, however, was liberalism, freedom of thought and speech, of faith, of association, all supported by laws that protected private property and human rights. In the context of 1919, both Chen and Hu were advocating ideals that would have made the 1911 Revolution more revolutionary and less Chinese.

Both Beijing professors were influential among the students, but the messages did not get very far. It is significant that, even today, the liberalism of Hu Shi, associated with total Westernization, remains suspect. As for Chen Duxiu's most famous defence of 'Science and Democracy', it is remarkable that in 1979 and again in 1989 scholars both in Taiwan and the mainland have repeatedly quoted it with approval — clearly emphasizing its relevance for today — because neither the spirit of science nor that of democracy was healthy in both parts of China. Chen Duxiu's influential statement was made about the time he was to become the first secretary-general of the newly-founded Chinese Communist Party. He wrote it in January 1919, a few months before the May Fourth demonstrations at his university, but his remarks became symbolic of the movement for the next seventy years. Let me quote his defence of his magazine, *New Youth:*

> Our magazine had done no wrong. Only because we defended the two gentlemen, Mr Democracy and Mr Science, did we commit some great crimes. In order to support Mr D, we could not but oppose Confucianism, the practice of rites, chastity, old morality, old politics. In order to support Mr S, we could not but oppose old art, old religion. In order to support both Mr D and Mr S, we could not but oppose 'national essence' and old literature . . .
>
> Westerners who supported Mr D and Mr S had to create much disturbance and spill much blood to rescue them both from darkness and bring them forth into the bright world. We now know that these two gentlemen can save China from the darkness of its politics, its morality, its learning. In support of these two, we will not decline to accept every oppressive action by the government, every attack and denunciation by society, even to bleed from our lopped off heads.

The fact this statement was made in 1919 is important. It was just after a disastrous World War I for the West and a little over a year after the October Revolution in Russia. Suddenly, the ideals of the 1911 Revolution and Sun Yat-sen's methods of seeking assistance from Western powers and Japan seemed suspect and even backward. For the next few decades, Western values associated with capitalism and imperialism were portrayed as flawed. An exciting world revolution was seen as being in the making. Liberal democracy of the Anglo-American variety was being rejected by the new Soviet Union, by Mussolini's Italy and then by Hitler's Germany. Why then should China waste time with gradualism and evolution? Why not leap forward to the advanced forms of collective revolutionary action? It was therefore understandable, if tragic, that most Chinese intellectuals were tempted by what they saw as short-cuts to achieve the *Chinese* national revolution and a revolutionary China. Chen Duxiu was quickly converted and turned to the Communist Party. Sun Yat-sen was half-converted and allied himself with the Soviet Union. Hu Shi alone remained with the small minority that continued to argue for liberal democracy and the scientific spirit — these few, largely intellectuals, were lonely voices trying to sustain the momentum of the May Fourth movement.

Yet, ironically, the May Fourth movement marked a watershed of a kind. Up to that time, everyone who claimed to be a revolutionary was inside the Chinese revolution, fighting for national salvation as patriots but prepared to be as radical as necessary. After 1919, Sun Yat-sen and his followers, who stood for the 1911 Revolution, saw themselves alone as being truly inside the *Chinese* revolution. To them, the Chinese Communist Party, which looked to Marx and Lenin and whose senior cadres were trained abroad by Stalin, were clearly outside. These communists might claim to be more revolutionary, but their revolution was certainly not Chinese! Hu Shi and his liberal friends who favoured modernization through learning directly from the West were rejected by both sides as being both un-Chinese and un-revolutionary. In short, the May Fourth movement marked a division into two major revolutionary groups.

This potted history and what follows may be over-simple, but I believe it reflects the course of events during most of the 20th century. The Chinese revolution led by Sun Yat-sen's successors turned away from his revolutionary ideals and became more intensely Chinese in the quest for national legitimacy and in the effort to survive against treacherous warlords, an expansionist imperialist Japan and an 'alien' Soviet-led Communist Party. During the period leading up to the Sino-Japanese War of 1937-45, these efforts became increasingly popular, appealing to a pervasive anti-Japanese nationalism all over China and among Chinese overseas. Saving China was the goal of China's nationalist revolution — almost nothing else mattered while China was in danger.

The pressure on the Chinese Communists to be nationalist was no less acute. For their own survival, they too had to play down their revolutionary ideals. They also needed to be inside the *Chinese* revolution, emphasizing both their patriotism and their concerns for the peasantry, who formed some 80 per cent of the population. Mao Zedong's success over the Stalinist cadres who had returned from the USSR in the 1930s marked the resurgence of the *Chinese* over the internationalist elements in their revolution. In fact, by the end of the Sino-Japanese War they had turned the tables on the KMT government by showing that the peasant nationalism which they had aroused, and which they now led, was far more Chinese than the nationalism of the classes of landlords and bourgeoisie who supported the KMT. The communists were ready to demonstrate that the KMT was not only reactionary (that is, against revolution) but also not really Chinese!

I will not go into the reasons why the CCP won and the KMT lost in 1949, nor argue here who was inside and who was outside the Chinese Revolution. Both parties obviously believed that theirs was the true Chinese revolution. Mao Zedong and his party believed that they had won because they were both revolutionary and Chinese, and that the KMT had lost because it was neither Chinese nor revolutionary. By their victory, it would appear to the CCP that the Chinese nation had spoken. The Mandate of Heaven was theirs. At the same time, they also thought theirs was a victory for world revolution and human progress. China was thus contributing, for the first time, to global history.

Mao Zedong and the CCP lost no time in resolving an inherent contradiction. Throughout the civil war in China prior to the CCP victory in 1949, only the *loyal* party members of each of the main contenders for power really counted as insiders. After their victory, however, the Communist Party quickly rectified this by a constitutional device. As noted in the chapter by John Fitzgerald, they defined the broad classes of peasants and workers as *renmin* ('people' as in People's Republic) and therefore, by constitutional right, *inside* the national revolution. This was also broadened to include sympathetic bourgeoisie and intellectuals who had supported the CCP at critical stages. Only the *enemies* of the people — that is, counter-revolutionaries, Kuomintang reactionaries who followed Chiang Kai-shek to Taiwan and abroad, certain classes of unrepentant landlords, compradores, and common criminals — were *outside* the revolution. By using this device to define who should and who should not legally be recognized as *citizens* of the *People's* Republic, they claimed that theirs was truly a revolution of the people.

In theory, China was under a visionary leadership guided by scientific Marxist ideology and functioning through what was called democratic centralism. Therefore, every citizen was about to experience revolutionary change. In reality, however, the revolution was determined and tightly controlled by the Party. It soon became clear that most people lived and worked under active members of the Party at every level and therefore were more the objects of education and indoctrination than active participants. Again, on paper, this meant that everyone so indoctrinated was accepted inside the revolution and, therefore, in time, everyone would become a revolutionary and share in the fruits of the revolution. Everyone ultimately would be inside and no one would be left outside. But this was not to be so for several reasons. Firstly, there were class enemies within, false revolutionaries and potential traitors, dissidents and recalcitrants who resisted education and indoctrination. Secondly, there was a dangerous world outside, of capitalists and imperialists, of socialist backsliders (even in the USSR) who wished to restore capitalism (the USSR as a whole even came to be seen as 'social imperialist' and 'hegemonist'), all of whom threatened the Chinese national revolution. And thirdly, there were millions of Chinese outside China who were potential sympathizers or enemies; or who simply wanted nothing to do with the Chinese revolution.

The net result of all these factors was that the revolution which had begun by being inclusive became, over the next thirty years until the end of the so-called Great Proletarian Cultural Revolution, more and more exclusive. Let me briefly explain. Mao Zedong discovered by 1956-57 that education and indoctrination by conventional means was not reliable. Intellectuals outside the Communist Party could never be trusted, and were always potential enemies of the revolution. They were therefore placed *outside* the national revolution, many of them jailed and sent to labour camps, others simply not allowed to work with the skills they had. And then it was discovered that hundreds of millions of peasants could be converted to revolutionary enthusiasm very easily — thus swelling the ranks of those inside the revolution. But in so doing, Mao Zedong also found that many of his colleagues within the Party did not agree with him, or thought he was going in the wrong direction. He was moving away from world revolution and 'sinicizing' it instead: that is, turning the revolution inward into a peasant-based and backward Chinese uprising. Mao, however, concluded that it was his comrades who were not true revolutionaries in that many were too timid and conservative, merely greedy for privileges and power, and that some were sympathetic with 'capitalist roaders' led by Soviet leaders under Khrushchev. It must have been disconcerting, if not disheartening, for him to find that so many of his comrades were not inside *his* national revolution, but actually distancing themselves from him. The Cultural Revolution of 1966-76, therefore, was the result of his effort to cleanse the Party from within. During that decade of unprecedented confusion, thousands were deemed to have been *outside* the revolution whilst millions of others were quickly brought inside the Party. No one was clear what the criteria for good communists entailed. A mixture of enthusiasm, boldness and native cunning, including the memorization of some key Maoist texts, was probably enough for most of the new members. Good education, advanced technical skills and even years of loyal work experience for the Party were denigrated if they were not accompanied by constant affirmations of Maoist loyalty.

With large numbers joining the Party during the Cultural Revolution decade, it might well be argued that more people were now inside the revolution than ever before. In fact, there was so much confusion that no one knew who was a revolutionary any more — and this was perhaps the one clear result of the Cultural Revolution. For those older members who managed to survive — the Old Guard — it must have been a great relief when Mao Zedong died in 1976 and they were able to restore everything to the conditions before 1957. To many, they had lost twenty years. But, at least for the Old Guard, the Party was not totally destroyed and there was the opportunity to rebuild a Party that had so nearly lost its way. But what was left of the 1949 Revolution for them to rebuild?

Deng Xiaoping and the remnants of the Old Guard led a dramatic new start after 1978. Swiftly, everything pertaining to Mao Zedong's mistakes since 1957 was swept away. Verdicts were reversed and those wrongfully jailed or dismissed were restored to their posts; old standards for education and Party membership were brought back; a socialist legal order, still largely modelled on that of the Soviet Union, was re-established. A new 'open door' policy was introduced that built bridges to the capitalist world. The initial results were stunning, at least at the economic level. Reforms in the countryside were accompanied by a resurgence of rural and then low-level urban entrepreneurship, the rise of new medium-sized industry in the urban centres and an increase in foreign trade — some of the developments were unbelievable, and most Chinese people were delighted with the changes. Slowly, somewhat uncertainly at first, and then more and more confidently, a new and more open kind of Chinese national revolution emerged.

But something else also became clear. On the one hand, Mao Zedong's efforts to place his revolution in the vanguard of world revolution had failed. He had, intentionally or not, taken the road back to something more Chinese, more traditionally peasant-based and unmistakably 'feudal' and pre-capitalist, and in effect *anti*-revolutionary. On the other hand, by changing gears and opening up China, Deng Xiaoping could not return to the ideals of world revolution of the 1940s and 1950s. The world itself had radically changed during the years when Mao had kept the PRC in isolation. By 1979, there was no world revolution to join or return to. Instead, it was a world of relative capitalist success, of remarkable advances in science, industry, communications and international trade, and a world increasingly aware of human rights as the globe grew smaller and smaller. And, not least, the face of East and Southeast Asia had changed and great things were now expected to happen in a vigorous and increasingly prosperous Asia-Pacific region.

In this new political and economic environment, Deng Xiaoping and his team, notably Hu Yaobang and Zhao Ziyang, were shaping a new start, not for a revolutionary society for the new socialist man, but for a more familiar *Chinese* revolution. Just about everyone, inside and outside China, wanted China to be opened up, wanted Deng Xiaoping to let in more light, and to let more minds be opened to new ideas coming from the outside in order to give the Chinese national revolution a new lease on life. In this context, recalling the 1911 Revolution and the May Fourth movement seemed perfectly natural — that was how the Chinese revolution had begun, and the 1949 Revolution had been meant to be that revolution's culmination. But partly because the 1911 Revolution was still very much the KMT and Taiwan's own special ancestor, and still regarded as too narrowly conceived in nationalist terms — that is, merely for China's unity, strength, and prosperity — it was the May Fourth movement that captured greater attention among Chinese intellectuals from the start.

It was not an auspicious start. In 1979, within months of Deng Xiaoping's return to power, when the PRC was preparing to celebrate its 30th anniversary, the intellectuals debated the meaning of the May Fourth movement on its 60th anniversary. It was immediately pointed out that the 'Four Modernizations' espoused by Deng Xiaoping did not include a fifth modernization, *political* modernization. There was no mention of the urgent need for democratic reform. Intellectuals in 1979 interpreted the 'May Fourth spirit' as meaning that they must learn from the outside world and turn to experiences outside Mao Zedong's revolution. It is now clear that many in China, especially young Chinese students, have taken a hard look *outside* since 1979 and have digested some of what they have found. Not least, among many other things, they have found that the two major slogans of the May Fourth movement, of 'Science and Democracy', are once again what China urgently needs. But during the past decade and a half their experiences have not been encouraging. Scientific thinking is being limited to technology and industrial productivity. Cries for democratic reforms have been brushed aside. The Democracy Wall came to an end and the leaders of the small democracy movement were incarcerated. Others were sacked from the Communist Party and otherwise punished. But so much else was being achieved during these years in the economic sphere that what protests there were were minimal and could, in fact, be safely ignored by the Party leadership.

All that has changed. Overall, the Chinese economy has done very well; but by the latter half of the 1980s corruption had become rampant. When Hu Yaobang's unexpected death occurred in 1989, the students in Beijing were in the midst of preparing for yet another decade's anniversary of the May Fourth movement to express their concerns. Suddenly, the calls for 'Mr Science' and 'Mr Democracy' seemed very appropriate again. And if they are indeed that appropriate, they show that the 1949 Revolution is no longer part of the world revolution the CCP had wanted to join, but is now very much an extension of the *Chinese* Revolution of 1911. And May 4, 1919 is the key link that confirms that there has only been *one* Chinese revolution and that the 1949 Revolution was really only a part of it. What had distracted us for three decades was Mao Zedong's bold but misguided effort to rise above that. When his revolution became a disaster during the Great Proletarian Cultural Revolution, it sealed the fate for a revolutionary China.

'Mr Science' and 'Mr Democracy' Revitalized

One consequence is that the May Fourth movement is now again a powerful symbol, especially in relationship to 'Science and Democracy'. The call for more science might on the surface be puzzling insofar as much praise had been heaped on scientific advances in the PRC, on how China has kept pace in many areas of technology and produced a number of fine scientists. There is, of course, much still to be done, and Chinese scientists are quick to admit that they are far behind in several fields of high technology and lack solid foundations in the basic sciences. The real problem, however, does not lie in advances in technology. Many Chinese now recognize that the much more complex issue is the reluctance to use the scientific method to think critically about society, culture, politics and economics.

This is a problem that is very difficult to unravel in China because it questions the foundations of Communist Party ideology. The problem arises because the PRC had started with the proposition that Marxism-Leninism was scientific and encompassed all the scientific thinking the Chinese Revolution would ever need. It also argued quite unconvincingly that all other forms of scientific thought were class-based (in particular, bourgeois) and therefore biased and ultimately unscientific. Only Marxism-Leninism was science. The continued acceptance of this premise in China would have made it very difficult to introduce new ideas about society, politics, economics and culture that do not start with Marxist premises and assumptions.

When the new 'open door' policy began in the late 1970s, there was a reluctant acknowledgement that capitalism had not only survived but had also brought great economic and technological progress to the countries that espoused it. It was also recognized that these advanced sciences and technologies would be invaluable for China. Catching up with the West in many areas was only a matter of time. Given the Chinese abilities in mathematics and basic sciences, few doubted that China would get there before long. But in fact, many Chinese today realize China needs more science than that. Scientific thinking and methods are equally important in economics and management, in social and political policy-making. And the hardest of all is the willingness to think about the humanities and the social sciences (however imprecise their results may be) beyond the Marxist-Leninist framework.

There is yet another aspect about science that has now been highlighted. This concerns national investment in education at every level. It is not only to ensure that the best talents are found for advanced studies and scientific work, but also for mass education, the broad base invaluable for modern industry. Science training and the early introduction of the scientific method in schools require an enlightened policy toward teachers and school curricula. This, the authorities in China now admit, has been pathetic, except in a small number of key schools, colleges and universities. Note what Chen Duxiu had said in 1919. He was not worried about technological advances but about 'old religion': that is, about superstitions, ignorance and the power of unscientific ideas on ordinary lives. Hence he talked about saving China 'from the darkness of its politics, its morality, its learning'. On none of these three has there been progress comparable to, say, China's defence sciences and military technology (to take but one obvious example).

Here is why 'Mr Science' has been seen in China as inseparable from 'Mr Democracy'. If Chinese intellectuals are given freedom only to advance technology and the natural and physical sciences, but not to apply scientific non-Marxist thinking to social, political, cultural and economic phenomena, there can be little progress in the kind of knowledge that supports and enlightens a modern society and environment and nation. 'Mr Science' needs freedom to think, to innovate, to challenge and criticize, to be free from obscurantist bureaucrats and rigid authoritarian systems, no less than 'Mr Democracy' does. Of course, not all these freedoms are found outside China. But when they are found, they have provided great assistance to the scientists that have advanced the wealth, as well as the quality of life, of so many democratic societies.

The Chinese have always had far greater difficulty agreeing on what kind of animal democracy is. The reasons are obvious. After experiencing for 2000 years a powerful system that centralized all power in the hands of the emperor and his mandarinate, how are they to think in democratic terms? Sun Yat-sen had begun to talk about this at the beginning of the century. Twenty years later, Chen Duxiu in 1919 identified the issue as one that was vital for China, and three-quarters of a century after that, the Chinese are still wondering how they can introduce more democratic institutions into China.

They have not been helped by the fact that the PRC since 1949 proclaimed that somehow the 'democratic centralism' that had been erected by the CCP was more scientific (because it is Marxist-Leninist) than any other form of democracy. Any other suggested form was therefore likely to be seen as anti-Marxist and unscientific. And if that form should come from outside China, it was also unpatriotic and treasonable.

Both these obstacles to democracy, the imperial tradition and Marxist-Leninist dogma, are well known. Together, they are so deep-rooted and so strong that it may well be that 'Mr Democracy' (as Chen Duxiu, Hu Shi and others knew it) may be impossible for China in the foreseeable future. It is understandable why Chinese intellectuals argue that it may not be essential to borrow democratic forms from outside China. What may be more important in the long run is the emergence of the democratic spirit, protected by a respect for human rights and freedoms that is embodied in a fair and efficient legal system. What to them is crucial is an environment where there is free speech, where there are checks and balances to counter corruption and maladministration, and where it is lawful to criticize those in power.

And here another difficulty may face the democrats in China. As Chen Duxiu put it, 'In order to support Mr D, we could not but oppose Confucianism, the practice of rites, chastity, old morality, old politics'. Within China, but often rejected by Chinese revolutionaries, are forces of tradition still alive today. These forces are not all inimical to the democratic spirit. Some are still greatly respected because they help progress: for example, there is the tradition of support for education, and there is the this-worldly attitude toward hard work, thrift, material success and entrepreneurship. What does stand in the way of democracy, however, is the traditional authoritarianism of emperor and father sanctioned by state Confucianism, which has been translated to the bureaucratic machinery of the modern state and political party. Criticisms of this aspect of the tradition are often rejected by those in power, with appeals for respect for all the traditions that made China a great civilization. It is therefore very easy to attack democrats who appear too eager for change by accusing them of being unpatriotic, unChinese and against tradition. One of the great ironies of the Chinese national revolution is that cultural values which may at times be severely condemned could, at different times, be defended because they are Chinese and therefore should only be judged by Chinese and not foreign standards.

The Revolution Outside

My thoughts have been for some time on whether more was achieved outside China and outside the Revolution than inside: that is, whether more revolutionary changes occurred *outside* the control of the PRC's leaders in Beijing than were achieved by their own efforts. How might we begin to evaluate what happened among Chinese inspired by Marxism-Leninism-Maoism as compared with what has been attained *outside* that revolutionary framework? Has the most important revolution been a smaller revolution, consisting of little modernizations, that has occurred among Chinese people elsewhere?

What, then, has been the odyssey of the Chinese Revolution outside the mainland? The revolution of 1911 had started, certainly, as a nationalist one to be achieved in a republic that would establish a prosperous, strong and united China. It was in time also expected to be democratic and scientifically advanced and to be able to re-distribute wealth to the poor. By 1928, some twenty years later, that revolution had achieved no more than a nationalist republic. And another twenty years after that, after 1949, it was struggling to rebuild its base in Taiwan, and had to depend on the support of old KMT members and anti-Communists all over the world. By that time, uniting China from Taiwan was widely seen as a myth, and all its initial nationalist revolutionary ideals seem to have been couched negatively in anti-Communist rhetoric. If the 1949 Revolution in the PRC had lost its way through Mao Zedong's romantic zeal, then the 1911 Revolution in Taiwan from 1949 was kept in a frozen state for more than twenty-five years. Only in the 1970s was it possible to think afresh about the consequences of comparative prosperity. Science and technology had developed to match manufacturing needs and stimulate new industries. And following that, with prosperity and confidence, more scientific thinking has been permitted to extend into examining China's great cultural traditions, and this in turn has opened more minds to the possibility of democracy.

Beyond Taiwan, there is Hong Kong, and there are the large communities in several cities in Southeast Asia and, more recently, growing communities in a few cities in North America and Australia. For most of them, there had been divisions between those Chinese who had identified with the 1911 Revolution and the KMT and those who had sympathized with the 1949 Revolution. But they had other things in common. Among the most important was the fact that they were free from traditional political and social norms. Many such Chinese, of course, are still deeply concerned for the goals that Chinese national revolutionaries have yet to achieve — namely unity, prosperity and strength for China — while many of the younger Chinese would call for the spirit of both science and democracy. Despite the fact that no Chinese outside can really do anything significant now for the Chinese revolution, their lives outside that revolution have given them rich insights into what their present adopted countries have done, with or without revolution. The one striking fact that all Chinese can now see is that Chinese outside China who had lived in, or still remain in, communist or so-called socialist countries (now very much fewer in number) had done very poorly. In contrast, those who live in liberal capitalist countries had done immeasurably better. This is not merely because these countries have either had their revolutions a long time ago or had never needed one, but also because these open and liberal societies have taught most of them to bring scientific inquiry and habits of mind into their daily family lives, into every aspect of their education, and have, in most cases, introduced them to the value of living in a democratic environment. They already have what the May Fourth movement wanted in 1919 and what the Chinese in China still want three-quarters of a century later.

Today, from the perspective of the mid-1990s, several points are clearer than they have been for some time. The Chinese revolution was much influenced by revolutionary ideas from the outside but (and this should not really surprise us) it has been far more Chinese than revolutionary. In the most painful and tragic ways, it has brought changes and some progress to the Chinese in China — but has yet to contribute to world civilization. However, there are signs that, *outside* the Chinese revolution (and I mean here both outside China and outside the idea of revolution as the Chinese have conceived it), progress among Chinese people elsewhere is having an impact on those within China. For this to have any lasting effect and ultimately transform China, there needs to be sustained openness to the world.

I would deeply hope that China has passed the stage of depending on a big-R revolution to achieve its nationalist goals. Its two-part revolution of 1911 and 1949 has brought to the surface what is possible and what is not, what can be fruitful and what is not. The experiences have been so rich and varied, and so much has been learnt by so many millions both inside and outside, that we can now hope that China will remain open to the world. I believe that most Chinese everywhere now realize that only through this openness, and the trials and changes that that would bring, can China fulfil the nationalist expectations its peoples have had for so long for the Chinese Revolution. Is there a message here? If there is, the message today would be something like this: Be open to the world and then you can be as Chinese as you like.

SIX

From Nationalism to Nationalizing: Cultural Imagination and State Formation in Postwar Taiwan

Allen Chun

The Invention of Nationalism

Cultural discourse and cultural policy have always been prominent features of Taiwan's postwar politics. Their significance, however, has not been well understood by scholars. Whether invoked as icons of national identity, myths of origin, shared social values, common ideologies or habits of custom, the 'renaissance' of traditional Chinese culture in Taiwan was part of a broader project by the Kuomintang government to realize its vision of the modern state. This construction of culture or invocation of tradition had roots in the politics of national survival but evolved over time into an all-encompassing ethos with ramifications for the moral conduct of everyday life. Institutions like the school, media, family, military and workplace played important roles in diffusing this culture from the realm of high politics to the level of everyday routine. The need to constantly reinforce a national frame of mind or imagined community through social practice represents the peculiarity of Taiwan's nationalizing process.

It reflected, though, a crisis of culture endemic to the emergence of the modern nation-state. This crisis was perhaps most clearly articulated by Ernest Gellner, who argued that the modern nation-state was founded upon bonds of solidarity among its 'citizens', which presupposed the universalization of a shared civilization or ethnic tradition in the minds of equal and autonomous individuals as a condition for its continued survival. Without elaborating upon the specific nature of what might constitute a 'national' culture, Gellner emphasized the role of education and the need for universal literacy as major prerequisites for realization of such a national culture.[1] Gellner's view of mass

---

[1]   Ernest Gellner, *Nations and Nationalism* (Basil Blackwell, Oxford, 1983).

education as the vehicle for bringing about a national culture and also for disseminating shared social values throughout the populace parallels Benedict Anderson's focus upon 'print capitalism' and the emergence of a common colloquial language.[2] Yet unlike Gellner's stress on progress in educational standards, for Anderson the construction of a colloquial language was simply a tool that enabled the allegorical imagery of the nation and its empty, homogenous notions of community to become engrained within the social imagination, especially via the medium of popular literature and mass culture. Thus, according to Gellner and Anderson, any notion of culture associated with this newly emerging nationalism had to be *reconstructed* and *forward-looking*, in spite of its origin, insofar as it had to be able to transcend what Clifford Geertz aptly termed the 'primordial sentiments' of traditional culture.[3]

This does not mean, of course, that traditional values could not be invoked or that there could be no recourse to the past (more often than not, there was) but rather that the basic imperatives of national culture reflected less upon the content of culture than upon the peculiar nature of the nation-state. That is to say, one is not dealing here simply with new *ideologies* of boundedness; one is dealing more precisely with a new kind of *boundedness*. The kind of boundedness that one now easily recognizes to be synonymous with the birth of the nation-state along with its concurrent notions of citizenship is in many respects incompatible with the elite culture of traditional societies. Where the high civilizations of past empires had been able to transcend political boundaries by embracing the totality of a broader cosmological vision, as in the case of a kingdom of God or the Sinocentric empire, the boundedness of the nation-state has demanded a different kind of totality, and this is what national culture has aimed to reflect. Thus, unlike the implicit hierarchy of traditional societies, the geopolitical reality of the nation-state has demanded that its constituent citizens should themselves be bound by a common identity and shared values, and this is the source of what Gellner and Anderson perceived to be bonds of horizontal solidarity intrinsic to

---

2   Benedict Anderson, *Imagined Communities: Reflections on the Origins and Spread of Nationalism* (Verso, London, 1983). While the genesis of a standard colloquial Chinese (Mandarin) has had important ramifications for the spread of nationalism throughout China, it is ironic to note that the terms for Mandarin used on the mainland, Taiwan and Singapore clearly reflect the ways in which language is used to serve different kinds of national sentiment. On Taiwan, Mandarin is called 'the national language' or *guoyu*, following early Republican usage which is itself a replacement for *guanhua*, literally 'the language of officials'. On the mainland, *guoyu* became *putonghua* or 'the common language', as if to stress universal egalitarianism. In Singapore, the use of *huayu* for Mandarin as 'the language of ethnic Chinese' conforms with the ethnic neutrality of national politics there.

3   Clifford Geertz, 'The Integrative Revolution: Primordial Sentiments and Civil Politics in the New States', in C. Geertz (ed.), *Old Societies and New States* (Aldine, Chicago, 1963).

modern nationalism. In the case of Taiwan, this solidarity involved an allegiance to a higher-level collectivity where territorial boundedness was itself a fiction prompted by a particular claim to legitimacy (namely, the Republic of China) and where the fiction of the nation was predicated upon the synonymity of one people, one culture, one family and one nation.

Anthropologists on the whole have been quick to point out that the crisis of culture is most acute in those nations emerging out of multi-ethnic settings or deeply rooted local traditions: that one either had to compromise ethnic divisiveness by appealing to cultural ideals based upon pan-ethnic values or evade ethnicity altogether by adopting politically neutral values or utopian ideologies. The point I wish to make instead is that the crisis of nationalism and of national culture transcends ethnicity simply because in principle it is trying to construct a radically different kind of bounded community called the nation-state. It should not only be endemic to multi-ethnic nations struggling to define a new basis of common identity; by its forward-looking nature, it should also be endemic to ethnically homogeneous nations struggling to replace a pre-existing cosmological totality with a sense of totality that did not exist before.

The case of postwar Taiwan is interesting in this regard, not only for the way the Kuomintang felt compelled to define national identity in terms of race, language and history but also in the way it attempted to invoke, resuscitate and reinvent tradition for the purpose of legitimizing its own vision of modern society. The radical vision of a modern (Nationalist) society can easily be traced back to the 1911 Revolution, which led to the overthrow of the Qing dynasty and the birth of the Republic. Prior to the 1911 Revolution, there was no cognate notion in Chinese of society or nation as a territorially distinct, politically bounded and ethnically identifiable group of people. Many terms had to be borrowed from Japanese.[4] Up until the mid-19th century, it was unusual for Chinese to call other ethnic groups 'ethnic groups', referring to them instead as barbarians. Only during the early years of the Republic did intellectuals begin to associate *zhonghua minzu* (Chineseness as an ethnic category) with *zhongguo ren* (citizens of China), in so doing making the ethnic population of territorial China synonymous with the concept of a single political community.[5] Moreover, Chineseness in terms of material culture,

---

[4]   Han Qinchun and Li Yifu, 'Hanwen "minzu" yizi de chuxian ji qi shiyong qingkuang' [The Appearance of the Chinese Term *Minzu* and its Circumstances of Usage], *Minzu yanjiu* [*Minzu* Research], vol.2 (1984), pp.36-43.

[5]   According to Peng Yingmin, full-fledged definitions of the nation as people (*minzu*) and nationalism as the principle of a common people (*minzu zhuyi*) were spelled out explicitly by Liang Ch'i-ch'ao and Sun Yat-sen and were later influenced by foreign writings, like those of Joseph Stalin. See Peng Yingmin, 'Guanyu woguo *minzu* gainian lishi de chubu kaocha [A Preliminary Analysis of the History of the Chinese Concept of *minzu*], *Minzu yanjiu*, vol.2 (1985), pp.9-12.

ethnicity or residence was never clearly defined.[6] Even the Kuomintang's rendition of nationalism (*minzu zhuyi*) as the 'principle of a common people' clearly underscored the notion of a bounded citizenry as the distinctive feature of nationhood (in contrast, for example, to the purely institutional characteristics of the nation-state).[7] This point was reiterated early on by Sun Yat-sen, who in a famous phrase criticized the traditional Chinese polity as being 'a dish of loose sand' (*yi pan sansha*). This explains why the raising of 'societal consciousness' (*minzu yishi*) and the promotion of spiritual values toward that end have been constantly emphasized in Nationalist Taiwan as the primary means of bringing about national solidarity, which in turn constitutes the primary weapon for combating Communism and imperialism.

One must explain then how culture has been used to embody the sense of bounded totality and perception of a spiritual sharedness that emerged with the nation-state. In this regard, it is important to see where culture has been invoked, what rhetorical forms it has taken and how the collusion between the state, party, institutional agents like the media, schools, family and local community in the promotion of national consciousness has worked to provide a certain coherence or systematic tenor to the concept of 'traditional Chinese culture'. The interrelationship of these different institutional agents suggests first of all that culture operates at many different levels of public discourse — for example, as a sense of history, feelings of national consciousness, shared political ideology, conceptual worldview, values of civilization, and customs. The way in which these various levels of discourse fit together to project a certain coherence must also be viewed as a consequence of a larger political vision which reflects the peculiar worldview of the KMT state.

At the simplest level, the primary problem which confronted the new Republic after its birth was that of constructing a bound polity drawn together by a set of master symbols, shared beliefs (or myths) and moral consciousness; that is to say, a set of horizontally universal values that could replace the hierarchically stratified values of Heaven and divine kingship that buttressed a previous cultural order. That the Chinese perceived nationalism or *minzu zhuyi* literally as 'the principle of a common people' rather than as the rationality of a set of sociopolitical institutions like the state or its bureaucracy is significant: for much of the ideological energy that was expended to create a sense of national community was focused upon the heightening of 'societal consciousness' (*minzu yishi*), especially in reaction to the domination of Western imperialism and the sense of political humiliation and cultural degradation suffered as a result. Thus, the struggle of nationalism which began with the collapse of the Chinese imperial system and has continued to be

---

6   David Y. H. Wu, 'The Construction of Chinese and Non-Chinese Identities', *Daedalus*, vol.120, no.2 (Spring 1991), pp.159-80.

7   This is similar to what Richard G. Fox calls 'ideologies of peoplehood' in his Introduction to *National Ideologies and the Production of National Cultures* (American Anthropological Association, Washington, DC, 1990), p.3.

fought to the present day essentially involved the construction of a set of conscious ideological or mythological beliefs that could be used to cultivate a sense of societal self-esteem as a form of resistance to the West. For the most part, this effort to use culture to create a heightened sense of societal consciousness (and *vice versa*) was the underlying strategy which linked nationalist discourse on both the mainland before 1949 and Taiwan thereafter.[8]

Yet modern as it was, the strategic call to tradition and culture in postwar Taiwan was also a specific response to the threat of Communism posed by mainland China. In terms of discourse, it is thus no coincidence that the invoking of tradition represented an ideologically conservative response to the radical visions of a Communist national polity. In this regard, the construction of tradition and culture had an explicitly political agenda from the beginning. At the same time, it is equally important to point out that the usages to which tradition was put and the diverse meanings invoked by culture were always changing. These changes reflected strategic positionings within a changing political order, but as meaningful responses these changing constructions of traditional culture throughout the postwar period had to reflect, more importantly, changing utopian visions of a modern Nationalist polity.

In short, the dilemma of nation-building that plagued the KMT government was not unlike the crisis of modernity in Europe or the impact of colonialism in the Third World that prompted the invention of tradition, the discovery of custom and the objectification of culture as general phenomena of the late 19th and early 20th centuries.[9] Such notions of tradition, custom and culture, insofar as they came to be politically contested, mythologized in

---

8   On the mainland, the elevation of the Great Wall to the status of a *de facto* national symbol is a case in point. Prior to the 19th century, the Chinese had little idea of it, much less a name for it. From the late 16th century to the late 19th century, when the Ming emperors expanded greatly upon the original Qin walls to ward off Mongol invasion, the Great Wall had negative connotations through its association with the excesses of despotic emperors. Yet despite its despotic connotations, nationalists like Sun Yat-sen and Lu Xun seized upon the Great Wall as a rallying point for Chinese national consciousness. This ambivalent relationship to the Wall continued throughout the Communist era, wavering constantly between periods of denigration and deification. See Arthur Waldron, 'The Great Wall Myth: Its Origins and Role in Modern China', *Yale Journal of Criticism*, vol.2, no.1 (1989), pp.67-90.

9   There is already a considerable literature on this subject, stemming independently from the work of, among others, Eric Hobsbawm and Terence Ranger (eds), *The Invention of Tradition* (Cambridge University Press, Cambridge, 1983); John Clammer, 'Colonialism and the Perception of Tradition in Fiji', in T. Asad (ed.), *Anthropology and the Colonial Encounter* (Macmillan, London, 1973); S. N. Eisenstadt, 'Post-Traditional Societies and the Reconstruction of Tradition', *Daedalus* (Winter 1973), pp.1-28; Roger M. Keesing and Robert Tonkinson (eds), 'Reinventing Traditional Culture: The Politics of Kastom in Island Melanesia', *Mankind*, vol.13, no.4 (1982), pp.297-305; Bernard S. Cohn, 'The Census, Social Structure and Objectification in South Asia', *Folk*, 26 (1984), pp.25-49; and Nicholas Thomas, 'Material Culture and Colonial Power: Ethnological Collecting and the Establishment of Colonial Rule in Fiji', *Man*, vol.24, no.1 (1989), pp.241-56.

ideology and ritualized in practice, were essentially local responses to changing global situations.[10]

As part of the KMT's effort to continue the legacy of the Republic in its retreat from the mainland and in the process to (re)nationalize Taiwan, the government embarked upon a program to resuscitate 'traditional Chinese culture'. By invoking 'tradition', the authorities appeared to resuscitate elements of the past, but they were clearly inventing tradition (by virtue of their selectivity). The government in effect played an active role (as author) in writing culture (by constructing discourses on tradition, ethnicity, ethical philosophy and moral psychology). It also inculcated these reconstructed notions of tradition (as culture) through the 'normative' machinery of the school, media, family and military in order to construct disciplinary lifestyles and ritual patterns of behaviour compatible with the underlying ethos of the state. Chinese culture ultimately became an object of discourse not only in a political sense but also through the construction of knowledge (as in the chronicling of history[11] and archaeological treasure hunting), market commercialization, and domestication of life routines (as a result of group socialization, pedagogical dissemination and public etiquette). Thus, the crisis of culture in postwar Taiwan was one which was predicated by the government's attempt to *nationalize* Chinese culture (by making the latter a metaphor or allegory of that imagined community called the nation-state) where no such culture (of the nation) previously existed. In concrete terms, it was driven by the perceived need to establish new foundations of spiritual consciousness, ideological rationality and moral behaviour that could conform to the dictates of the modern polity or nation-state in ways that primordial notions of Chineseness could not. Insofar as tradition was invented or reconstituted, by nature it also had to be a kind of mystification which coincided with the hegemonic process of state formation. In other words, a need to forge a new kind of *hegemony* was what prompted these mystifying discourses on culture.[12]

---

[10]   See Jocelyn S. Linnekin, 'Defining Tradition: Variations on the Hawaiian Identity', *American Ethnologist*, vol.10 (1983), pp.241-52.

[11]   See Nicholas B. Dirks for a discussion of modern historical writing in 'History as a Sign of the Modern', *Public Culture*, vol.2, no.2 (1990).

[12]   See Philip Corrigan and Derek Sayer, *The Great Arch: English State Formation as Cultural Revolution* (Basil Blackwell, Oxford, 1985); Geoffrey Benjamin, The Unseen Presence: A Theory of Nation-State and Its Mystifications, Working Paper, Sociology Department, National University of Singapore, Singapore (1988); Bernard S. Cohn and Nicholas B. Dirks, 'Beyond the Fringe: The Nation-State, Colonialism and the Technologies of Power', *Journal of Historical Sociology*, vol.1, no.2 (1988), pp.224-9; Nicholas Thomas, 'Sanitation and Seeing: The Creation of State Power in Early Colonial Fiji', *Comparative Studies in Society and History*, vol.32, no.1 (1990), pp.149-70; Bruce Kapferer, 'Nationalist Ideology and a Comparative Anthropology', *Ethnos*, vol.54, nos 3-4 (1989), pp.161-99; and Roger M. Keesing, 'Creating the Past: Custom and Identity

Tradition as Hegemony

In contrast to both socialist China and the world-at-large, Nationalist China as promoted by the KMT regime appealed to traditionalism. However, an appeal to traditionalism was merely one of many possible metaphors of culture, just as it represented one of many possible faces along a wide political spectrum. That is to say, 'Chinese traditional culture' not only involved a multiplicity of *things* (markers of national identity, habits of custom, icons of patriotic fervour and national treasures), it also involved the authority of different kinds of rhetorical *statements* (through the codification of discursive knowledge as shared myths, beliefs and values, common language, ethnicity and history) whose coherence and systematic quality ultimately reflected the larger utopian vision of a Nationalist state.

In Taiwan, while it is difficult to find an iconic symbol to equal the stature of the Great Wall in nationalist sentiment, the KMT government, in clear contrast with the mainland, has consistently maintained its role as the guardian of traditional Chinese culture. This notion of guardianship was reflected not only in its proprietary attitude toward the possession of various 'national treasures' (*guobao*), which included artifacts of high culture such as those belonging to the National Palace Museum, classic texts and objects of historical or archaeological antiquity, but was also reflected in its conservative attitude toward the preservation of language (against the simplification of characters), thought and other fruits of Chinese civilization. Despite their rhetoric, these icons of identity were all rallying points for shared national sentiments.[13] They portrayed the unique achievements of the nation (*vis-à-vis* other nations) and in the process enhanced feelings of national pride.

Underlying the imagination of a cultural China as signifying the nation was an appeal to sacred origins and the myth of a continuous history, as captured most powerfully in the concept of *huaxia*, *hua* here referring to a general sense of Chineseness emanating from the mythical Xia dynasty. Rooted in the sanctity of a primordial past, the legitimacy of history has often served in China to vindicate the mandate of Heaven despite the actual history of repeated dynastic upheaval, barbarian conquest and alien religious influences. Yet this myth of sacred communion with the past was more importantly a definition of culture or civilization that transcended considerations of ethnic identity and the realities of political affiliation. In premodern times, attachment to this notion of *huaxia* was key to the inclusiveness of a Sinocentric world order that could assimilate distinct nations, heterogeneous customs and diverse beliefs. In postwar Taiwan, the appropriation of this notion of *huaxia* had quite different meanings. In the context of the modern world system, *huaxia* epitomized the uniqueness of

---

in the Contemporary Pacific', *The Contemporary Pacific*, vol.1, nos 1-2 (1989), pp.19-42.

13   Icons of national identity need not be limited to obvious political symbols like the flag, nor do they merely invoke patriotic feelings.

China *vis-à-vis* other nations, as though rooted to its origin in civilization. Pitted against the People's Republic, *huaxia* represented the defence of a traditional past that contrasted with the forward-looking radicalism of a communist worldview. Within Taiwan, *huaxia* also served a different function by anchoring Taiwan to the Chinese nation-state as a whole.

During the first twenty years following the takeover of Taiwan in 1945 by the KMT government, these notions of culture as 'national treasure' and 'historical sanctity' were already obvious dimensions of government policy. This period could be called an era of 'cultural reunification', characterized by the need to reconsolidate Chinese culture by purging it of the vestiges of Japanese influence after fifty years of colonial rule and by suppressing any movements toward local Taiwanese cultural expression. The main tool of cultural reunification was the forced imposition of standard Mandarin as the language of everyday communication and the medium for disseminating social values. A ban on colloquial Taiwanese and Japanese in all avenues of mass communication such as radio, film, television and newspapers, which were government controlled, along with the prohibition of all publications originating from Japan and mainland China, remained in effect throughout the period of martial law. The imposition of standard Mandarin upon an indigenous Taiwanese population, who had been left out of the Nationalist experience that gripped China proper in the early 20th century, represented a kind of colonialism which was no less 'foreign' than the Japanese interregnum that preceded it. In effect, the reunification of Chinese culture on Taiwan, glossed in language and steeped in the virtues of history and civilization, was a process of political domination by the Chinese state that coincided with the suppression of Taiwanese ethnicity.

Given the heavy-handed attempts to impose Chinese culture from on high and the intense politico-military confrontation that characterized the early postwar era in Taiwan after the retreat of the Nationalist government from the mainland, there was really no concerted effort to programmatically reconstruct culture. Given the 'war of manoeuvre', in Gramsci's terms, and the priority of national reunification, the strategic deployment of 'culture' underscored the primacy of political survival and economic reconsolidation.

The political character of Chinese culture during the first twenty years of Taiwan's 'glorious restoration' (euphemistically termed *guangfu* by the KMT) functioned to legitimize the Republic of China in at least three aspects — as a separate nation (*vis-à-vis* other nations) rooted in its own history, as a standard bearer of traditional values (*vis-à-vis* the PRC), and as a cultural ideal (as distinct from ethnic reality). However, cultural discourse went beyond the strategic deployment of master symbols and the rhetoric of appropriation or domination and gave way eventually to elaborately written master narratives of culture. By *invoking* tradition, cultural discourse and cultural policy in Taiwan engendered ideologies of various kinds, which included not only sweeping notions of civilization but also political ideology, scholarly knowledge, moral philosophies and standards of custom. By (*re*)*inventing* tradition, cultural policy in Taiwan had to rewrite the content of tradition in order to suit new rhetorical forms and new political agendas. In the service of national unity, these various icons and narratives of Chineseness provided the basis of a cultural hegemony that had not existed in the past.

During the 1960s, although the hysteria of war had not waned measurably, the sociopolitical infrastructure was sufficiently established to permit a 'war of position', in Gramsci's terms, with regard to the role of ideology in national development. In 1966, coinciding with the 100th anniversary of the birth of Sun Yat-sen but principally in reaction to the Cultural Revolution on the mainland, the Kuomintang initiated a large-scale 'Cultural Renaissance movement' (wenhua fuxing yundong). This was officially inaugurated by a speech delivered by Chiang Kai-shek, an arcane four-page essay containing no fewer than eighty-six footnotes.[14] In 1967, a committee was established at the level of the provincial government, which in turn set up smaller regional committees at the level of urban district and rural township administration to carry out the work of the Cultural Renaissance movement, primarily through the local agency of the elementary and middle schools. Called upon to serve as active nerve centres for the promotion of cultural learning and awareness, both as part of the daily curriculum and in extracurricular activities, the schools served as a focal point for government efforts to extend the level of public consciousness to the local level.[15]

The Cultural Renaissance movement was not a spontaneous discovery of traditional culture. It was a systematic effort to redefine the content of these ideas and values, to inculcate widespread societal consciousness through institutional promotion, and to use organized social movements as the spiritual framework for national development in other domains. In other words, not only was there an organized effort to cultivate a spirit of national solidarity through recourse to tradition but an attempt was also made to lead people to believe that this spirit of cultural consciousness was the key to the fate of the nation in all other respects. In other words, achievements as diverse as economic progress and athletic success were all deemed to be consequences of (and causes for) this spirit of national unity. The cultivation of cultural consciousness was also explicitly linked to an all-encompassing culture

---

[14]   Chiang Kai-shek, 'Zhongshanlou zhonghua wenhuatang luocheng jinian wen', reprinted in Taiwan Provincial Government (ed.), Zhonghua wenhua fuxing lunji [Essays on China's Cultural Renaissance] (Gaizhao chubanshe, Taipei, 1967).

[15]   The scope was far-reaching and was motivated by four explicit guidelines: '1) allow the media to sow the seeds of public dissemination and incite education to take the initiative, 2) exemplify and actively lead through the expression of social movement, 3) use the schools as activity centres for the extension of the Cultural Renaissance movement to the family and society-at-large, and 4) use the full network of administration to step up coordination and supervision'. See the Provincial Government News Agency (ed.), Taiwan guangfu ershiwu nian [Twenty-five-year Retrospective of the Glorious Restoration of Taiwan] (Provincial Government Printer, Taichung, 1970), section 18, p.2.

industry, through the extension of ties with overseas Chinese and foreign cultural agencies; the financing of grassroots cultural groups; the development of the tourist industry; increased publication of the classics; preservation of historical artifacts; large-scale promotion of activities in science, ethics, and social welfare; development of sports; and wider cultural coverage in the mass media, incorporating an intensified anti-communist propaganda.[16] Cultural Renaissance was simply the first step in a long-term process to objectify (and 'commodify') culture.

Within the schools, Cultural Renaissance was an important part of both curricular and extra-curricular programs. Courses on society and ethics as well as citizenship and morality were taught at the elementary and middle-school levels. At the high-school level, introduction to Chinese culture, military education, and thought became a staple part of the curriculum. Outside the classroom, essay and oratory contests on topics pertaining to Chinese culture were regularly held as well as study sessions to discuss current speeches and writings. These were supplemented by activities in other aspects of traditional culture, such as music, dance, folk art, painting, calligraphy and theatre. Moral education, moreover, was not limited to the schools and children. The schools were meant to be a cultural training ground that extended eventually to the family and local community in the form of family training groups, social work teams as well as women's and neighbourhood associations. Local organizations usually awarded prizes to model youth, model mothers, model teachers, model farmers and other deserving Samaritans on convenient occasions like Martyr's Day, the birthdays of General Yuefei, the Ming dynasty naval hero Koxinga, the consummate teacher Confucius, and others. Even teachers underwent moral supervision and training by periodically participating in study groups and attending various talks given by scholars on topics pertaining to Chinese culture.

In sum, two dimensions of culture were relevant to the nationalizing experience in postwar Taiwan. The first, which was an overt aspect of cultural policy during the phases of both cultural 'reunification' and 'Renaissance', assumed a need to develop a sense of spiritual consciousness that could directly engender national solidarity. The second, which was an aspect of the Cultural Renaissance movement, necessitated the inculcation of traditional social values through socializing practices (moral training) in the conduct of everyday behaviour. Within an institutional setting, the KMT state attempted to instill moral and cultural precepts through active dissemination of ideology (that is, Confucianism, Nationalist ideology, democracy and science).

In historical terms, the KMT's cultural policy arose from the politics of national survival in a rapidly changing global situation. Cultural discourse was

---

16   See Taiwan Provincial Government (ed.), *Zhonghua wenhua fuxing yundong shi nian jinian zhuanji* [Commemorative Essays on the Tenth Anniversary of the Cultural Renaissance Movement] (Committee for the Promotion of the Chinese Cultural Renaissance Movement, Taipei, 1978).

literally synonymous with cultural policy in the sense that throughout the postwar era, the government designated itself as the sole voice of culture. This authority was backed by the imposition of martial law, which reinforced the impression that culture was itself a matter of national defence. In effect, culture was made into a kind of *totalizing* force insofar as its fate was perceived to be synonymous with national destiny itself. On the other hand, culture was an *individualizing* force insofar as it was perceived to be inseparably linked to the minds and actions of its constituent citizens. Taken together, these totalizing and individualizing tendencies of cultural authority were operational features peculiar to the KMT's vision of the modern polity in a way that viewed the continued survival of the nation as being dependent upon the solidary actions of all individuals in society. While the efficacy among the general populace of mass movements inspired by Cultural Renaissance is debatable, the efficacy of cultural hegemony, as the following section will show, resulted from its de-politicization, secularization and institutional dissemination within the process of socialization.

Hegemony as Process

It is through the state's 'unseen presence' that the modern state has attempted to exercise power and render the mystifications of its collective ideology acceptable to the populace.[17] Political domination has depended less upon the state's physical presence or threat of force than upon a set of institutions designed to diffuse the spectacle of its authority throughout the body politic. This echoes the hegemonic functions that Louis Althusser, following Antonio Gramsci, has attributed to the state's ideological apparatus in modern capitalism.[18] Hegemony here refers not just to the functions of political ideology but also to the existence of institutions devoted to ideological investment. Philip Corrigan and Derek Sayer have thus pointed to the importance of 'moral regulation' in the rise of the modern state in England.[19] Only in the process of modern state formation did the conception of the nation as a collective body emerge along with correlative institutions like the census, statistics and national identity (ID cards) devoted to comprehending society

---

[17]   On this point, see Benjamin, 'The Unseen Presence'.

[18]   Louis Althusser, 'Ideology and Ideological State Apparatus', in his *Lenin and Philosophy* (New Left, London, 1971); Antonio Gramsci, *Selections from the Prison Notebooks*, edited and translated by Q. Hoare and G. Nowell Smith (Lawrence and Wishart, London, 1971).

[19]   Philip Corrigan and Derek Sayer, 'From "The Body Politic" to "The National Interest": English State Formation in Comparative and Historical Perspective (An Argument Concerning Politically Organized Subjection)', Paper presented at the Mellon Foundation Symposium on Modernity and the Nation-State, California Institute of Technology, Pasadena, 1987.

and its population, which became objects of gazing, discourse and control.[20] Consistent with the concept of moral regulation was the need to maintain social well-being and the attempt to construct behaviours or lifestyles that could conform to the perceived interests of the collective whole.[21]

Corrigan and Sayer's discussion of moral regulation resembles, at least superficially, the traditional Chinese emphasis upon moral cultivation which was at the heart of the KMT's organized mass campaigns to heighten national consciousness. Underlying the very idea of moral cultivation was not only a set of social values which had a basis in traditional Chinese thought but also a code of conduct or behaviour which formed the basis of a shared ethos that could be replicated in the minds of each citizen. In this regard, the notion of one language, one race, one origin, and one spirit provided the basis for defining a set of ethical values and rites of everyday etiquette which were to be consistent with this larger vision of society.

In order to understand how this larger ideology of national culture was transformed into everyday practice, one must look first at the way in which certain traditional values, especially those of Confucianism, were used to give meaning to Nationalist ideology, so as to provide a kind of secular ethos for social life. One must then look at the way in which political ideology itself, such as The Three Principles (*Sanmin zhuyi*) of Sun Yat-sen was meaningfully rooted in 'science', 'democracy' and traditional ethics.

Insofar as culture in Taiwan has invoked tradition, it represented a defence of Confucianism as the conceptual basis of Chinese tradition. Like other discourses of tradition, Confucianism was invoked essentially as a set of stripped down ethical values which had a specific role in the service of the state. As a generalized moral philosophy or a kind of social ethics that could be easily translated into secular action, Confucianism entailed here a devotion to filial piety, respect for social authority, and everyday etiquette. This was a far cry from the variations of Confucian orthodoxy that emerged in the different schools of Confucian learning and which through the practice of

---

20   Corrigan and Sayer (ibid., p.100) point to the state as an explicit locus of regulatory power, following the insights of Michel Foucault – particularly in *Discipline and Punish: The Birth of the Prison* (Pantheon, New York, 1977) – who showed how disciplinary institutions created new forms of knowledge like criminology, the social sciences and statistical method as the means by which individuals came to be more effectively regulated in modern society. Similarly, Bernard S. Cohn, in 'The Census, Social Structure and Objectification in South Asia', *Folk*, 26 (1984), pp.25-49 has argued that the census, cadastral surveys, historical knowledge and other forms of 'local knowledge' were important instruments of colonial power which helped put into place modern mechanisms of social control.

21   In this regard, Michel Foucault points to the welfare-state and liberal democracy (instead of the regime of authoritarianism) as the eventual products of modern disciplinary power. See Foucault, *Discipline and Punish*, and more explicitly his 'Politics and the Study of Discourse', in C. Gordon (ed.), *The Foucault Effect: Studies in Governmentality* (University of Chicago Press, Chicago, 1991).

government developed as theories of imperial statecraft, with emphases upon sage-kings, moral cultivation and ritualist ethics. The 1911 Revolution was in many ways a reaction to the conservative, ritualist foundations of late Qing-dynasty Confucianism and its ties to the mandate of Heaven as the cosmological basis of the empire. By overthrowing the imperial system, the Republic was in principle a rejection of the theoretical underpinnings which made Confucianism a political orthodoxy to begin with. Thus, in spite of its appearance as a Confucian state, the KMT nation-state had to be something quite other. Recourse to Confucian tradition in the post-imperial period, especially in its emphasis upon filial piety, was actually an attempt to extend feelings of family solidarity to the level of the nation, which as a political entity was, on the other hand, founded upon a rationality that was by definition modern, and hence non-traditional.

The divergent positions taken by the KMT and the mainland with regard to Confucianism split precisely over their opposing viewpoints with regard to filial piety. While the KMT opted to view national unity as an extension of primary family ties, the mainland chose to reject Confucian filial piety by subordinating the family to the good of greater society, as defined by the state. This divergence in policy toward Confucianism was an explicit point of difference between the two regimes and clearly manifested itself at many levels of rhetoric and text.[22] At the primary-school level, the classical text *Ershisi xiao* [Twenty-Four Stories of Filial Piety] emphasized social etiquette and personal health. At a higher educational level, the study of Confucian ethics was taught using selected classical works and was combined with the teaching of political ideology in a way that lent to Nationalist moral philosophy a generally Confucian flavour.

The teaching of Nationalist ethics and political ideology is a further example not only of how culture (as nationhood) was rewritten at all levels of interpretation but also of how the writing of culture had to be viewed as the collective labour of various agents of the system insofar as it involved the regulation of public behaviour at all levels of everyday practice. In this regard, it is widely known that although canonized as the founding principles of the Republic, The Three Principles of Sun Yat-sen was not a formal treatise written by the author but a collection of essays compiled and edited posthumously, then credited to him. Nonetheless, these lectures became the point of departure for continued writing and formulation of The Three Principles, and perhaps like the case of Confucianism it was really these post-hoc discourses and their ongoing mutations that became the basis not only of Nationalist ideology *per se* but more importantly a broader view of 'traditional Chinese culture'. One might even argue that the two supplementary chapters

---

22   Roberta Martin, in 'The Socialization of Children in China and on Taiwan: An Analysis of Elementary School Textbooks', *The China Quarterly*, vol.62, no.2 (1975), pp.244-9, shows that differences in ideology were systematically written into school children's textbook narratives and fables.

on the principle of livelihood appended by Chiang Kai-shek to the original text of The Three Principles helped transform Sun's thought into a general treatise on ethics, democracy and science which made it conducive to the overall climate of Cultural Renaissance. Given the flurry of writings by scholars expounding upon the underlying principles of Sun's political and cultural philosophy as well as the explicit attempt by the KMT government to institute the teaching of The Three Principles as part of the mandatory curriculum at all levels of education, it is clear that Nationalist party ideology constituted an object of *ideological investment* and *institutional normalization* in ways that were relevant to cultural discourse as a whole.

The *malleability* of Nationalist ideology to suit the needs of different sociopolitical conditions rather than its textual *authenticity* was what ultimately enabled The Three Principles to be transformed from political doctrine, strictly speaking, into a broadly conceived cultural ideology consistent with all other representations of the imagined community. For much of the early history of the Republican era after the 1911 Revolution, Nationalist political ideology was intended to serve an important function as a revolutionary agent of sociopolitical change.[23] The transformation of Nationalist ideology away from revolutionary pragmatism had much to do with Chiang Kai-shek's New Life Movement and his particular interpretation of The Three Principles.[24] As the Chinese Communist Party increasingly saw The Three Principles as a revolutionary doctrine written from a pre-Communist petty bourgeois perspective, the ideological split between the two parties intensified correspondingly. However, it was really during the Cultural Renaissance movement and its anti-Communist fervour that the systematic transformation of The Three Principles into a doctrine of cultural traditionalism took place.

---

[23]   Tsui Tsuiyen argued that the influences of pragmatism and empiricism were clearly implanted in Sun's Three Principles as a result of his Western training overseas. See Tsui Tsuiyen, in 'Sanmin zhuyi wei minsheng daode zhi biaoxian' [The Three Principles as the Manifestation of the Morality of Livelihood], in his *Minsheng shi guan lun cong* (Jindai zhongguo, Taipei, 1979), p.3. In a similar vein, Chang Hao noted that the focus of The Three Principles was largely upon the revolutionary character of nationalism and anti-imperialism in relation to which the emphasis upon democracy (*minquan*) and livelihood (*minsheng*) was secondary. See Chang Hao in 'Sanmin zhuyi de yuebian — you zhengzhi zongjiao zou xiang gailiang zhuyi' [The Transition of The Three Principles — From Political Religion to Reformism], in Chen Yishen and Liu Ahrong (eds), *Sunwen sixiang de lilun yu shiji — cankao ziliao xuanji* [Sun Yat-sen's Thought in Theory and Practice — A Selection of Source Material] (Hungwen guan, Taipei, 1987), p.189. See also Chen Yishen, 'Zhengzhi yishi xingtai de liubian — yi sanmin zhuyi wei li' [Shifts in Political Ideology — The Case of The Three Principles], in Chen Yishen and Liu Ahrong, *Sunwen sixiang de lilun yu shiji*, pp.742-3.

[24]   This was most clearly spelled out in a 1952 lecture entitled 'The Essence of The Three Principles' (*Sanmin zhuyi de benzhi*), which is reprinted in Chen Yishen and Liu Ahrong, *Sunwen sixiang de lilun yu shiji*, pp.107-20.

It was determined early on that public education would be primarily devoted to political training and that the KMT would be an active agent in the writing of the curriculum.[25] The guideline underlying the mapping of the curriculum was clearly spelled out in government directives: the focus at the elementary-school level would be upon the application of concrete practice, in middle school upon the correct learning of concepts, and in high school upon the understanding of underlying principles. Even after the explicit teaching of nationalist principles shed the title of 'party ideology', it continued to be diffused throughout all levels of education and expanded in content to include other aspects of social life, ethico-moral values, and personal conduct — that is, ultimately all aspects of public behaviour. By the time this course on 'citizenship' was renamed 'The Three Principles (of Sun Yat-sen)' in 1944 and again in 1950, the government had already begun to systematically program the focus of education toward the long-term cultivation of a Nationalist worldview.

This systematic program coincided with the publication of Chiang Kai-shek's 'Two Amendments to the Cultivation of the Principle of Livelihood' (*Minsheng zhuyi yulo liang pian bushu*) in 1953. Standardized textbooks on The Three Principles issued by the Ministry of Education began to appear around this time, followed by fifteen years of experimentation in course offerings. In 1968, the curriculum was revised more or less permanently, with courses at the elementary level focusing upon 'life and ethics' and courses at the secondary level focusing upon 'citizenship and morality'.[26]

The systematic reconstruction of The Three Principles at all levels of education was the direct historical consequence of an explicit program to politicize education from the point of view of the KMT. On the other hand, the range of courses on personal conduct, moral behaviour and civic values made

---

25   The idea of a party-based education was actually a continuation of prewar educational policy. In 1929, the Ministry of Education formally implemented a course on 'Party ideology' (*dangyi*) as the nucleus around which the government aimed to define and achieve its goal of Nationalist education. In 1932, this course was renamed 'citizenship' (*gongmin*) and widened to include topics on ethics, morality, politics, law and economics. This was taught as a required course in high school. In addition, other complementary courses on 'common sense', 'health training' and 'civic training' were instituted at the elementary and middle-school levels.

26   The explicit emphasis in all these courses upon the cultivation of a higher national collective conscience cannot be overemphasized. In chapter 72 of volume 6 of the textbook 'Citizenship and Morality' used at the elementary-school level, no less than 1,387 references can be found to words invoking nationhood, China, patriotism, society, and world (not even counting less exact references to Chinese culture, the people, and so on). In contrast, only 298 references are found to words invoking individuals and individuality. See Cheng Rongzhou, *Guomin zhongxue daode jiaocai de yishi xingtai zhi pipan yanjiu* [A Critical Study of Ideology in Middle School Morals Textbooks], MA thesis, Three Principles Institute, Taiwan National Normal University, Taipei (1989), p.40.

clear that the successful acquisition of correct political ideology was founded equally importantly upon the cultivation of an ethico-moral lifestyle in all other respects. Thus, piety, etiquette and deference were not just limited to family virtues, as might be inferred from Confucian notions of filial piety, narrowly defined. They were supposed to be the moral foundation of all societal relationships. The cultivation of these values in the practice of everyday life was as much the precondition for successfully inculcating the broader vision of Nationalist society as was the explicit teaching of correct political ideology. In other words, to achieve this goal of politicizing education, it became important to see how political ideology in abstract terms represented the 'natural' culmination of moral education and the normal practice of everyday social life.[27]

The writing of national ideology in the context of education has been from the outset a crucial dimension of the KMT's attempt to define culture and to use the symbols of a common culture as the basis by which to cultivate a unitary societal consciousness and thus perpetuate or reproduce the nation-state. While the government's political authority to construct and define culture was backed by the power of the totalitarian state, the construction of an ideology (culture) of the nation (in all its flavours) through the writing and dissemination of political ideology (ethics and philosophy) and the promotion of master symbols of the body politic and various rituals of state was predicated upon a different kind of politics altogether — namely cultural hegemony. Underlying the overt politicization of the Cultural Renaissance and the dissemination of political ideology through education was the internal transformation of political values into neutral or sublimated form — that is, by invoking tradition and by appealing to ethical virtue and moral conduct. Hegemony was thereby the end result of a complex process of ideological transformation, and it was really the latter that has been actively promoted through social movements as culture.

The writing of ideology and culture in the process of constructing a hegemony ultimately represented part of an even larger project of socialization in institutional terms. For it was really within this larger framework of socialization that the active promotion of culture served a crucial role in the government's project of constructing rites and routines of disciplinary lifestyle

---

27   Liu Dingxiang phrased it clearly when he remarked, 'from the goals and aspirations of this kind of education, it would appear that 'party-based education' (*danghua jiaoyu*) did not have any strong intent of creating an ideological regime; on the contrary, one could even say that enlightenment about democracy (*minzhu qimeng*) and the development of rationality (*lixing de zhankai*) were the means to promote the education of political liberation. In this regard, the primordial meaning of party-based education was to view education as the agent of revolutionary change, democratization, scientific progress and socialization'. See Liu Dingxiang, in *Zhengzhi yishi xingtai yu guomin zhongxue 'gongmin yu daode' jiaocai zhi yanjiu* [A Study of Political Ideology and Textbook Materials in Middle School 'Citizenship and Morality' Courses], MA thesis, School of Education, Taiwan National Normal University (1989), p.65.

in various domains of social interaction. In this regard, filial piety, national ideology, codes of ethical conduct, work ethics and civic obligations were all manifestations of a larger set of life principles which had as their ultimate goal 'the making of a moral person' (*zuoren*). Literally speaking, the concept of *zuoren* simply meant displaying proper conduct, and in the context of different institutions it became in practice a code word for conformity to the routines and behaviour of the institution, whatever they were. The practice of everyday life thus depended on moral correctness in the same sense that upward mobility within the system was often accompanied by moral training (*shouxun*).

In practice, such moral regulation depended upon the collusion of many institutional agents at the local level, the most important being the party and the military. Given the single-party politics of the state, the line separating party from government was always ambiguous to begin with. All civil servants were strongly persuaded to be active members of the party. Party units were set up in each institution, and members not only actively engaged in recruitment of new members but were constantly on the outlook as well, supervising the actions and thoughts of colleagues.[28] Similarly, the appointment of military personnel as *jiaoguan* (school officers) or enforcers of proper moral behaviour was an extension of the state into the disciplinary apparatus of secondary schools and universities. One responsibility of the *jiaoguan* was to oversee the activities of the China Youth Corps (literally Anti-Communist China Youth for National Restoration Corps, a party-sponsored group to which many students belonged). The presence of the military, while seen in some ways as a direct imposition of the party and state in the operation of the school, was also portrayed as part of the overall civilizing environment of the school. For males, the socializing function of military training became most evident during the two years of mandatory conscription, where military training was combined with political indoctrination, moral teaching and daily discipline.

Officially speaking, the government has never declared an end to the Cultural renaissance movement, and promotion of these activities continues to the present day in the schools, military and other institutions under the direct supervision of the government or the party. However, emphasis upon cultural renaissance began to diminish from about 1977 onward with the promotion of cultural reconstruction (*wenhua jianshe*).[29] The call for cultural reconstruction

---

28   Lin Yuti, in *Taiwan jiaoyu mianmao sishi nian* [Forty Years of Education in Taiwan] (Zili wanbao, Taipei, 1985), p.29, notes that one earned merit points on one's achievement report (*chengji kaohe*) for such activities.

29   I prefer to translate *wenhua jianshe* as cultural reconstruction instead of cultural development, as it is translated officially, in order to accent its historicity as something which emerged in the aftermath of the Cultural Renaissance movement and to suggest that the work of the government in this regard should really be classified as a kind of

was the last of twelve recommendations put forth by President Chiang Ching-kuo to the Legislative Yuan on 23 September 1977 as part of his package for national development and complemented new policy initiatives to stimulate economic progress and raise standards of living.

A Committee for Cultural Reconstruction was established in November 1981 under the aegis of the Executive Yuan to take responsibility for the management of cultural affairs. Its work was meant to coordinate with that of the Committee for Cultural Renaissance and focused predominantly on the 'fine arts', such as music, art, theatre, expressive culture and heritage conservation. Like the earlier work of cultural renaissance, cultural reconstruction was concerned with actively promoting culture to advance society. Unlike cultural renaissance, by placing national culture within the context of the arts, cultural reconstruction was meant to be explicitly 'non-political' in orientation and as such regularly sponsored cultural interchange of various sorts. Cultural centres (wenhua zhongxin) were set up in each township to organize and promote cultural activities. They were responsible not only for cultivating the broader view of Chinese tradition but also for promoting interest in and preservation of local traditions. The domestication of culture during this era of reconstruction coincided with the development of 'the culture industry' in Taiwan in other Regards — such as tourism, media commercialization, public festivals and popular arts.[30] Following an era of unprecedented economic growth, cultural reconstruction was viewed as an index for measuring social progress at a time when threats to national security became increasingly removed from everyday life.

The promotion of cultural reconstruction represented a significant transition in the politics of culture in Taiwan. However, far from 'depoliticizing' culture, as might be interpreted from the apparent blooming of culture and the arts in the age of newfound prosperity, this trend toward the secularization of culture was consistent with the KMT's overall attempt to indigenize Nationalist ideology and to defuse the mainland-Taiwanese ethnic tensions that had plagued most of Taiwan's postwar history. This trend can be attributed largely to the vision of Chiang Ching-kuo, which contrasted sharply with the staunch Cold War rhetoric of his predecessor and father Chiang Kai-shek. In this regard, the establishment of a Chinese cultural hegemony, rooted in the origins of civilization, its sense of continuous history, Confucian ethical legitimacy, and the spiritual consciousness of one people that had been inculcated over previous decades, was an important precondition for the reinvention of local tradition and the full-fledged development of cultural

---

cultural construction. I also avoid 'development' so as not to confuse it with the Chinese word fazhan.

[30]   One can argue here that Max Horkheimer and Theodor W. Adorno's notion of a culture industry, as originally spelled out in 'The Culture Industry', in their The Dialectic of Enlightenment [orig. 1944] (Continuum, New York, 1972), is characteristic more generally of the modern nation-state.

values. Instead of instilling meaning into the notion of an autonomous Taiwanese culture, it served even more firmly to anchor local folkways within the larger cultural stream of Chinese history, language and civilization. Moreover, during this era of 'liberalization' of culture, there was little indication that the government had actually relinquished its *authority* over the writing and practice of culture.[31] The culture industry remained very much a state enterprise. If anything, its authority over culture was enhanced by its success in extending the legitimacy of Chinese culture to encompass all Chinese cultures.

During this period, the mass media continued to play an important role in disseminating public culture. Controlled by the government's News Bureau (*xinwen ju*) and its various arms, the mass media had always been an important voice for official information about culture. Rigid censorship was enforced in all forms of mass media, such as television, radio, newspapers and other printed literature, to ensure the suppression of Communist sentiment and of views generally unfavourable to the government so as to reinforce the consensus of a unified people and the harmony of an ethical worldview, all of which were seen as crucial to the maintenance of a stable society.

The work of the News Bureau covered the publication of foreign-language journals like *Free China Review* and *Sinorama* as well as weekly newspapers like *Free China Journal*, five small-scale magazines and 178 occasional pamphlets and monographs, many of which were sent free-of-charge to public agencies and select individuals, both domestically and abroad. As these publications included both propagandistic information and writings on the 'softer' side of cultural, artistic, 'folk-popular' and touristic interest, displayed in glossy format and written for easy consumption, they also grew with the evolution of an increasingly diverse and refined culture industry.

Similarly, cultural centres not only served as local activity centres for artistic, musical and folk programs but also sponsored research on local society. Each cultural centre was staffed by research personnel, who in collaboration with local scholars regularly produced monographs on local history, folk customs and traditional arts. Like the cultural publications produced by other government agencies, these monographs were distributed free-of-charge among interested agencies and persons as though to underscore the importance of redistributing cultural capital among a broad range of consumers, in the name of heightening national consciousness and at the expense of profit-maximization. Yet this kind of cultural promotion was no

---

[31] To exemplify the coordination between state agencies in relation to the work of culture, Li Yih-yuan notes that the head of the Committee of Cultural Reconstruction also serves nominally as the general secretary of the Committee of Cultural Renaissance. Li Yih-yuan, *Taiwan guangfu yi lai wenhua fazhan de jingyan yu pinggu* [The Experience and Assessment of Cultural Development Since the Restoration of Taiwan], in *Wenhua de tuxiang* [Images of Culture], vol.1 (Yunchen, Taipei, 1992), p.20.

less hegemonic than the culture industry found elsewhere. Within this hegemonic scheme, the commodification or objectification of culture was the inevitable result of a deliberate process of demystifying the traditional (sacred) aura of culture as a precondition for making it a tangible entity accessible to all citizens.

With the transition to cultural reconstruction, one begins to see the emergence of a well-organized and diversified culture industry. By depoliticizing national culture and institutionally diffusing the hegemony of the whole onto a local level (through cultural centres), reconstruction enabled culture to become *categorized* (as an object of gazing, discourse and practice), *commodified* (for public consumption), and *totalized* (through universal accessibility) in a way which was not previously possible.

Politics of the Unreal

Much commotion has been caused in the literature on nationalism since Ernest Gellner first put forth his radical thesis that (the ideology of) nationalism created (the phenomenon of) nations everywhere instead of *vice versa*.[32] This is not to say that the idea of the nation alone or the diffusion of nationalism as political ideology was a sufficient criterion for the adoption of the nation-state as social institution but rather that the conceptual underpinnings of that institution, whatever they were, constituted an important basis for its continued existence. While Gellner in later writings stressed the significance of culture as a phenomenon that often succinctly embodied aspects of this new national identity defined in terms of language, custom, history, ethnicity, and the like, he also opened up the possibility that other kinds of ideological constructions were at work.

One notable example is Benedict Anderson's often cited notion of the modern nation as 'imagined community'. In his attempt to explain the rapid rise and spread of nationalism, especially in countries where the idea of a homogeneous community bound by equal, autonomous individuals was totally foreign to local societies bound by traditional ties of familiarity and kinship, Anderson's attention was largely focused, as noted earlier, upon how abstract notions of national identity had been made possible by the creation of a colloquial language and disseminated through the medium of popular literature and mass culture. By virtue of its radical departure from pre-modern culture, where the sacred aura of a hierarchical, cosmological order and esoteric rites of state were usually set apart from the provincialism of local custom and language, the emergence of the nation had to be by definition a fictive or imaginative construct that had to be constantly realized and reproduced as a condition for its continued existence.

While Gellner and Anderson have rightly pointed to certain ideological imperatives that have led to the emergence of nationalism — that is, its

---

[32] Ernest Gellner, *Thought and Change* (Routledge, London, 1964).

possibilities of being — they have on the other hand been relatively less concerned with the nature of cultural construction in the aftermath of nationalist revolution and with the ways in which cultural discourses have necessarily responded to ongoing sociopolitical change. In other words, how does any one nation deal with its ethnicity, customs and tradition, and how do changes in cultural definition reflect back on the agents of change?

Political scientists like Louis Althusser and Antonio Gramsci, writing in a Marxist tradition, and historical sociologists like Philip Corrigan and Derek Sayer, commenting upon the historical novelty of the nation-state, have spelled out certain institutional characteristics of the state in a way that sheds light upon the functions of these imaginative constructions of culture. By emphasizing the role of hegemony, ideological mystification and collective misrepresentation in the state's inherent overall project of disinterested domination, they have reiterated the position that the state cannot thrive by domination alone and that its dominance depends upon the extent to which it is able to make intrinsic fictions of (cultural) ideology real (that is, socially acceptable) in the minds of individuals, and in the process sublimate the violence of political domination.

The case of postwar Taiwan shows that cultural construction has been a complex process of writing, socialization and politicization in ways which have always been intricately tied to ongoing sociopolitical conditions. Yet at this point, one must ask, how *successful* has this elaborate cultural construction been in legitimizing the Republic of China in the minds of individuals? The recent resurgence of Taiwanese ethnic consciousness during the post-1989 era of democratization after decades of martial law has shown that the history of political domination and hegemony has not been able to eradicate local cultures of resistance, despite the state's lofty intentions. Yet, on the other hand, the failure of the Democratic Progressive Party to rally support for Taiwanese independence among a predominantly Taiwanese population, as evidenced by the results of the first popular elections after the lifting of martial law, presents us with a curious dilemma.

While it is too early to predict the future of Taiwanese independence, it is important to note that Taiwanese nationalism represents a critique of the Republic of China as nation-state construction in two possible senses — that is, as cultural imagination (nation) and as societal polity (state). Aided by the KMT's gradually weakening claim of political guardianship over all of China and its subsequent retreat from its previous insistence upon recovering the mainland, the Taiwanese independence movement has attempted to capitalize upon the need to recognize instead the political reality of a predominantly ethnic Taiwanese nation, by using the cultural reality of a Taiwanese nation as the basis of a new societal polity.

Without denying the reality of a predominantly Taiwanese population, the issue of ethnic nationalism has been influenced less by a failure to demonstrate the reality of Taiwanese ethnicity than by a failure to unmask the hegemonic fictions of traditional Chineseness that have been inculcated as a result of decades of cultural discourse. Anchored still to a cultural China by the myth of shared origins (*huaxia*), the independence movement has refused to separate nation (as ethnic community) from state (as political apparatus), choosing instead to seek alternative cultural origins in the imagination of an indigenous (pre-Japanese, pre-KMT) past.

In the span of a few decades, the KMT has attempted to naturalize the imagination of a Chinese nation-state, founded upon the imposition of a common language and ideology, routinized in the ritual of everyday life, and orchestrated though social movements. One may doubt the effectiveness of these mass movements to engender any genuine feelings of patriotic fervour, but these superficial sentiments are clearly secondary to the unconscious cultural fictions that are at the root of the state's project of hegemonic domination. Equally important, the history of the modern nation-state shows that while the writing and practice of culture were in fact novel creations by the state to maintain its ongoing existence, the phenomenon of hegemonic construction has at the same time been largely the privilege of those in power. It certainly may be possible for the advocates of Taiwanese independence and other repressed voices in history to stake their cultural claim in a contested political arena, but it remains to be seen whether those operating outside institutional power, namely the rest of civil society, can meaningfully reformulate the content of culture as a means of successfully effecting societal change (this being the naiveté of Gramsci). I think much more would be gained in the long run by questioning the nature and authority of the nation-state itself. By controlling the course of culture, the changing nature of politics is the key to its own future.

SEVEN

'Special Things in Special Ways': National Identity and China's Special Economic Zones

George T. Crane

In April 1992 Vice-Premier Tian Jiyun gave a speech at the Central Party School in which he ridiculed 'leftism'. He invoked the Special Economic Zones (SEZs) to deride conservative opponents of economic reform:

> Couldn't you establish a special economic zone for leftists? . . . Salaries would be low, you would rely on coupons, you would have to stand on line to buy everything and suffer everything else that goes along with leftism . . . If we actually set up [such] a place . . . would anyone want to go?[1]

His audience of aspiring Party bureaucrats laughed at the absurdity of a leftist SEZ and the idea of willingly returning to the economic stagnation of the past.

Tian's speech was notable for its political import in support of Deng Xiaoping's 1992 southern offensive to accelerate economic growth and quicken the pace of reform.[2] It also demonstrated a transformation of Chinese economic discourse. Although Tian's target was 'leftism', not socialism *per se*, his rhetoric deflates the socialist myth. He suggests that state socialist alternatives to SEZs, areas that by definition allow for exceptions to socialist practice, are so backward and hurtful as to be virtually unthinkable: 'Would anyone want to go?' The SEZs, by contrast, are now an accepted model for what China should be, perhaps already is, economically. Foreign firms, consumer goods, Hong Kong fashions, business deals, stock markets — these are the implicit signs of China's economic sense of itself. The vision of the

---

[1] Quoted in Sheryl WuDunn, 'Bootleg Tape of Aide's Jab is Hit in China', *The New York Times*, 31 May 1992, p.7.

[2] Roderick MacFarquhar, 'Deng's Last Campaign', *New York Review of Books*, vol.39, no.21 (17 December 1992), pp.22-8.

national economy implicit in Tian's comments is clear: China has moved away from the inefficiencies and poverty of late Maoist 'leftism' and embraced the free-wheeling practices of the SEZs, a change for the better in his reckoning. Although his evaluation may be contested by Chinese critics of the reforms, it is significant as an assertion of an economic identity.

Articulating an economic identity is no small matter. Reform advocates expend a great deal of energy describing the character of China's economy — from 'socialist commodity economy', to 'primary stage of socialism', to 'socialist market economy' — most likely in the belief that reframing the official rhetoric and paradigms will influence political opinions and policy agendas. Ideological issues loom large in the debate over the nature of the Chinese economy but, as will be discussed below, a national economic identity cannot be reduced to ideology alone. State leaders, and other prominent image makers, employ a wide array of concepts and rhetoric, not strictly confined to ideological orthodoxy, to construct understandings of a national economy that will inspire people to produce, consume and invest in ways supportive of growth while preserving extant political institutions.

This chapter explores China's economic identity as revealed in debates surrounding the establishment and expansion of Special Economic Zones. The concept of 'national economic identity' will be developed in a discussion of how national identity is expressed in economic matters. The language used in China to define and criticize the SEZs is then examined for insights into the formation and reformulation of Chinese economic identity.

National Economic Identity

National identity is often defined in political terms. Recent theorizing holds that nations are not primordial groupings but modern creations forged from a variety of historical sources, including ethnicity, race, language, religion, shared experience and geography. The impetus for shaping national communities is rooted, argues Ernest Gellner, in the social strains of industrial society, with its complex division of labour that cuts across narrower collective identities, and the rise of the bureaucratic state.[3] These macro-historical processes demand, in Gellner's words, cultural homogeneity, a broadening of social ties that unifies parochial communities and eases the dislocations of economic and political transformation. 'Nationalism' is an ideology of this endeavour to expand the collective identity, and it 'holds that the political and the national unit should be congruent'.[4] 'National identity' is more diffuse than the political program of nationalism.[5] The 'nation' is the cultural object with which people identify and which the state strives to bound and secure. For Eric Hobsbawm, 'Nations do not make states and nationalisms

---

[3]   Ernest Gellner, *Nations and Nationalism* (Cornell University Press, Ithaca, 1983), ch.3.

[4]   Ibid., p.1.

[5]   Anthony Smith, *National Identity* (University of Nevada Press, Reno, 1991), p.vii, ch.1.

but the other way around'.[6] It would seem, then, that specific definitions of a nation are fragile, an unsurprising outcome if, following Hobsbawm's argument, the project of national identification is understood as an attempt 'to fit historically novel, emerging, changing and, even today, far from universal entities into a framework of permanence and universality'.[7]

National identity, however unstable its meaning, reaches beyond politics and culture to economic life as well. In the first instance, as argued by Gellner, economic transformations condition the rise of nationalism and, through nationalism, the nation. As states draw political boundaries around newly created nations, they also delineate territorial economies that in turn provide material sustenance for the national community. Production, exchange, consumption and investment are more than just foundation stones of the national home, however; they are also expressions of the national self. Harry Johnson, in his landmark study of economic nationalism, hints at this facet of the relationship of nation and economy: 'Nationalist economic policy will tend to foster activities selected for their symbolic value in terms of concepts of national identity and the economic content of nationhood'.[8]

A national economy can be envisioned in any of a number of ways, each of which is bound up with malleable understandings of national identity. Just as the 'nation' arises from a complex of elements — ethnicity, race, geography, historical experience, language — so, too, is a national economic identity multi-dimensional, drawing upon, though by no means limited to, interpretations of predominant economic practice (industry versus agriculture), position in the world economy, and the economic role of the state. Economic identity is, as Hobsbawm suggests for national identity, a 'dual phenomenon'; that is, interpretations come from the 'top down', the purview of state managers, and from the 'bottom up', the realm of social forces and movements.[9] It is of acute importance for state elites because the efficient and predictable extraction of economic resources from society requires mass acceptance of certain economic ideas, or at least popular quiescence in the face of meaningful economic symbols.

The political utility of economic identity can be seen in the case of Taiwan. In recent years Taiwan has been portrayed as a newly industrializing, semi-peripheral, economic success with a strong state that embraces the syncretic ideology of Sun Yat-sen and turns Chinese cultural practices to

---

6   E. J. Hobsbawm, *Nations and Nationalism since 1870: Programme, Myth, Reality* (Cambridge University Press, Cambridge, Mass., 1990), p.10.

7   Ibid., p.6.

8   Harry Johnson, *Economic Nationalism in Old and New States* (University of Chicago Press, Chicago, 1962), pp.13-14.

9   Hobsbawm, *Nations and Nationalism Since 1870*, pp.10-11.

economic advantage.[10] This definition is, of course, time-bound. In the early 1950s it was not clear that Taiwan was an economic success waiting to happen, and in the early 1990s domestic political change and extensive ties with China are inspiring new economic identities.[11] More importantly, Taiwan's national economic identity has figured prominently in its politics, as state managers have sought to define and defend the island's economy by creating inspirational images. Yet the picture of Taiwan as 'Free China', upholding the principles of free market liberalism, was, in the 1950s especially, empirically false. The domestic market was heavily protected, the state dominated the economy, and prevailing economic ideology was closer to Friedrich List than Adam Smith. But the liberal economic image was politically significant in a number of ways. It helped to cement the relationship with the United States, a key to economic transformation, and it held out a promise of economic opportunity to the politically excluded Taiwanese majority.[12] In Taiwan, as of the early 1960s, the prospect of economic liberalism enhanced the state's legitimacy and prolonged KMT hegemony.

Quite the opposite has been the case in China, where an economic identity crisis of sorts has periodically exploded in wrenching realignments of policy and practice. The Great Leap Forward, for example, was a rejection of the dichotomous characterization of predominant economic activity as either agriculture or industry. Instead, Mao Zedong embellished the institutional interests behind Leap policies with a utopian rhetoric of far-reaching social transformation and the rapid attainment of a new position in the world economy — catching up with Great Britain — not as another advanced capitalist country but as a modern communist power.[13] The Great Leap also attempted to create its own economic culture, in which functional specializations would be subsumed by a universalizing collectivism. Although

---

10   Thomas Gold, *State and Society in the Taiwan Miracle* (M. E. Sharpe, Armonk, 1986); John C. Fei et al., *Growth with Equity: The Taiwan Case* (Oxford University Press, New York, 1979); A. James Gregor, *Ideology and Development: Sun Yat-sen and the Economic History of Taiwan* (Center for Chinese Studies, Berkeley, 1981); George T. Crane, 'The Taiwanese Ascent: System, State and Movement in the World-Economy', in Edward Friedman (ed.), *Ascent and Decline in the World-System* (Sage, Beverly Hills, 1982).

11   Julian Baum, 'Independence Crusade Gains Impetus', *Far Eastern Economic Review* vol.155, no.41 (15 October 1992), p.15

12   Thomas Gold discusses the legitimacy of the KMT state in terms of a changing 'pact of domination' inherent in the move to export-oriented industrialization around 1960. See Gold, *State and Society in the Taiwan Miracle*, pp.18, 95-6, 123-5.

13   David Bachman discusses the institutional interests behind Leap policies in *Bureaucracy, Economy, and Leadership in China: The Institutional Origins of the Great Leap Forward* (Cambridge University Press, New York, 1991). For a critique, see Frederick C. Teiwes, 'Leaders, Institutions, and the Origins of the Great Leap Foward: Review Article', *Pacific Affairs*, vol.66, no.2 (Summer 1993).

its tragic failure was not enough to undo the legitimacy of the Communist Party, the Leap's far-reaching effort to reinvent China's economic identity set the stage for the Cultural Revolution and has haunted post-Mao reformers as they struggle to script the future.

The experiences of the Great Leap Forward and Taiwan suggest the importance of national economic identity and also reveal its subtlety and complexity. Economic liberalizers in Taiwan in the 1960s saw themselves as solving specific problems, not as defining national visions.[14] But in the very specificity of their acts they were recasting the economic facet of Taiwan's collective identity, turning it from an inward-looking agricultural backwater to an export-oriented industrial dynamo. On the other hand, the Great Leap was, especially for Mao, a conscious effort to redefine the character of China's economy. In this case, however, the project failed; China would not become what Mao wanted it to be. The lesson here may be that an identity that strays too far from people's lived experience may be unsustainable over time:[15] the reality of famine simply overwhelmed the promise of communist utopia. Economic identity is, then, beyond the absolute control of political leaders. It can crystallize from the cumulation of many seemingly insignificant actions and it can dissolve even when strengthened by the grandest gestures.

How, then, can state managers fix the meaning of economic circumstances and construct a collective identity that bolsters their legitimacy and heightens their capacity to rule? To a certain degree, they are constrained by the conditions they are trying to interpret. If the economy is sliding into disaster, optimistic claims of success will ring hollow and possibly undermine the credibility of the claimants. Nonetheless, political leaders do have some room for manoeuvre in defining and redefining the economic milieu. What is most remarkable about the Great Leap is the very limited extent to which it damaged the authority of the Communist Party. The leadership, though increasingly divided, deftly diffused the semantic tension between rhetoric and reality. Scapegoats were found to carry the blame, policies were revamped to ease the agricultural emergency, and the language of planning and consolidation was invoked more prominently, even as Mao was developing a very different agenda of Cultural Revolution. What this suggests is that skilful manipulation of public language and political action can overcome people's economic fears and preserve a sense of national community.

The construction of economic identity thus hinges on the interplay of collective economic experience and the representation of that experience in the public utterances and actions of political officials. The process is grounded in perceived circumstances: an identity cannot be invented out of whole cloth, but is complicated by polysemy, a multiplicity of plausible meanings that can

---

[14]   K. T. Li, *The Evolution of Policy Behind Taiwan's Development Success* (Yale University Press, New Haven, 1988), pp.142-3, 145-6.

[15]   William Bloom, *Personal Identity, National Identity and International Relations* (Cambridge University Press, Cambridge, Mass., 1990), pp.59-65.

be assigned to any specific fact. What does China's recent 13 per cent annual growth rate mean? Was it an indicator of a dynamic transformation that will make China a global economic power in the near future? Or was it a dangerous overheating, indicative of a loss of control and impending chaos? Was it a sign of the economic efficacy of Chinese culture or a validation of a particular strategy of reform that may be replicable in other countries? How some meanings come to hold more evocative power than others is the crux of national identity, economic or otherwise.

An exploration of all facets of national economic identity is well beyond the scope of this chapter. My project will be confined, therefore, to examining the 'top-down' aspect of Chinese economic identity as it plays itself out in a single policy: the Special Economic Zones. The zones are an apt focus because their short history is marked by controversies over definition and interpretation. By limiting my study to the debates among state managers, the political significance of national economic identity will be highlighted. The principle questions are: what do the SEZs mean to China's political leadership and how have SEZ images informed China's national identity?

China Constructs SEZs

SEZs are both products and producers of China's new economic identity. They emerged from the crisis of late Maoism. Hua Guofeng's definition of China's economy left no room for 'special' efforts beyond the repertoire of Maoist theory and practice, but the sense of economic failure articulated by various other leaders instigated reform and legitimized SEZs. Without a national economic identity of failure and decline, the idea of a 'special zone' could hardly have arisen in China in 1979. Once created, however, the zones have come to symbolize a new identity that in turn is shaping representations of the national economy. SEZs are models for a China transformed, rejecting socialism but resisting an unequivocally capitalist personality, and aspiring to be an East Asian success story.

Late Maoism bequeathed to China a structural economic crisis. Excessive investment in heavy industry had taken resources away from agriculture and light industry; the 'Third Front' strategy had forced industrialization into costly inland locations; foreign trade was befuddled by Byzantine pricing practices; and entrepreneurial social forces had been smashed by an over-developed state.[16] China's problems were not wholly structural, however, because structures are not completely autonomous from the practices they enable. Structures are given meaning and life by the human agents who

---

16   Carl Riskin, *China's Political Economy: The Quest for Development Since 1949* (Oxford University Press, Oxford, 1987); Nicholas Lardy, *Foreign Trade and Economic Reform in China, 1978-1990* (Cambridge University Press, Cambridge, Mass., 1992); Barry Naughton, 'The Third Front: Defense Industrialization in the Chinese Interior', *The China Quarterly*, no.129 (September 1988), pp.351-6.

understand them, in one manner or another, and who work through or around them.[17] China's crisis, therefore, was and continues to be interpretative as well as objective. The meaning of economic circumstances is contested by various influential actors, a process that parallels the definition of problems and the formulation of policies. National economic identity is the object of this struggle for meaning and the SEZs are sites for such contention.

Since 1979 the definition of SEZs has been keenly disputed and never finally settled.[18] The zones did not emerge fully formed, the product of a comprehensive policy review; rather, they evolved gradually, buffeted by shifting political and economic fortunes. Modelled loosely on export processing zones in other developing countries, the SEZs were originally envisioned as areas where foreign investment would be both permitted and controlled in an effort to gain national economic advantage from world markets. As such, the zones were a decisive break with past economic practice, though the full extent of their novelty would not be evident for years. From their inception, however, the SEZs represented a national economic identity at odds with the language of the Hua Guofeng interregnum.

For Hua Guofeng, Mao's immediate successor, China's economic identity was rooted in the past, the era of socialist construction and autarky.[19] He understood China's dominant economic practice to be heavy industry and he was not worried by imbalances in light industry or agriculture.[20] While calling for dramatic increases in agricultural output, Hua saw no need for structural reforms to improve productivity. Regarding China's position in the world economy, he clung to an image of self-reliance that resisted thoroughgoing integration into global markets.[21] The state's role in the economy was not

---

17   'Social structures, unlike natural structures, do not exist independently of the agents' conceptions of what they are doing in their activity'. See Alexander Wendt, 'The Agent-Structure Problem in International Relations Theory', *International Organization*, vol.41, no.3 (Summer 1987), p.359.

18   George T. Crane, *The Political Economy of China's Special Economic Zones* (M. E. Sharpe, Armonk, 1990), ch.2.

19   Roderick MacFarquhar aptly sums up Hua's political-economic understanding as 'an unlikely combination of mid-60s radicalism and mid-50s economics'. See 'The Succession to Mao and the end of Maoism', in Roderick MacFarquhar and John K. Fairbank (eds), *The Cambridge History of China, Volume 15, The People's Republic, Part 2: Revolutions Within the Chinese Revolution, 1966-1982* (Cambridge University Press, Cambridge, Mass., 1978), p.376.

20   The summary of Hua's economic thinking in the following paragraphs is taken from 'Unite and Strive to Build a Modern, Powerful Socialist Country', *Peking Review*, vol.21, no.10 (10 March 1978); and 'Hua Kuo-feng's Speech at Taching Conference, 9 May 1977', in Harold C. Hinton (ed.), *The People's Republic of China, 1949-1979: A Documentary Survey*, vol.5, (Scholarly Resources, Wilmington, Del., 1980).

21   He recognized the need for expanded foreign trade but avoided full integration into world markets. See Colina MacDougall, 'Policy Changes in Foreign Trade Since the

over-developed, in Hua's view, and only minimal decentralization of decision-making power was needed to improve administrative efficiency. In short, Hua defined China's national economy as structurally sound, poised on the cusp of greatness.

Optimism pervaded Hua's assessment of China's economic performance. Although he would on occasion describe current conditions as 'backward', he dwelt much more on the progress made since 1949 and what was to be accomplished by the year 2000. Shortcomings were blamed on 'interference and sabotage by Liu Shaoqi, Lin Biao, and the Gang of Four'. In light of the 'fine political and economic situation' ushered in by the downfall of the 'Gang of Four', Hua predicted 'gigantic' achievements in the near future. Ideologically, the new Chairman largely adhered to Mao's populist and voluntarist vision, emphasizing that proper political orientation and the sheer force of popular will, aided by modest material incentives, would drive economic expansion.[22] Culture was subsumed by ideology in Hua's discourse, economic success was more a function of socialist principles than traditional practices, and Confucian values were not explicitly invoked because they were politically debased.

Hua's definition of China's economy thus afforded no rationale for 'special economic zones'. If the economy was structurally sound, self-reliant, well planned, rapidly modernizing, and ideologically correct, then special efforts aimed at fundamental change were unnecessary. 'Reform' was a *non sequitur* in Hua's economic thinking because, for him, China was not in crisis.

Alternative renditions of China's economic circumstances coexisted uneasily with Hua Guofeng's imagery. Political leaders of various ranks and outlooks — Deng Xiaoping, Chen Yun, Hu Qiaomu, Zhao Ziyang, and Hu Yaobang — have disagreed with one another, in complex and fluid ways, on the meaning of China's economic identity, but what united them in 1978 was a sense of economic failure. Using Hua's rhetoric (the political context did not allow for a new economic idiom right away), their critique undermined his optimism. The national economy was out of balance, they argued, excessive investment in heavy industry distorting development of agriculture and light industry. Agriculture was 'very weak on the whole', a situation requiring structural reform.[23] Isolation from world markets had proved inefficient and wasteful, cutting China off from dynamic global forces of growth and transformation. The distended scope of state power was suffocating economic initiative; administrative decentralization and a recalibration of plan and

---

Death of Mao, 1976-1980', in Jack Grey and Gordon White (eds), *China's New Development Strategy* (Academic Press, London, 1982), pp.149-71.

[22] 'The broad masses have inexhaustible creative power and are fully capable of making a great leap forward in science and technology by relying on their own strengths'. See 'Speech at Fifth NPC', in Hinton, *The People's Republic of China, 1949-1979*, p.2829.

[23] 'Communique of Third Session of Eleventh Central Committee Plenum', *Peking Review*, vol.21, no.52 (29 December 1978).

market were needed. Standards of living were low and had to be improved. And the misplaced emphasis on ideological correctness subverted 'objective economic laws'. China was thus represented as economically inadequate, threatened by deepening poverty and backwardness.

The language of economic failure provided a medium for framing SEZ policy. Officials in Guangdong and Fujian argued in 1979 that their provinces had been gravely injured, even purposefully under-developed, and they pressed for 'special policies and flexible measures' to overcome their plight.[24] It became an easy conceptual leap from the idea of doing something special to the notion of having a place, a zone, where the special something would be done. Spatial constraints on economic practice have long been a part of Chinese experience, running from the foreign concessions of the nineteenth century to the base areas of the revolution, to the 'Third Front' of the 1960s, to the export commodity production bases of the 1970s. The conception of a 'special economic zone' thus draws upon the familiar convention of economic territoriality and infuses it with a new meaning, leading in turn to a re-invention of China's economic identity.

Identity hinges on difference, the image of an 'other' against which a self is measured.[25] As the significant 'other' of Hua Guofeng was overcome, economic difference has been reconstituted in various ways. Interior others, the bad examples among 'us', have taken a variety of forms. For fiscal conservatives the antagonist is in the shape of irresponsible agents of economic imbalance and disorder; for internationalists, the antagonist is conceived of as nativist champions of autarky; for anti-imperialists, as compradore builders of new foreign concessions; for radical reformers, as gerontocratic defenders of decrepit state enterprise. Exterior others, foreign 'thems' that serve as counter-identities for 'us', are also numerous. Neo-authoritarians invoke politically repressive but economically dynamic East Asian states as protagonists of sorts, positive others that China should emulate. Those worried over 'peaceful evolution' cast the United States as a threat to the economic integrity of socialism. Conversely, for iconoclastic modernizers, the United States serves as a symbol of progress. The Soviet Union figures as a cautionary tale for more circumspect Chinese reformers. The plethora of significant others, both interior and exterior, has fragmented Chinese economic identity into a host of competing interpretations.

SEZs have been swept along in this protracted and complex economic identity crisis. They have been many things to many people. Much of the

---

24   Lawrence C. Reardon, 'The Bird in the Cage: Chinese Export Promotion Policies and the Development of the Special Economic Zones, 1960-1982', PhD Dissertation, Columbia University (1991), pp.195-205.

25   This is the central theme of William Connolly in *Identity/Difference: Democratic Negotiations of Political Paradox* (Cornell University Press, Ithaca, 1991). The following reference to interior and exterior 'others' is taken from this same source (p.40).

debate over the meaning of SEZs, and how they relate to China's national economy, has been conducted in ideological terms. Disputes about their 'nature' (*xingzhi*) raged in the early 1980s until an orthodoxy of sorts emerged, viewing the zones as a politically safe combination of capitalism and socialism.[26] This state capitalist interpretation distinguished China's SEZs, made out as contributors to socialist construction, from various other zonal development policies found in putatively capitalist countries. Although such ideological definitions are important, helping to diffuse some political assaults, what is most striking about these formulations is how irrelevant they are in the practice of China's open international policy. When Deng Xiaoping travelled to Shenzhen in 1984 and again in 1992, his trips were remembered as endorsements of more reform and faster change, not as validations of state capitalism. So, too, people from all over China are drawn to the SEZs because the zones symbolize something more than ideological innovation.

Of course, for some the zones symbolize all that is wrong with China. The critical rhetoric overlaps with the ideological but its appeal does not rely upon references to Marxism-Leninism-Maoism.[27] Representations of SEZs as 'concessions', imitations of the nineteenth-century imperialist treaty ports, appeal to patriotism as much as to socialism. Depictions of Shenzhen as a parasitic enclave 'making money from the rest of the country' play on regional inequalities as well as doctrinal impurities. Worries about creeping 'Hong Kongization' are consistent with ideological condemnations of capitalist excess but they also reflect anxieties over the loss of traditional values. The most powerful critical devices resonate with demotic expressions of unease inspired by the tumult of economic change.

The criticism, however, has not been powerful enough to dominate interpretation of SEZ identity. This is due in part to the political weaknesses of the critics themselves. Only at certain times — most notably mid-1985, early 1987, and mid-1989 — have they been able to muster enough clout to threaten

---

26   Li Kehua (ed.), 'Yijiuba'er nian Guangdongsheng jingji tequ xueshu taolunhui jiyao', [Outline of the 1982 Guangdong Provincial Special Economic Zone Symposium], in Sun Ru, *Qianjinzhong de Zhongguo jingji tequ* [China's Advancing Special Economic Zones] (Zhongguo caizheng jingji chubanshe, Guangzhou, 1983); Jing Tou, 'Guangdongsheng jingji tequ xueshu taolunhui ruogan wenti de butong jianjie' [Several Different Opinions on the Guangdong Provincial Special Economic Zone Symposium], *Jingji kexue* [Economic Science], no.4 (1982).

27   Critical assessments of SEZs are drawn from Chen Yong, 'Guowai chukou jiagongchu he woguo jingji tequ de zhengzhi falu diwei' [Foreign Export Processing Zones and the Political-Legal Position of China's Special Economic Zones], in *Guangdongsheng jingji tequ, falu diaocha baogao* [Guangdong Province Special Economic Zones, Legal Investigation Report] (internal document, no publisher, n.d. [1982?]); Yao Yilin's interview in *Ming bao*, 4 June 1985; 'Report on Hu Qiaomu's Fujian Inspection', *Fujian ribao*, 2 February 1986, in FBIS CHI-86-049; Joseph Fewsmith, 'Special Economic Zones of the PRC', *Problems of Communism*, vol.35, no.6 (November-December 1986), pp.75-85.

SEZ policy seriously. But language does matter and key figures of speech of zone detractors are fraught with ambiguity, to such a degree that they connote the opposite of what is intended. 'Hong Kongization' is the most curious in that, in other contexts, Hong Kong is an icon of modernity revered by state officials. Deng Xiaoping is the most prominent, and far from the only, leader to hold up Hong Kong as a vision of China's future. Although the 'concessions' image may evoke xenophobic feelings, it may also appear anachronistic, especially when China enjoys international status, with a permanent seat on the United Nations Security Council and a nuclear armoury. 'Making money from the rest of the country' may be read not as a denunciation but as an indication of where, and how, money is being made, prompting inland administrators to copy zone policies. The polysemous rhetoric of SEZ criticism does not produce unequivocally negative images.

⟫ Ambiguity is also found in the language of SEZ advocacy, though uncertainty in this context seems to further a reformist, even transformational, project. Zone supporters have created a rhetoric of SEZ exceptionalism that has been used at crucial moments to reassert the zones' identity. The name itself marks them as 'special', and this notion has been interpreted to justify new and extraordinary reform efforts. Hu Yaobang coined an oft quoted slogan in 1983: 'New things should be dealt with in new ways, special things in special ways; adopt completely new methods while not changing position [of opening to the outside]'.[28] Liang Xiang, former mayor of Shenzhen, similarly argued that his zone must enact 'new mechanisms, new systems, new regulations, and new work styles. Otherwise, the "special" will not emerge from the SEZs'.[29] The meanings of 'special' and 'new' are open-ended and context-dependent but their assertion, in all of their vagueness, renders virtually all economic practices in the SEZs liable to change. The new, the different, the experimental are valued above all else. In the language of SEZ exceptionalism, categories of socialism and capitalism are less important than the imperative of the new, ideological rationalizations notwithstanding.

More subtle exceptionalist symbolism also deflates ideological claims. Adorning the Shenzhen Municipal Government Building is a statue of a buffalo straining to uproot a gnarled tree stump. This monument is pictured in various publications about Shenzhen and is meant to capture the spirit of the place. Its title, *ruzi niu*, literally 'to serve as an ox for the children', was used

---

28   Hu Yaobang promises here to maintain the official policy of 'opening to the outside', the one constant in a world of change. See *Zhongguo jingji tequ nianjian, 1983* [Yearbook of China's Special Economic Zones, 1983], (SEZ Yearbook Publisher's, Hong Kong, 1983), pp.89-90.

29   Liang Xiang, 'Nuli ba Shenzhen jingji tequ bande genghao' [Work Hard to Run Shenzhen SEZ Even Better], in *Jin'er Shenzhen* [Shenzhen Today], (People's Daily Press, Beijing, 1984).

by Lu Xun in his poem 'Laughing at My Own Predicament'.[30] Mao Zedong interpreted this poetic line as 'serving the proletariat'.[31] Thus it would appear that the Shenzhen buffalo conveys the ideologically correct message of self-sacrifice and egalitarian concern. But in a 1985 book co-edited by the Editorial Board of *Red Flag*, the Party theoretical journal, and the Shenzhen SEZ Policy Research Office, reference is made to the 'wasteland-reclaiming-buffalo' that signifies 'making strenuous efforts to scale new heights, conducting reforms and innovations and charging ahead in a pioneering spirit'.[32] Socialist values are minimized in favour of the rhetoric of the new and path-breaking. Although novelty and transformation are generally consonant with Marxist historical materialism, in the context of post-Mao China they are assaults upon Party authorities, the conservative defenders of political and economic stasis. It is the avant-garde, not socialism, that is reclaiming the wasteland.

As might be expected, assertions of SEZ exceptionalism are common in good times, when the national political and economic context authorizes experimentation. And when national circumstances are working against reforms, the specialness of SEZs has again been invoked to preserve their identity. In 1985 the zones came under heavy criticism at both the National People's Congress and the People's Political Consultative Conference, where they were linked to the Hainan automobile scandal and censured for insufficient exports and industrial development.[33] Gu Mu took the lead in defending zone policy in a series of newspaper and magazine articles in which he argued that China would 'unavoidably encounter some unexpected situations and commit some mistakes' due to the 'entirely new' experience of opening to the world economy.[34] Newness here provides a certain dispensation from economic sin; SEZs should be excused from routine policy evaluation

---

[30] For an analysis of 'Laughing at My Own Predicament' and the meaning of *ruzi niu*, see Jon Kowallis, *The Lyrical Lu Xun* (University of Hawaii Press, Honolulu, forthcoming).

[31] *Selected Works of Mao Zedong, Volume III* (Foreign Languages Press, Beijing, 1967), p.96.

[32] *Shenzhen tequ xinmao* [The New Look of the Shenzhen Special Economic Zone] (Economic Information and Agency, Hong Kong, 1985), pp.1-2. Inside the back cover of this same book, *ruzi niu* is directly translated as 'reclaiming buffalo'.

[33] 'Vice Premiers Yao Yilin and Others [Li Peng] Answer Questions from Hong Kong and Macao Reporters', *Wen wei bao* (Hong Kong), 29 March 1985, p.1, in FBIS CHI-85-061. For a similar critique, see Pan Zhaozong, 'Report on Hu Qiaomu's Fujian Inspection', *Fujian ribao*, 2 February 1986, in FBIS CHI-85-049.

[34] Gu Mu, 'Opening Up to the Outside World: A Strategic Decision Reinvigorating China', *Shijie jingji daobao* [World Economic Herald], 8 July 1985, in FBIS CHI-85-149. The themes of this article are reiterated in Gu Mu, 'Opening Up to the World — A Strategic Decision to Make China Strong and Prosperous', *Kaifeng*, no.9 (8 September 1985), in FBIS CHI-85-197, 10 October 1985; and 'Gu Mu Discusses Open Policy', *Liaowang*, no.38, 23 September 1985, in FBIS CHI-85-201, 17 October 1985.

because they are a category unto themselves. Moreover, Gu contended that the failings of the new could not be corrected by the measures of old. 'Tightening control' in a state socialist manner would simply be 'returning to the beaten path and not studying new methods to solve new problems'.[35]

The power of the new is insidious. In 1987 the anti-bourgeois liberalization campaign roiled Shenzhen. Three local papers were closed by Party authorities, and a member of the Discipline Inspection Committee called for tighter control over the SEZs. It seemed that zone policy might be redefined by critical interpretations. Oddly enough, the reformist cause was saved by Peng Zhen, a leading defender of ideological orthodoxy. Peng's public utterances during a May visit to Shenzhen and Zhuhai included his usual references to upholding the 'four basic principles' and cultivating 'socialist spiritual civilization'. But rather incongruously, he also employed exceptionalist imagery, even paraphrasing the slogan made popular by Hu Yaobang: 'special things must be done in special zones'.[36] Such phrases suggested a certain licence for experimentation and diluted Peng's conformist message. Most likely, Peng did not want to eradicate SEZs, but bringing them into line with his conservative principles was confounded by the current description of zones as privileged sites of non-socialist practice. Whatever his intention, Peng's choice of words was constrained insofar as exceptionalist rhetoric had become the vernacular of SEZ interpretation.

To summarize the argument thus far, SEZs arose out of struggles to define China's national economic identity at the start of the post-Mao era. Initially, the sense of economic failure, articulated in opposition to Hua Guofeng's portrait of China, provided the grounds for 'special' policies such as SEZs. As the debate on China's economic identity fragmented, however, several different, albeit interrelated, rhetorics — ideological, critical and exceptionalist — have been employed to frame the meaning of SEZs. Exceptionalist interpretations appear to have had the greatest power in defining the zones. To a significant degree, this reflects the political effectiveness of SEZ advocates, who have been able to resist attempts to weaken zone policy. Language and connotation, however, are also important. Ideological depictions lack evocative power and critical images contain conflicting messages. Exceptionalist renditions, by contrast, produce exciting visions of newness, opportunity and progress.

The defining power of exceptionalism may be rooted in its simplicity. It is an elaboration of a tautology, 'special zones are special', which is both ambiguous (what is 'special'?) and unequivocal (they must be 'special'!). Yet as shall be observed, they have also opened the way for a reversal of identification: instead of China defining SEZs as new and different, SEZs have come to define China.

---

35   Gu Mu, 'Opening up to the Outside World', p.K13.

36   *Xinhua* [New China News Agency], 7 May 1987, in FBIS, 8 May 1987, pp.K22-4.

SEZs Construct China

By 1983 it was clear that influential state agents wanted to apply particular aspects of SEZ policy to other parts of China[37]. In so doing, they seemed to believe that an essential Chinese economic identity, centred on one or another understanding of 'socialism', could be preserved. They thought they could control the ways in which zones would serve as models 'for' China.[38] This has not been the case, however. As SEZ-like practices have spilled across the country, the economic meaning of 'socialism' has been attenuated to near literal insignificance, a sign without a referent. Exceptionalist representations of SEZs have filled the void and are becoming a national economic identity antagonistic to the socialist other. The new identity is hotly contested by elder statesmen, who resist the demeaning of socialism, while it is hardly acknowledged by pragmatic reformers, who try to avoid political controversy with rote invocations of tired ideological tropes. SEZs are not the only authors of identity transformation — the reform project has produced several — but they are perhaps the most provocative.

The expansion of SEZ practice has come in four waves. The opening of fourteen coastal cities in 1984 was the first step, creating zonal enclaves all along China's eastern seaboard from Dalian to Beihai. In 1985 larger territorial units — the open deltas of the Yangtze and Pearl Rivers, and southern Fujian — were refashioned in the image of SEZs. Further spatial extensions of specialness came in 1988 with Zhao Ziyang's open coastal policy and the redefinition of Hainan island as a provincial SEZ. The entire coast, consisting of twelve provinces and over 40 per cent of China's population, would follow the lead of Shenzhen, ironically making it ever more difficult for the original SEZS to maintain their 'special' status. The most recent spurt of zone expansion was inspired by Deng Xiaoping's southern tour in early 1992, where he urged an intensification and speed-up of economic transformation, sparking a veritable 'zone fever' among administrators all

---

[37]   Crane, *The Political Economy of China's Special Economic Zones*, ch.4

[38]   The distinction of models 'of' and models 'for' is from Clifford Geertz, *The Interpretation of Cultures* (Basic Books, New York, 1973), p.93. A model 'of' provides for the 'manipulation of symbol structures so as to bring them, more or less closely, into parallel with the pre-established nonsymbolic system'. In other words, they render complex realities apprehensible. A model 'for' allows for the 'manipulation of the nonsymbolic systems in terms of the relationships expressed in the symbolic'. They are 'a model under whose guidance physical relationships are organized'. Chinese reformers, looking to change the economy, saw in SEZs models 'for' China; the zones, as symbols as well as policies, would help to 'liberate thinking' — a reformist shibboleth — and hasten transformation. But many reformers thought they could control the symbolic interpretation so as to keep the image of SEZs within the realm of 'socialism', thus preserving the PRC's essential economic identity. It is argued below that the reformist architects of zone policy have lost symbolic control and that the connotations of SEZ practice cannot be monopolized by them.

over the country.[39] Economic zones began to be built as far afield as Tibet and Xinjiang, while the development of Shanghai's Pudong zone has become a national obsession. SEZs are hardly special any more because the exceptionalist rhetoric central to their identity has crystallized into a model for China, at the expense of socialism.

The transference of SEZ identity to the economic nation at large can be seen in key moments of the territorial expansion of zone policy. The 1984 decision to open fourteen coastal cities invested SEZs with national symbolic significance. Shenzhen and its Shekou Industrial District were especially singled out for praise.[40] At a critical meeting, Liang Xiang, then mayor of Shenzhen, revealed the secrets of SEZ success: 'We have exceeded the limits of the current system and boldly reformed the economic and management systems'.[41] Exceptional measures had made Shenzhen a model worthy of emulation. In the same context, Gu Mu suggested that classes be organized in Shenzhen for cadres from the soon-to-be-opened coastal cities, where Liang Xiang and Yuan Geng, leader of Shekou, would lecture on the dos and don'ts of exceeding 'the limits of the current system'. Zhao Ziyang reportedly urged people from Shanghai to go to Shenzhen to learn how to 'open their field of vision'. In all of these pronouncements little was explicitly said about socialism, though the notion that the coastal cities would build small, physically segregated development zones implied that the contagion of non-socialism could be quarantined and controlled. What is clear, however, is that the coastal cities initiative was infused with the ethos of SEZ exceptionalism.

Similarly, the specialness of SEZs informed Zhao Ziyang's 1988 proposal to transform the entire seaboard economically.[42] What was most striking was his unattributed acceptance of so much of what was special about SEZs. In laying out the particulars of his open coast vision, he generalized from the experience of the SEZs while mentioning them only in passing. Seaside provinces should, in Zhao's view, encourage more foreign investment, promote export-oriented industrialization, import materials and components,

---

[39] David Zweig, 'China's New Economic Warlords', *Asian Wall Street Journal*, 3 August 1992, p.8.

[40] Zeng Jianhui, 'The Birth of an Important Decision — A New Step in Opening the Country to the World', *Liaowang*, no.24 (11 June 1984), in FBIS CHI-84-118, 18 June 1984, pp.K1-7, provides a quasi-official account of the Coastal Cities Forum that hammered out the essentials of the new policy in early 1984: 'The experience of Shenzhen and Shekou industrial zone attracted the attention of the comrades attending the forum. This is because they took the lead and their experiences were of great and guiding significance' (p.K5).

[41] Ibid., p.K5. All attributions in this paragraph are taken from this same source.

[42] Zhao was quite explicit on this point in comments he made in Shenzhen following his extensive inspection tour of coastal provinces in 1987-88: 'Shenzhen should serve as an example for the coastal areas to further open up to the outside world'. See FBIS CHI-88-037, p.10.

take advantage of opportunities in labour-intensive processing and assembly, and decentralize economic power.[43] These are the stock in trade of SEZs, but now the exceptional was to be made routine. Socialism did not figure prominently in Zhao's discussion of opening the coastline; indeed, it had been pushed far into the background by the 'primary stage' formulation articulated at the 13th Party Congress in November 1987.

The growing insignificance of socialism to Chinese economic identity and the increasing salience of SEZs as models for China is evident in Deng Xiaoping's 1992 southern tour. The trip was provoked by conservative criticism of reform, including an indictment of SEZs as capitalist hotbeds of 'peaceful evolution' that ought to be abolished because they are threats to the 'socialist structure'.[44] In response, Deng went to Shenzhen and argued that planning and markets are merely 'economic measures' employed by socialist and capitalist countries alike, not truly distinguishing features of a national economy.[45] With these words he dissociated the idea of socialism from the whole range of economic practices from planning to markets. Deng's defense of Shenzhen is coupled with a literal demeaning of socialism.

Deng reduces the economic meaning of socialism to the development of productive forces and the achievement of an ultimate common prosperity. He does not specify how productive forces should be built and how or when common prosperity will be attained, tacitly legitimizing a very broad range of economic behaviour. The political limits of Deng's socialism are regularly reiterated with invocations of the 'Four Basic Principles' and repression of dissent but the economic possibilities appear ideologically unbounded. For Deng, SEZs are locations where 'socialism' and 'capitalism' are largely irrelevant to everyday economic action, an imagery consistent with the exceptionalist rhetoric of zone advocates. Yet while effectively denying the interpretive utility of the socialism-capitalism dichotomy, Deng tries not to relinquish all socialist aspiration. His telos continues to be a common prosperity at some unspecified time far in the future. This residual egalitarianism is overwhelmed, however, by his preeminent pragmatism.[46]

---

43 See Zhao's discussion with *Xinhua*, 22 January 1988, in FBIS CHI-88-015, 25 January 1988, pp.10-15. For an analysis of the open coastal policy, see Dali Yang, 'China Adjusts to the World Economy: The Political Economy of China's Coastal Development Strategy', *Pacific Affairs*, vol.64, no.1 (Spring 1991), pp.42-64.

44 'Deng's Struggle Against Conservatives Described', *Kyodo*, 9 March 1992, FBIS CHI-92-046, pp.26-7; *Ming bao* (Hong Kong), 6 March 1992, in FBIS CHI-92-046, 19 March 1992, pp.26-7.

45 'Full Text of Document Number 2', *Zheng ming*, no.174 (April 1992), in FBIS CHI-91-063S, pp.1-7.

46 Arif Dirlik comments on the inherent contradiction of pragmatism and egalitarianism in post-Mao Chinese ideology: 'Unable to integrate these two languages into a new language of socialist progress, socialist ideology in China has ended up for the most part speaking two languages at once, which has confounded the speakers no less than the

Therefore, even if Deng wants SEZs to be models for a 'socialist' China, his rhetoric and public spectacles have promoted an interpretation of zones as something outside the categories of socialism and capitalism.

Deng's economic vision, which has been given wide currency, values the process of change more than the destination of change, authorizing the new and neglecting the orthodox. SEZs have long been represented in precisely these terms. And if these theoretical subtleties are too esoteric, Tian Jiyun makes plain how SEZs serve as summary symbols for China's economy, calling for a nationwide SEZ that will break up 'forbidden areas' and open them to global interchange.[47] Although official discourse holds that China can maintain its socialist identity by using capitalism to serve collectivist ends, a formulation presaged in the earliest discussions of SEZs, the meanings given to these terms do not allow for such clear-cut distinctions.[48] Socialism is articulated in terms of capitalism, stripped of any distinguishing characteristics, but asserted as being superior to capitalism. China thus appears to be both but neither, the ambiguous position of SEZs.

Ideology is obviously important to state managers struggling to define China, but it is not the only facet of national economic identity. Co-acting with ideology is the image of SEZs as models for a neo-authoritarian China. This identity emerges from the explicit comparisons made between the 'East Asian Tigers' and China's SEZs as well as from economic and political practices within the zones themselves. Shenzhen, from its inception, has been closely associated with Hong Kong; and Xiamen with Taiwan. Hong Kong investors provide the bulk of the 'foreign' investment in Shenzhen, Hong Kong architecture sets the style of its buildings, and Hong Kong currency freely circulates in its economy. Although these connections may be a strategy to reunite 'Greater China', they also affect China's sense of itself, linking sections of the mainland to the idea of East Asian economic success. A significant part of China thus becomes, symbolically as well as empirically, a newly industrializing economy highly integrated into world markets through a dynamic export-oriented manufacturing sector, brimming with growth and success, where entrepreneurial social forces are liberated by the recalibration of state power, where ideology is subsumed by pragmatism, and where modern vestiges of Confucian culture — thrift, hard work and education — are economic advantages. The description of an 'East Asian model', and its aura of positive accomplishment, now makes sense for China.

---

listeners'. See Arif Dirlik, 'Revolutionary Hegemony and the Language of Revolution: Chinese Socialism between Present and Future', in Arif Dirlik and Maurice Meisner (eds), *Marxism and the Chinese Experience: Issues in Contemporary Chinese Socialism* (M. E. Sharpe, Armonk, 1989), p.28.

47   *Hong Kong Standard*, 4 June 1992, p.1, in FBIS CHI-92-109, 5 June 1992, pp.17-18.

48   Fang Sheng, 'Opening Up and Making Use of Capitalism', *Beijing Review*, vol.35, no.12 (23-29 March 1992), pp.18-20.

The emerging East Asian Chinese economic identity is reinforced by the political experience of Shenzhen. True to the neo-authoritarian project, even pretenses of democracy and mass participation have been elided for many years in the leading SEZ. Shenzhen went for a decade without a local people's congress until the municipal government finally organized elections in December 1990 and created legislative institutions.[49] Prior to that time the local administrative apparatus was relatively autonomous from even the modest level of political participation possible within China's National People's Congress system. The message is clear: politics should not be allowed to interrupt economics.

Although Shenzhen represents the political exclusion and economic dynamism of East Asia's newly industrializing countries, its language continues to avoid the characterization of 'capitalism'. An outgrowth of the ideological reinventions outlined above, this taboo is a powerful vestige of the socialist past. 'Capitalism' connotes pain and suffering, the brutal exploitation of hapless workers. To include it in any Chinese self-description would be to admit to a sinister side and sully the reputation of East Asian dynamism.

Of course, the SEZs (and China) have no shortage of victims and losers. Shenzhen realities include monotonously dehumanizing labour with little chance for effective organization and representation; a large 'floating population' whose prospects hinge on capricious bureaucratic and business decisions; and a crass materialism that generates prostitution and crime.[50] These experiences get little play in SEZ discourse because they corroborate neither the state's reform project nor the popular hope for something better. Critics who cite SEZ flaws have been unable to make their voices heard above the positive overtones of zone success. To a large degree they have been silenced by the state-controlled media. Moreover, negative stories that get out are still susceptible to multiple interpretations. The Shenzhen stock market riot of 1992 can be understood as an example of reform-inspired corruption and chaos that delegitimates economic change. But it also reveals the popular desire for economic innovation and access to the wealth so conspicuously on display.[51] Corruption is real and failure is common, but the predominant imagery of SEZs, and the meaning they convey to China at large, is prosperity, novelty and liberation.[52]

---

49   *Xinhua*, 24 June 1992, FBIS CHI-92-123, 24 June 1992, p.18.

50   For an extensive critque of social conditions in Shenzhen, see 'Decade of Suffering — A Chronicle of 300,000 Temporary Workers at Shenzhen', *Zhongguo zuojia* [China's Authors], no.3 (June 1989), pp.176-207, in Joint Publications Research Service, China Report, CAR 90-083, 9 November 1990, pp.6-38.

51   The dual nature of the incident is discussed in Mark Clifford, 'After Shenzhen Chaos: China Mulls Better Way to Allocate Shares', *Far Eastern Economic Review*, vol.155, no.34 (27 August 1992), p.53.

52   For example, the brief mention of SEZs in the television series *He shang* [River Elegy] pictures them as transformative and progressive; Stanley Rosen and Gary Zou (eds),

Ironically, then, SEZs have returned to Chinese economic identity the optimism of Hua Guofeng's rhetoric, albeit in a radically different form. They are not, however, a final resolution of identity struggles. In constructing a distinct national economic identity, SEZs reconstitute economic difference; they create new 'others' as mirrors for themselves. Where once 'capitalists', 'landlords' and 'imperialists' were antagonists, the 'other' can now be conceived of in terms· of the poor, the unemployed and the unsuccessful. SEZ advocacy, in hiding inequalities and failings, rationalizes inequality and redefines failure. If zones and the free-wheeling economic practices they instill are taken to be grand opportunities for prosperity and progress, then anyone who founders in them is liable to be represented as inherently inferior. SEZs thus authorize a discourse drawn more from traditional ('peasants are backwards') and market ('your economic failure is your own fault') languages than from socialist ideology, languages that justify the gap between rich and poor.

Conclusion: The Language and Significance of National Economic Identity

The emergence of China's SEZs sheds light on the construction of national economic identity, illuminations that may clarify the process in other places at other times. Economic identity was described above as multi-dimensional and historically contingent. The various possible components of economic identity (predominant economic practice, position in the world economy, ideology, and so on) can be interpreted and combined in a variety of ways. Each category is polysemous in itself as well as in relation to others; though grounded in experience and circumstance, meanings are fluid and variable. As debates on China's SEZs suggest, the meaning of economic identity is unsettled, varying with the specific language employed in its construction. The language used to create meaning is the medium for identity formation and reformation, even in the seemingly objective realm of economic practice. Rhetorical devices and images provide connotation and tone to interpretations of economic conditions. And these have the power to capture the imagination of political leaders and mass constituencies alike. Connotation and tone may make the difference in how people identify themselves and their surroundings. Ideological depictions of SEZs appear to lack evocative power, as 'state capitalism' is hardly inspirational. Many critical portrayals contain conflicting messages; 'Hong Kongization' may be understood as a good thing to some Chinese. Exceptionalist rhetoric, by contrast, seems to both create and resonate with a positive sense of acceptance of SEZ practices. The way in which identity is articulated is a critical element in what identity is taken to be, a point suggested by Benedict Anderson: 'Communities are to be

'The Chinese Television Documentary "River Elegy"', *Chinese Sociology and Anthropology*, vol.24, no.2 (Winter 1991-92), pp.85-6.

distinguished not by their falsity/genuineness, but by the style in which they are imagined'.[53]

Although identity construction may be caught up in Wittgensteinian language-games, this is not to suggest that it is without real consequence.[54] Quite to the contrary, national identity, however contingent and malleable, is known to move people to war. In less dramatic ways, the new economic identity of SEZs is shaping Chinese politics and society.

SEZ exceptionalism complicates the state's capacity to manage the national economy. At one level, nettlesome though by no means incapacitating problems are created. The perception of economic zones as engines of growth, prosperity and progress enhances their popular appeal. Everyone, everywhere, wants to have a zone so that they too will be associated with East Asian dynamism. The resulting zone fever has outrun state policy. The land taken for zone development cuts into agricultural acreage in some areas, prompting the state to close unauthorized sites.[55] Regulating foreign capital is made much more difficult by the multiplication of SEZ-like enclaves. The reach of the state is simply insufficient to evaluate all of the far-flung foreign-funded projects. The generalization of the SEZs' experience, fuelled by their exceptionalist imagery, thus requires that administrative resources be used to rein in renegade zones.

The economic identity constructed by SEZs could also exacerbate centrifugal forces within the Chinese state, playing on regional distinctions. To a significant degree, the East Asian Newly Industrializing Country (NIC) ethos is a phenomenon of southern China, with Guangdong and Fujian provinces as its heart. The 'other' constituted by this identity is largely northern and inland, areas that economically prosperous southerners consider backward. The spread of zone policies may offset the potential North-South identity divide but if inland northern zones do not work out they may become reminders for people there of just how different they are from their coastal southern cousins.[56] A geographical bifurcation of economic identity, even well short of complete division, would hamper the centre's capacity to manage the national economy.

---

[53] Benedict Anderson, *Imagined Communities: Reflections on the Origin and Spread of Nationalism* (Verso, London, 1991), p.6.

[54] Lugwig Wittgenstein, in demonstrating the indefiniteness of language, argues that meaning is established through 'language-games'; see *Philosophical Investigations* (Basil Blackwell, Oxford, 1958).

[55] 'Coastal Areas Cut Development Zones by Over 75 Per Cent', *Xinhua*, 11 August 1993, in FBIS CHI-93-161, 23 August 1993, p.41; 'Economic Zones to be Approved in a "Planned" Manner', *Xinhua*, 16 August 1993, in FBIS CHI-93-156, 16 August 1993, pp.31-2.

[56] Edward Friedman, 'Reconstructing China's National Identity', *Journal of Asian Studies*, vol.53, no.1 (February 1994), pp.67-91.

The identity politics of SEZs could also influence the framing of economic policy. To a certain degree, the Chinese state is losing control over the definition of the national economy. The socialist language of state is nearly meaningless in economic terms. Although the East Asian identity that is arising from the SEZs serves the state's interest in projecting a strong and prosperous nation, the state cannot monopolize the meaning of economic conditions. By emphasizing economic modernization above all else, unfettered by official ideology, state managers empower non-state individuals who can claim expertise in economics and business. Professional economists, managers, entrepreneurs, engineers and financiers from outside the Party-state apparatus are able to gain a greater voice in describing China's economic circumstances and framing policy debate. At present, the 'private sector' is structurally disadvantaged, especially through government control of the means of communications, but it is legitimized, even encouraged, by China's new NIC identity. As they take advantage of the space provided for them, private entrepreneurs and experts could undermine the state's capacity to define issues and, concomitantly, manage national economic affairs.

This possibility of shifting power relations appears, at first glance, to confirm the 'peaceful evolution' critique of China's open policy.[57] But while the conservative argument that openness will change China seems irrefutable, it neglects the critically important internal impulse for transformation. While Western 'capitalist' ideas are entering China and shaping its economic identity, 'China' itself is not a singular unproblematic thing. The economic meaning of China to the Chinese people has been unsettled for many decades. The definition of identity and the constitution of difference do not simply stop at a certain historical moment, but are regularly re-enacted and re-invented. The 'West' and how it relates to China are matters for reinterpretation, holding different meanings for different Chinese writers and speakers. Thus 'peaceful evolution' is a vastly oversimplified construct, assuming an essentially fixed 'China' and 'West' that neglects the fact that Chinese identity, economic or otherwise, is contested from within as much as from without.

---

[57]   Analyses of the politics of 'peaceful evolution' can be found in John W. Garver, 'The Chinese Communist Party and the Collapse of Soviet Communism', *The China Quarterly*, no.133 (March 1992), pp.1-26; Zhao Suisheng, 'Deng's Southern Tour: Elite Politics in Post-Tiananmen China', *Asian Survey*, vol.33, no.8 (August 1993), pp.739-56.

EIGHT

A Democratic Chinese Nationalism?

Edward Friedman

The most frenzied moments in the Mao-era propagation of a national identity — one in which all of China's people and resources had to be mobilized to fend off foreign forces so as to preserve a pure and socialist China — emerged in the period between 1964 and 1970 when Third Front and Cultural Revolution policies culminated in the anointment of Minister of National Defense Lin Biao as Mao's successor. Lin Biao, the Chinese people were taught, knew best how to save the Chinese nation by keeping out all polluting and dangerous imperialist forces. However, Lin's sudden demise in 1971 and his subsequent discrediting in 1972 helped traumatically to explode the exclusionist notion of Mao's original nationalist revolution. Chinese began to be receptive to reimagining in more open terms who they were and what they could become.[1]

The Chinese Struggle Re-Conceived as Democratic

Starting in the 1970s, especially after Lin Biao's fall, ever more Chinese found Mao's notion of patriotism, one of mobilizing all resources to keep out foreign pollutants, ever less compelling. Mao's anti-imperialist nationalism came to seem more a problem — even a cause of China's problems — than a solution. That is, Leninist anti-imperialism looked ever less like an accurate analysis of the source of China's poverty and ever more like a counter-productive rationale for perpetuating the arbitrary power of an outmoded Party caste whose ways kept China backward. For most politically proud Chinese at the end of the twentieth century, especially for those who still imagined Mao as a great Chinese patriot, the question posed by this newly subverted national identity came to be: Where did the great Mao go wrong? And how is it that a

---

[1]   Edward Friedman, *National Identity and Democratic Prospects in Socialist China* (M. E. Sharpe, Armonk, 1995).

struggle to liberate China from humiliating occupation by Japanese militarists ended up imposing this dilemma?[2]

One popular answer among Chinese was that Mao's struggles were initially correct. In this view, Maoism until 1952 had involved a proper sinification of Marxism. Power was not seized, as Lenin had done by a direct assault on the capital, but instead Mao had won national power by gradually surrounding the polluted city with a liberated, purified Chinese countryside, an experience of nationalism that, as Lucian Pye describes in this volume, made an open port city such as Shanghai seem a threat to true Chineseness. Mao was seen as a patriotic innovator in imagining a truly Chinese road to power. In addition, Mao's words and deeds on people's war inspired millions of other would-be liberators the world over. These perceived achievements created a proud Chinese nationalism.

But unfortunately, Mao and his colleagues, after conquering state power, wrongly took for granted that the economic institutions constructed by Lenin, Stalin and the Bolshevik party in Russia embodied a true economic science of socialism. The collectivization of agriculture, five-year plans premised on the physical control of quantity-oriented production, and the over-concentrated and economically irrational super-centralization of a command economy had not been mentioned by Karl Marx, who left the institution-building of socialism up to the revolutionaries who one day would conquer state power. What was built by Lenin's cadres turned out, however, to be a very Russian form of state, a replication and indeed intensification of Czarist tyranny and its military-oriented industrialization, emphasizing hierarchy, subordination, dependency, gigantism and extreme centralization. That is, Lenin as a Russian had built on institutional bases of the czarist regime such as the *nomenklatura*, a dependent service caste, and concentration of power in part through a pervasive secret police and internal passports. Increasingly, Mao's 1952 surrender of the policies of China's short period of New Democracy and his embrace of Russia's way of building socialism is imagined in the post-Mao years as abandoning a Chinese way and adopting a Russian way.[3] As explained by the Japanese scholar Okobe Tatsumi, 'Having abandoned "New Democracy" and rushed towards socialism in the 1950s, China . . . failed [in the Mao era] to benefit from the modernizing effects of capitalist development and is now trying to return to "New Democracy"'.[4]

---

[2]   Lowell Dittmer and Samuel Kim (eds), *China's Quest for National Identity* (Cornell University Press, Ithaca, 1994).

[3]   Wang Haibo, 'A Study of Mao Zedong's "On the New Democracy"', *Jingji yanjiu*, no.12, 20 December 1993, pp.16-25, translated in JPRS-CAR-94-011, 16 February 1994, pp.3-10.

[4]   Kyoko Tanaka, 'Research in Japan on China's Economy and Foreign Trade 1978-1992', in *The Development of Contemporary China Studies* (Centre for East Asian Cultural Studies for UNESCO, Tokyo, 1994), pp.99-114. It is natural that Japanese analysts of international communism are especially sensitive to this set of polar oppositions — Mao

Unfortunately for the Chinese people, when Mao in the early 1950s set China on the Russian road, he imagined the pre-1952 era not in terms of that New Democracy but rather as a form of war communism, a Jacobin-Leninist project that institutionalized the policies that a Robespierre might have used to consolidate power. Turning his back on the popular New Democracy, Mao instead promoted 'a mixture of Stalinist central planning and Yanan-style military communism'.[5]

Given the pervasiveness of these bipolar categories, which pit a good early Mao against a tragic late Mao, the post-Mao project of dynamizing China's economy is readily experienced as a break with Mao's Stalinist *cum* war communist disasters and a return to a relegitimation of the New Democracy as the truly Chinese way. Mao is reimagined in terms of his great success in the 1938 to 1952 era, as a democrat, as the Mao of the New Democracy. This reimagining of Mao and of the recent past facilitates a reinterpreted Chinese nationalism and a very different vision of a Chinese future.

This transition came as a surprise to most foreign scholars because, among other reasons, they had misunderstood Mao's supposedly populist Cultural Revolution as democratic and as having been inspired by Marx's and Lenin's supposedly democratic thoughts on the socialist promise of the Paris Commune of 1871. This interpretation was wrong in all three regards: be it Marx on the Paris Commune, Lenin's view of Marx on the Paris Commune, or Mao's understanding of Lenin on the Paris Commune. Clarifying this intellectual error is crucial if one would see how the tyrannical Mao of the Great Leap and the Cultural Revolution can be apprehended in the post-Mao era as unrelated to the democratic project that Marx (but not Lenin) actually promoted and that the Chinese people increasingly embrace at the end of the twentieth century.

---

versus Stalin, China versus Russia, indigenous versus alien, authentic versus artificial, good versus bad. After all, Japan's Second World War era Communist Party leader Nosaka Sanzo had been with Mao at his Yanan guerilla base headquarters at the end of the anti-Japanese war fought by a Chinese resistance in terms of the ideals of a New Democracy. 'Nosaka contended that the changed conditions of occupied Japan made the call for violent revolutionary change on the Bolshevik model . . . no longer necessary. Now that the JCP could operate openly as a competitive political party . . . the party should emulate the Chinese example and seek a broad base of support . . . '. But then 'the Soviet Union's overwhelming influence on the party' led it to redefine the American occupation of Japan as bringing, not the prospects for a New Democracy, but, 'only chains and slavery' that could be smashed only by 'violent revolution'. Germaine Hoston, *The State, Identity and the National Question in China and Japan* (Princeton University Press, Princeton, 1994), p.425. In 1958 the Moscow-Beijing rift allowed the JCP to abandon this Soviet Stalinist anti-democratic dogma and again enter democratic politics in Japan. Mao apologized to the JCP for backing Stalin's postwar imposition of a destructive Soviet way on the Japanese comrades.

5   Okobe Tatsumi, cited in Tanaka, 'Research in Japan on China's Economy', p.102.

As is well known, Marx had little to say about the socialist future in his writings on the Paris Commune — except for such matters as praising the end of night work for bakers. What Lenin learned from the Paris Commune came mainly from the history of the Commune written by a Russian participant, Peter Lavrov, who criticized the Commune from a Blanquist perspective because, Lavrov believed, waiting for socialist conditions to ripen meant allowing capitalist oppression to continue.[6] The Bolsheviks came to believe that the Paris Commune was too soft on its counter-revolutionary enemies and that a vanguard of conspirators, to win and hold power, would have to be far more ruthless than the Communards had been.[7]

Marx's promotion of democratic elections and the Commune's actual multi-party democracy were ignored or dismissed by Lavrov, Lenin and the Bolshevik revolution. What mattered for Leninists was all power permanently in the hands of the revolutionary vanguard. The Commune was a history book of *negative* lessons on how *not* to consolidate power. Trotsky summed this all up in his writings on the Paris Commune:

> We can thus thumb the whole history of the Commune, page by page, and we will find in it one single lesson: a strong party leadership is needed. Those fighters of '71 . . . lacked . . . clarity in methods and a centralized leading organization. That is why they were vanquished.[8]

---

6   Alex Kimball, 'The Russian Past and the Socialist Future in the Thought of Peter Lavrov', *Slavic Review*, vol.30, no.1 (March 1971), pp.28-44; Philip Promper, *Peter Lavrov and the Russian Revolutionary Movement* (University of Chicago Press, Chicago, 1972). Lenin redefined Blanquism to mean barricade fighting so that Lenin could present his Blanquist conspiratorial vanguard seeking total power as anti-Blanquist — that is, at one with Marx's condemnation of Blanquism. Nonetheless, the Bolsheviks in fact derived Blanquist lessons from the Commune, not democratic ones.

7   According to Lenin's wife, 'Closely studying . . . the Paris Commune . . . Ilyich remarked on the pernicious effect of the mild attitude of the . . . workers' government towards their manifest enemies. And therefore . . . Ilyich always "tightened the screws"'. Dmitri Volkogonov, *Lenin: A New Biography* (The Free Press, New York, 1994), p.21. In 1908 Lenin concluded that 'two mistakes destroyed the fruits of victory' of the Communards: 'The proletariat stopped halfway; instead of setting about "expropriating the expropriators"; it allowed itself to be led astray by dreams of establishing a higher justice . . . .The second mistake was excessive magnanimity . . . instead of destroying its enemies, it sought to exert mo.al influence on them'. Tamara Deutscher (ed.), *Not By Politics Alone — The Other Lenin* (George Allen and Unwin, London, 1973), p.150. In 1911 Lenin offered a cause for these failures of the Paris Commune: '[T]here was no workers' party' (p.155).

8   *Leon Trotsky on the Paris Commune* (Pathfinder Press, New York, 1970), pp.41, 44, 61.

The same points were made by Nikita Fedorovsky, writing officially in the Soviet Union. The Communards lost because they lacked an authoritarian organization and were too soft on enemies and potential enemies.[9]

Mao was heir to this Jacobin-Blanquist-Leninist understanding of the lessons of the Paris Commune. The Chinese participants in the Cultural Revolution who understood both the Paris Commune and the Cultural Revolution as experiments in direct democracy, while evincing their own very decent aspirations, missed the actual anti-democratic content of the Leninist and Maoist comprehension of the Paris Commune. And yet, whatever the misapprehension, these democratic aspirations in China did persist.

Chinese National Identity as Democratic

Today a democratic national identity is becoming hegemonic in China. According to well-known theorists of national identity, such a major sea shift should be virtually impossible. European analysts such as Ernest Gellner and Liah Greenfield have argued that Western versus Eastern nationalisms, democratic versus authoritarian identities, individualist versus collectivist cultures, and Anglo-American versus all the other civilizations create bipolar options for a society the way the x and y chromosomes imprint male or female gender on all of life. Consequently, 'democracy may not be exportable. It may be an inherent predisposition in certain nations . . . yet entirely alien to others, and the ability to adopt and develop it in the latter may require a change of identity'.[10]

Indeed, a cultural pessimism about democratic possibilities pervaded the thinking of educated Chinese at the end of the 1980s. No shift toward democracy seemed to lay in China's cultural cards. And yet only a few years later, more and more Chinese are imagining themselves and their future in most democratic ways. Real events have falsified these European hypotheses of a culturally genetic nationalism and call our attention to the work on national identity of constructivists and instrumentalists such as Benedict Anderson, Anthony Appiah and Crawford Young.[11] They have found, in opposition to primordialists and binary Eurocentrist thinking, that national identity is constructed anywhere and everywhere to serve the interests of rising political groups. The Chinese south, the marketeers, the mobile, open-

---

9   Nikita Federovsky, 'Marx's Civil War in France', in Karl Marx and V. I. Lenin, *Civil War in France: The Paris Commune* (International Publishers, New York, 1988 [1940]), pp.154-5, 158, 181.

10   Liah Greenfield, *Nationalism: Five Roads to Modernity* (Harvard University Press, Cambridge, Mass., 1992), p.10.

11   Benedict Anderson, *Imagined Communities* (Verso, London, 1991 [1983]); Kwame Anthony Appiah, *In My Father's House: Africa in the Philosophy of Culture* (Oxford University Press, New York, 1992); Crawford Young, *The Politics of Cultural Pluralism* (University of Wisconsin Press, Madison, 1976).

minded, and tolerant are on the rise in China. One should expect this rising group to be the bearer of a distinct national identity.

In this light, we can similarly see since the 1980s, in a so-called post-modern era, a previously self-consciously unique and insular Japan re-imagining itself as Asian and global.[12] In the United States, the country's civic culture is being reconceived as democratic because it is the fruit of multicultural roots rather than of purely English, Protestant or European seeds. Australians increasingly link past and future more in terms of Asia than Britain. In like manner, in tune with global imperatives of reconceiving the national project to suit a world of globalized interdependence, Chinese similarly are reimagining a successful future.

Here one sees an explicit politico-cultural struggle over the meaning of Asianness, with the conservatives and authoritarians in China embracing a notion of Confucian authoritarianism touted by Singapore's senior patriarch Lee Kuan Yew,[13] while Chinese reformers and democrats transcend the boundaries and promote a China thought of as tolerant and confederalist, the product of Tang-Song commercialization, of an openness to borrowing and sinicizing Buddhism, and of a long and ever returning capacity to incorporate the best the world had to offer into a Chinese synthesis.

Chinese no longer look to Beijing to imagine their future project. Thus when cultural Chinese (*Zhonghuaren*) say the twenty-first century belongs to the Chinese, they are referring not to the old-fashioned, over-centralized, corrupt, bureaucratic state of Chinese (*Zhongguoren*) run from Beijing in north China but instead are calling to mind a Chinese society that includes an open diaspora, Taiwan, Hong Kong, Macao and the Chinese abroad (not old fashioned *huaqiao* but contemporary *huaren*). The reactionary alternative of imposed centralization that is rejected in this reimagined Chineseness, according to Beijing University history professor Wang Tianyou,[14] discussing China's complex history of division and despotic reunifications at a 1994 conference in Taiwan, is a negative image in which Chinese 'return to the times of Kublai Kahn or Nurhaci', foreign warriors from the north in the 13th and 17th centuries whose over-centralized despotism suppressed the Chinese people.[15]

China is now increasingly felt as a plural noun. It is peopled by the various descendants, Chinese archeologists now show, of perhaps nine distinct cultural regions, definitely not one core northern-plains origin, a Mao-era tale now known to be a lie. Some Chinese scholars also advocate that the Chinese should imagine their Chineseness in terms of pre-Qin scholarship, before the

---

12   Carnegie Council on Ethics and International Affairs, *The Call for a New Asian Identity* (New York, 1994).

13   Friedman, 'Confucian Leninism and Patriarchal Authoritarianism', *National Identity and Democratic Prospects in Socialist China*, ch.9.

14   Wang Tianyou, 'Historical Lessons', *Free China Review* (October 1994), p.45.

15   Ibid.

despot Qin Shi Huang established a shaky system that brought Chinese unstable 'despotism and the domination of "alien races"'; thereafter, 'charlatan Confucians' invented legitimations for 'a dynasty of imposters'. Confucian scholars 'betrayed the nation'. Before the reign of Qin's despotism (read: Mao's despotism) and Confucian apologetics (read: official post-Mao apologetics), China was open, democratic and dynamic. And so it must be again.[16]

This plural identity is increasingly an experiential reality within the Chinese mainland. A singular bond to rulers in Beijing can no longer be taken for granted. In the southeastern province of Fujian, in regions still ruled by sent-down northerners in the post-Mao era, long-suffering village people (*min*) would not serve privileged and alien officials (*guan*). Unless local people came to the fore, 'no villager wants to be recruited'. Rather than speak the north's Mandarin language (*guan hua*) of distant officials, people insisted on the *minnan* language and 'tuned in to Taiwan's [television] stations'.[17]

Further south, in Guangdong, in the Mao era speech in the language of the northern capital had been rewarded; it was the language of status, power and careers. Today, in contrast, merchants in Canton pretend not to comprehend Mandarin, humiliating northern visitors, turning them into peripheralized outsiders. The southern view, as expressed in 1992 to a *New York Times* reporter, is that 'China is like Europe, and we want to speak our own language just as in France people speak French'. In place of a Mao-era nationalism that privileged poor, hinterland, Yellow River, north China peasants as the source of nation-building, national success by the late 1980s was identified with the market-oriented activities of southerners who had joined with Chinese capital from diaspora Hong Kong, Macao and Southeast Asia to produce world-competitive products, building a prosperous China. In the new southern narrative, northern peasants were re-categorized as backward, ignorant, superstitious, insular and static. Increasingly, southerners presumed that nothing of great worth could grow in that hinterland, while the south had long been enriched by absorbing the good of the world.[18]

Anthropology, archaeology and history have been revolutionized by southern scholars over the past decade so that Chinese are no longer imagined as a people descended from an isolated northern-plain culture but instead as an intermingling with the southern Chu and other cultures, each involved with influences outside of China. Increasingly, the Chinese are conscious that there

---

[16] Zheng Shiqu, 'Cultural Outlook of the Late-Qing *Guocui* School', *Social Sciences in China* (Autumn 1994), pp.180-90, translated from *Lishi yanjiu* [Historical Research], no.6 (1992).

[17] Huang Shu-min, *The Spiral Road* (Westview, Boulder, 1989), pp.195, 196.

[18] This paragraph draws on Edward Friedman, 'Reconstructing China's National Identity: A Southern Alternative to Mao Era Anti-Imperialist Nationalism', *The Journal of Asian Studies*, vol.53, no.1 (February 1994), pp.67-91, which contains considerably more detailed information on the southern perspective.

was not a single northern Han people who filled an empty space but a land long peopled by plural Chinese groups. Given this reconstruction of national identity, the southern narrative may be poised to become a self-fulfilling prophesy. 'Guangzhou should be the cradle of China's new culture', proclaimed a Cantonese analyst in 1984. The city's glory, wrote historian Ye Chansheng, came from its distance over the centuries from northern 'feudal influences'.[19] The focus now is on the normality of decentralization, the power in local creativity, a need for confederation premised on federal divisions of power rather than military concentrations of power.

Post-Mao mobility has strengthened regional identities. The many millions of people from one region who moved to urban areas in another region found themselves cursed by strangers, harassed by local police and helped only by their own kind. They qualified for no state benefits. Regional ties became matters of life and death. You could, people agreed, only trust your own kind, and that definitely did not mean all Chinese or all Han.

Urban people, especially in the north, see the transient labourers as migrants, a culturally backward people who bring crime and disorder. Urban governments are restricting immigration by instituting a system of official permits, often available only at a high price. Thus administrative records increasingly distinguish and discriminate against Chinese who are from another region. The migrants consequently feel a need for a government from their region that would stand up for its own people. And, in fact, provinces have begun to negotiate migration pacts. There is a shared feeling that such action is needed because life is so out of control that society could disintegrate. Confederation may come to be experienced as the alternative to chaos caused by an impotent centralization. Regions need the political power to protect their own kind. If regionalism is not to be divisive, it must be harnessed in new decentralized political forms that confer legitimacy on bounded regionalisms, on new notions of Chineseness.

A debate on national identity is being carried out among Chinese on a daily basis. They argued in 1994 about women's ping-pong champion He Zhili. She had been outraged by a 1987 order to throw a match at the World Championships in New Delhi, India. She disobeyed, won and was therefore barred from the Chinese team sent to the 1988 Seoul Olympics. Upset by the corrupt, centrally controlled athletic system that even forced Chinese athletes to lose to foreign players to further Beijing's foreign policy objectives, He Zhili married a Japanese, emigrated to Japan and took the name Chire Koyama. In October 1994, at the 12th Asian Games held in Japan, Chire Koyama defeated the reigning Chinese champion and won the women's singles title.

---

[19]   These citations come from Lynn White and Li Cheng, 'China Coast Identities: Regional, National, and Global', in Dittmer and Kim (eds), *China's Quest for National Identity*, pp.164-5.

The Olympics touch explosive national sensitivities. The water polo championship in Melbourne, Australia, pitting Russians against Hungarians after the Soviet Union crushed the 1956 Hungarian rebellion, turned pool water blood red. The ice hockey championship between the Soviet Union and Czechoslovakia after the USSR crushed the humanistic Prague Spring also provided a moment of painful national passions. During the 1984 Los Angeles Olympics, I viewed the first days on television in China. China was dominant. Then I flew to Japan and watched the Japanese perform brilliantly. Finally I returned to the United States where the USA seemed to prevail. Had I viewed the Olympics on television in Soviet Russia, Western Europe or Latin America, no doubt I would have been introduced to three yet different patriotic experiences.

Hence, it is not surprising that Beijing journals, loyal to conservative leaders such as Chen Xitong and Li Peng, denounced Chire Koyama for forgetting that Chinese blood ran in her veins and for betraying her Chinese motherland. What was extraordinary was that so many Chinese, despite seeing the 'rising sun' flag ascend, defended her.

Many Chinese said in 1994 that it was natural to abandon a closed and corrupt system and go wherever the market rewarded success. In fact, hundreds of Chinese athletes have already gone overseas. Most intriguingly, Cultural Revolution-era men's ping-pong champion Zhuang Zedong has become Chire Koyama's coach in Beijing, preparing her to represent Japan at the 1996 Atlanta Olympics. A Chinese newspaper editorialized about the players who have left China: 'Their achievements should be the pride of the Chinese people as long as they contribute to peace and progress in the "global village"'.[20] The popular rejection of the claim that Chire Koyama was a traitor is testimony to a most striking change in Chinese identity — in an open, pluralist and tolerant direction.

Rejecting Authoritarian Unity

Increasingly, not only independent intellectuals but even government officials in China conclude that China can only hold together if it loosens up. Unless China constructs a decentralized federalism or a confederated system, regional conflict will explode. Books have been written on a federalist solution to China's national identity crisis and conferences have been held to discuss federalism. I sometimes get the impression that every politically committed Chinese intellectual has his or her own pet plan for federalism. A thin repressive veneer laid down by the conservative leaders of China's over-

---

20   Anthony Kuhn, 'Ping-Pong Politics', *Far Eastern Economic Review*, 8 December 1994, pp.44-5.

centralized system confronts a growing federalist commitment among thoughtful Chinese (*Zhonghuaren*).[21]

In response to this legitimation of an anti-centralization political project, China's conservative rulers make political appeals to the Chinese as citizens (*Zhongguoren*), as in a 1994 *People's Daily* article, to persuade them that only a centralized dictatorship can bring prosperity to China.[22] Conservatives argue that only an authoritarian Confucian China, emulating the East Asian authoritarianism championed by Singapore's Lee Kuan Yew, can be both prosperous and orderly — that this has been the secret of material success in Singapore and South Korea. Lee Kuan Yew has been chosen honorary chairman of China's official International Confucian Association.

On Deng Xiaoping's famous 1992 southern tour that redynamized China's commitment to reform and openness, Deng promoted Singapore's Confucian way. He invited in a top economic aide of Lee Kuan Yew to advise on how to organize the new Pudong economic zone of Shanghai and other similar spots so that they too could enjoy the order achieved by Singapore. As explained by Singapore Professor Chan Heng Chee, the Chinese share a 'Confucian heritage which emphasizes hierarchy, respect for authority, communitarianism, Confucian humanism, and the cultivation of virtuous enlightened leadership. The Marxist-Leninist state buttressed these values and possibly Communism took root in China because the system of thought found echoes in China's traditions'.[23] The *People's Daily* contends that 'this culture better fits the future era', so that it will 'in the next century . . . replace modern and contemporary Western culture'.[24]

> In 1991, Deng Xiaoping chose the Singapore government to build and manage 'Singapore II', a 30-square-mile industrial town to house 700,000 people at Suzhou . . . Singapore proudly boasts that it will transfer its 'development software' of social control to China, Chinese officials have said they want to develop 60 Singapores . . . [25]

And yet, the conservatives' promotion of East Asian Confucian authoritarianism has not swept the mainland of China. The notion that authoritarianism alone can resolve economic dilemmas and guarantee economic progress seems too weak a contention. Responding to Lee Kuan Yew's silly suggestion that the Philippines should go authoritarian to solve its

---

[21]   Peter Kien-hong Yu, 'Federal System May Ease Coming Mainland Change', *Free China Journal*, 25 November 1994, p.6.

[22]   *Renmin ribao* [People's Daily], 31 October 1994.

[23]   Robert Bartley et al., *Democracy and Capitalism: Asian and American Perspectives* (Institute of Southeast Asia Studies, Singapore, 1993), p.21.

[24]   Frank Ching, 'Confucius, the New Savior', *Far Eastern Economic Review*, 10 November 1994, p.37.

[25]   Jim Hoagland, 'Singapore's Great Helmsman', *Washington Post Weekly*, 31 October to 6 November 1994.

economic problems, a perplexed Philippine President Fidel Ramos had riposted that the authoritarian Ferdinard Marcos had taken the Philippines from the richest to the poorest Southeast Asian nation. President Ramos explained that Singapore's authoritarian 'prescription fails to consider our ill-fated flirtation with authoritarianism not so long ago'.[26] Many Chinese tend to feel the same way — which is not to deny that Chinese authoritarians have a real base of support. The struggle over national identity is very much a political struggle.

Politically cynical Chinese, however, see through the official propaganda. Chinese conservatives are perceived to be manipulating Confucianism to reverse Deng's political project of reform and openness. At the same time, some of the Chinese who see a need for more political reform also evoke Confucius, but not as an authoritarian project. This Confucius is a thinker who advocated education and promotion by merit,[27] such that his way discredits the nomenklatura-based political cronyism of the ruling Chinese Leninist system. Notably, Confucian authoritarianism has not progressed in China despite its propagation by a regime that supposedly dominates the media. This failure suggests that the democratic national identity in China has grown quite resistant to Party propaganda.

A Democratic Future?

This is not to suggest that authoritarians must lose and democrats must win. The Chinese do fear chaos and civil strife. They do crave order and national greatness. The regime, however, seems reduced to defining the greatness it can deliver in chauvinist militarist terms.[28] Party leaders seem to believe that China may have to depend on heavy-handed rule in Hong Kong, on military action in the oil rich Xisha island waters of Southeast Asia, or on hostile action toward the emergent independence-oriented forces on Taiwan.

It is possible that repression, anxiety, inertia and chauvinism could combine to permit authoritarianism to continue in China. But it also seems quite possible that desperate chauvinist measures would, as with the Confucian campaign, seem to be so obviously narrowly political and self-serving as to backfire (as did the Argentine invasion of the Falkland/Malvinas Islands). My reading of China's political culture suggests that the conservative regime's use of chauvinist language to legitimate its fragile, yet still over-centralized authoritarianism, has instead boomeranged to further an open, democratic and federalist political project and concomitant national identity.

---

26 Book review, *The Journal of Asian Studies*, vol.53, no.3 (August 1994), p.891.

27 Yang Yingshi, 'Symposium on Confucius Hears Views on Education', *China Daily*, 15 October 1994.

28 Lieutenant General Mi Zhenyu, 'The Hundredth Anniversary of the First Sino-Japanese War Naval Battle and Contemporary Maritime Concepts', *Guofang*, 15 September 1994, translated in JPRS-CAR-94-056, 13 December 1994, pp.91-4.

The focus of China's post-Mao leadership on reintegrating Taiwan into China as a priority task to be achieved before the death of the surviving members of the original Maoist revolutionary generation may be significant instead in redefining national identity in the Chinese (*Zhonghua*) cultural region, especially because Beijing's desire for ever closer economic relations with Taipei has highlighted the reality of Taiwan's *de facto* independence. Taiwanese like to recite a popular litany that Taiwan has more people than two-thirds of the members of the United Nations and that Taiwan is the world's twelfth largest trading economy. Similar types of statistics would describe Guangdong and other Chinese regions, too. Can the regions fail to notice?

Officially, Taiwan favours peaceful unification with the mainland of China. But that requires an atmosphere conducive to trust. The only political form that will foster such trust is a democratic China with tremendously decentralized powers, perhaps even going beyond federalism to confederation, more like the European Union than like the United States of America. This projected future, as seen from Taiwan, accepts the idea that there is one Chinese (*Zhonghua*) civilization as there is also a European civilization. Separate state (regional) identities are compatible with a notion of one China (*Zhonghua*) if China is comprehended in the political and cultural forms just mentioned. In this perspective, Beijing would be worse than Tokyo if it still stubbornly claimed the right to run Taiwan because of a short period of political reunification (1945-49) at the end of the Japanese colonial era. To be morally superior to Japan, which is a political imperative for a Chinese nationalism that grew out of the resistance struggle against Japanese invaders, Beijing cannot insist on coercively imposing unification and Taipei cannot insist on absolute independence. That is, democratic confederation is the projected content of a greater Chinese (*Zhonghua*) nationalism that can contain all of China's challenging diversity.

The Parts and the Whole

The long-term logic of the situation leads toward heightened consciousness of Chinese regionalism. Indeed, for the first time in the history of the People's Republic, scholarly work on contemporary regionalism is being published. Yang Dongping of Beijing Science and Technology University, in his 1994 book *Chengshi jifeng* [Urban Monsoon], contrasts the closeted palace intrigues of Beijing with a socially cohesive Shanghai that is open to the ways of the entire world. The Shanghai-type nationalism that Lucian Pye, in a prior chapter, shows was buried by Mao's anti-imperialist nationalism has risen once again. The north is seen to lack the qualifications and the capacity to run all of China in the twenty-first century. In fact, increasingly the real Chinese character is deemed to have originated in the silk route and in the Yangtze River-oriented Tang and Song dynasties from which Japan and Vietnam and

Korea all borrowed. Increasingly, Chinese do not look to a unifying, centralizing Qin emperor or his newest embodiment in the capital Beijing.

This regionalist reconceptualization of Chinese identities makes clear, even to the reactionary writer He Xin, that there can be more obvious differences among the different types of so-called Han than between a Han and a so-called national minority group.[29] The Chinese press comments about how different regions prefer different teas or celebrate holidays differently. It is difference that catches public attention. That now-widespread perception is testimony to a Chinese national identity very different from Mao-era Han chauvinism.

Notable, too, is an explosive growth of Buddhism and Daoism.[30] These religions perceive patriarchal Confucianism as a narrow familial morality which, in its ethical essence, all can accept. Yet Confucianism defines all non-kin as strangers, all non-Confucians as beyond the reach of a common morality. In contrast, at the end of the twentieth century, Buddhism and Daoism point toward a larger human commitment that offers help to all contemporaries in need, including, as in Taiwan, sufferers from environmental poisons. It is an ethos suitable to the post-modern world. Buddhism and Daoism thus appears as societally-rooted, while Confucianism — even when proudly embraced as ethical truth — is relegated to a merely private realm and role.

Still, it is claimed that Chinese political leaders tend to be ultra-nationalist. For them to accept this new national identity (*Zhonghuaren*), they would have to find confederated openness conducive to a Chinese future of greatness. Strangely, they may well be persuading themselves of precisely this. The ruling group embraces any foreign stamps of approval for a vision of twenty-first century China as a world leader. Indeed, the rulers have circulated foreign books such as Paul Kennedy's *The Rise and Fall of Great Powers* and Allen Tofler's *Third Wave*, which envision just such future Chinese greatness. John Naisbitt's *Global Paradox*, the 1994 contribution to the futurological genre of techno-optimism, projects the twenty-first century as 'The Dragon Century'.[31]

Naisbitt defines China's success as its oneness with the 'Global Paradox', that economic union for great prosperity must now be premised on political and cultural independence. Naisbitt projects 'The Chinese Commonwealth — Gaining Power From Its Parts', a world in which 'the provinces go their own way with or without Beijing's approval' such 'that sometime in the next century China could become a confederacy of dozens of regions or countries held together by economic self-interest'.[32] It is APEC, NAFTA, GATT/WTO

---

29   Friedman, *National Identity and Democratic Prospects in Socialist China*, p.105.

30   Personal observation from travelling and interviewing in China.

31   John Naisbitt, *Global Paradox* (Avon, New York, 1994), ch.5.

32   Ibid., pp.249, 38, respectively.

and the European Union that seem to define a better future. Ever more, in this view, Chinese openness will combine with greater decentralization to produce ever stronger economic growth. In this light, chauvinistic Chinese leaders could well be on their way toward imagining future Chinese greatness in harmony with open confederation.

If this essay correctly captures some crucial aspects of the still somewhat hidden and maturing ·politics of identity formation among Chinese peoples, then it helps explain why the conservative (reactionary?) Confucian authoritarian identity propagated by Beijing has not taken hold and cannot be popular. Still, an analyst should be cautious about projecting from observable opinion in China. The Communist Party does not foster an atmosphere permitting public opinion to be the consequence of a give and take that comes from openly trying on and debating — or hearing debated — various identities. Public opinion in such systems is highly volatile. In the Ukraine, 90 per cent of the people, when polled under the rule of the Soviet Union dictatorship, chose the Soviet Union over an independent Ukraine. But a 90 per cent margin voted, one year later, for Ukranian independence. It is likely that the surface opinion one finds under the Beijing dictatorship is far more favourable to the regime's notion of Confucian, authoritarian, centralized unity than will be the case when political liberalization begins.

Even so, already the old statist institutions are weakening. People more and more identify with their local community. In other words, the extent of manifest change under the old order offers good reason to conclude that an extraordinary transformation in Chinese national identity is already under way and that it holds far more promise for achieving democratic political forms than is believed possible by superficial realists still mesmerized by the former hegemony of Mao's anti-imperialist nationalism or by Deng's and Lee Kuan Yew's concocted, palpably political East Asian Confucian authoritarianism.

That confederalist, regionalist, open identities can facilitate a peaceful democratic system in no way guarantees the transition. The politics of such a transition will be full of high risks, fraught with dangers. But it is certain that a new Chinese national identity is already being contested to define a more open and culturally richer twenty-first century China (*Zhonghua*).

The reactions by various Chinese to ping-pong scandals or the mistreatment of internal migrants are not what is crucial. The particulars come and go and can be forgotten. What matters far more is the mind-set which permits Chinese to keep interpreting facts, new and old, real or imagined, in a way that supports an open, plural and tolerant Chinese identity, as the cultural basis for a democratic Chinese nationalism.

NINE

To Screw Foreigners Is Patriotic: China's Avant-Garde Nationalists*

Geremie R. Barmé

In 'A Beijing Man in New York' (*Beijingren zai Niuyue*), China's popular 1993 tele-series, the protagonist Wang Qiming, a man on his way to making a fortune after a train of failures and betrayals, hires a New York prostitute. She is white, blonde and buxom. Wang decides to take some of his frustrations out on her. While thrusting himself onto the prostrate prostitute, Wang showers her with dollar bills. As the money swirls around the bed, Wang demands that she repeatedly cry out: 'I love you'.

Reportedly, this was an extremely popular scene with mainland audiences, in particular with the Chinese intelligentsia.[1] It is also the type of encounter that has a certain paradigmatic significance about it. It could be argued that by having his way with an American whore while buying her endearments with a shower of greenbacks, Wang Qiming's action is the most

*   In 'Zhunbei haole ma?' [Are you ready?], a recent emigré Chinese interviewee tells the writer Sang Ye that Chinese students and other Chinese mainlanders she had encountered in Australia 'think that to screw foreign cunt is a kind of patriotism' (*cao waiguo bi ye suan aiguo ma*). See Sang Ye, 'Zhunbei haole ma?, translated by Barmé with Linda Jaivin in Sang Ye, *The Year the Dragon Came* (Queensland University Press, Brisbane, forthcoming, 1996). Some of the material in this essay appeared in Barmé, 'Soft Porn, Packaged Dissent, and Nationalism: Notes on Chinese Culture in the 1990s', *Current History* (September 1994), pp.273-5. My thanks to the reviewers of *The China Journal* — Chris Buckley, Frank Dikotter, Michael Dutton, Andrew Nathan and Jeffrey Wasserstrom — who offered a number of insightful comments and suggestions on the draft of this chapter, as well as their encouragement. I am also grateful to Jonathan Unger and Anita Chan for their editorial work on the piece.

1   Zha Xiduo, 'Youse yanjinglide xiyangjing — Beijingrende Niuyue meng' [Looking at the West through Coloured Glasses — Beijing People Have New York Dreams], *Jiushi niandai yuekan* [The Nineties Monthly], no.2 (1994), pp.16-17. In relation to the market and cultural significance of white flesh in China today, see Louisa Schein, 'The Consumption of Color and the Politics of White Skin in Post-Mao China', *Social Text* (Winter 1995), pp.146-7.

eloquent recent statement (and inversion) of the century-old Chinese-foreign dilemma.[2]

This tele-series appeared at a time when both the Chinese authorities and segments of the population were becoming increasingly irate about their (perceived) inferior position in the New World Order and the attitude of the United States.[3] To an extent the series is a reprisal of the Boxers without any belief system. It represents the coming of age of Chinese narcissism, and it bespeaks a desire for revenge for all the real and perceived slights of the past century.[4]

In their representation of China as a nation ruthlessly violated by Western imperialism after the Opium Wars, from the mid-19th century onward many literati pointed out that China's military and spiritual weakness had made it an easy prey to aggressive foreigners. Questions of racial and political impotence have been central to Chinese thought and debates ever since.[5] Reformist and revolutionary movements in China over the past century have been born of a passion for national independence and strength. Most of the ideologically contending groups in China have, despite ideological clashes and heated debates, essentially pursued similar nationalistic goals.[6] A number of issues

---

2   Another choice scene occurs when Wang's lover, the Taiwanese restauranteuse Ah Chun, says: 'They [the Americans] can quite easily imagine a world without China, but could never conceive of a world without themselves'. Wang responds angrily: 'Fuck them! They were still monkeys up in the trees while we were already human beings. Look at how hairy they are, they're not as evolved as us. Just 'cause they have a bit of money!'

3   At the same time it should be noted the series belongs to a tradition in which history or things foreign are manipulated in an attempt to comment on contemporary Chinese political and social realities. The plot and characters of 'A Beijing Man in New York' are to a great extent concerned not with the fate of Chinese in the United States as such, but with the Chinese themselves and their endless in-fighting. Apart from the elements of the series discussed in this essay, there are many other complex issues raised in it that also relate to contemporary attitudes of self-loathing (see below). That the action of the piece takes place in New York is at times coincidental to the central concerns of this often-incoherent and crudely-made production.

4   See Linda Jaivin, 'Life in a Battlefield', *Asian Wall Street Journal*, 24-25 December 1993.

5   See, for example, Frank Dikotter, *The Discourse of Race in Modern China* (C. Hurst & Co., London, 1992), pp.75-7, 107-15; and 'Racial Identities in China: Context and Meaning', *The China Quarterly*, no.138 (June 1994), pp.404-12.

6   This point is made very forcefully by the noted writer and translator Dong Leshan in 'Dongfangzhuyi dahechang?' [An Orientalist Chorus?], *Dushu* [Reading], no.5 (1994), pp.99-102. For some of the basic texts in these century-old debates, see, for example, *Zhongguo jindai wenhua wenti* [The Question of Culture in Modern China] (Zhonghua shuju, Beijing, 1989); Chen Song (ed.), *'Wusi' qianhou Dong-Xi wenhua wenti lunzhan wenxuan* [Selected Works from the Debate on Eastern-Western Culture from the Time of 'May Fourth'], expanded edition (Zhongguo shehui kexue chubanshe, Beijing, 1989);

central to debates of the late Qing, in particular those that unfolded during the two reform periods (the Hundred Days Reform of 1898 and the Qing Reform of 1901-07), including such questions as political change, limiting central power, new economic policies, and so on, have been the object of interest since the late 1980s.[7] So, too, it is argued by some mainland academics that the overwhelming popularity of lengthy fictional works related to late Qing figures like Zeng Guofan in recent years stems from a mass yearning for a new strongman to lead China.[8] To an extent the early 1990s nostalgia for Mao Zedong is also a reflection of these mass sentiments.

The end of the Cold War has seen the revival throughout the world of national aspirations and interests; developments in China have certainly not occurred in isolation. The rapid decay of Maoist ideological beliefs and the need for continued stability in the Chinese Communist Party have led to an increased reliance on nationalism as a unifying ideology. But whereas throughout the 1980s the Communist Party emphasized its role as the paramount patriotic force in the nation,[9] mobilizing nationalistic symbols and mythology to shore up its position, by the 1990s the situation had altered. Patriotic sentiment is no longer the sole province of the Party and its propagandists.[10] Just as commercialisation is creating a new avaricious social contract of sorts, so nationalism is functioning as a form of consensus beyond the bounds of official culture. But it is a consensus that for the time being at least benefits the Party. Both economic realities and national priorities call for a strong central state and thus tend to give an ideologically weakened Communist Party a renewed role in the broader contest for the nation.

---

and Luo Rongqu (ed.), *Cong 'xihua' dao xiandaihua* [From 'Westernization' to Modernization] (Beijing daxue chubanshe, Beijing, 1990).

[7]   In 1988-89, a number of articles in the journal *Xin qimeng* [New Enlightenment] and the Shanghai paper *Shijie jingji daobao* [World Economic Herald], for example, made comparisons between the late Qing and Deng's reform era. From the early 1990s, there has been a renewed interest in the Qing reforms (*xinzheng*) among intellectuals and the reading public. See Lu Jia, 'Wan-Qing zhengzhire ranshao quan Zhongguo' [A Fad for Late Qing Politics Sweeps China], *Zhongguo shibao* [China Times], 29 November 1994; and Yang Ping, 'Zeng Guofan xianxiangde qishi' [Revelations of the *Zeng Guofan* Phenomenon], *Beijing qingnian bao* [Beijing Youth News], 28 May 1994.

[8]   This view is expressed by Sun Liping of the Sociology Department of Beijing University in Lu Jia, 'Wan-Qing zhengzhire ranshao'.

[9]   This was contested a number of times, as in the case of the anti-Hong Kong soccer riot in Beijing of May 1985 and the anti-Japanese demonstrations of the same year (aimed against what many perceived as national economic capitulationism).

[10] See James L. Watson, 'The Renegotiation of Chinese Cultural Identity in the Post-Mao Era', in Jeffrey N. Wasserstrom and Elizabeth J. Perry (eds), *Popular Protest and Political Culture in Modern China* (Westview Press, Boulder, 1992), pp.67-84; and Edward Friedman, 'Reconstructing China's National Identity: A Southern Alternative to Mao-Era Anti-Imperialist Nationalism', *The Journal of Asian Studies*, vol.53, no.1 (February 1994), pp.67-91.

Since 1989 there has certainly been an erosion of the authority of the Party-state, but it could also be argued that attempts are being made to reformulate and broaden the basis of national authority as the ambit of what constitutes 'patriotic' becomes greatly expanded. This is obvious in the Party's strenuous efforts at patriotic indoctrination and 'state-of-the-nation education' (*guoqing jiaoyu*),[11] aimed particularly at workers and the young. This movement was launched by Party General Secretary Jiang Zemin after the Tiananmen protests[12] and climaxed in late 1994 with the publication of the Party's 'Outline for the Implementation of Patriotic Education'.[13] Enterprising business people from Hainan and Beijing reacted to the official patriotic outpouring in a manner in keeping with present Chinese economic realities by announcing that they were planning a patriotic theme park in the capital.[14]

---

[11]   The term *guoqing*, literally 'national situation' (or *Zhongguo qingkuang*), has a venerable history in post-19th century Chinese cultural and political debate. The term has been variously deployed: to reject the influence of the West last century because Western institutions and practices did not 'conform to China's national situation', to being used in the 1930s to oppose Communist ideology as 'unsuited to China's situation'. Since 1981 the Party has employed the term as a propaganda device as, at times, have oppositionists, and a formidable literature on the subject has developed, in particular from the late 1980s onwards. See, for example, Lu Nian, 'Guoqing zhuanzhu gailan' [An Overview of Specialist Books on *guoqing*], *Wenhui dushu zhoubao* [Wenhui Reader's Weekly], 11 August 1990. See also the short-lived Beijing journal *Guoqing yanjiu* [Studies in *Guoqing*], published in 1989, and *Zhongguo guoqing guoli*, which started publication in 1992; and Wu Jie et al. (eds), *Guoqing jiaoyu shouce* [A Handbook for *Guoqing* Education] (Huaxia chubanshe, Beijing, 1990). A useful volume of leaders' remarks on the subject is Zhonggong zhongyang zhengce yanjiushi dangjianzu (ed.), *Mao Zedong, Deng Xiaoping lun Zhongguo guoqing* [Mao Zedong and Deng Xiaoping on China's *Guoqing*] (Zhonggong zhongyang dangxiao chubanshe, Beijing, 1992).

[12]   See Jiang Zemin's speeches in Zhonggong zhongyang zhengce yanjiushi (ed.), *Zai xinde lishi tiaojianxia jicheng he fayang aiguozhuyi chuantong — shiyijie sanzhong quanhui yilai youguan zhongyao wenxian zhaibian* [Carry on and Develop the Tradition of Patriotism in New Historical Circumstances — Extracts from Important Documents Since the Third Plenum of the Eleventh Party Congress] (Hongqi chubanshe, Beijing, 1990), pp.301-9, 319-26, 329-51, 373-81, 387-401. Li Ruihuan, the first post-Tiananmen ideological commissar in the Politburo, launched his own campaign to 'enhance national culture' (*hongyang minzu wenhua*) both to fit in with the strategic shift in propaganda requirements and to counteract attempts by rabid ideologues to purge the cultural sphere. See Li's 'Guanyu hongyang minzu youxiu wenhuade ruogan wenti' [Some Questions Relevant to Enhancing the Outstanding Elements of the National Culture], *Renmin ribao* [People's Daily], 10 January 1990.

[13]   See 'Aiguo zhuyi jiaoyu shishi gangyao', *Renmin ribao*, 6 September 1994.

[14]   'China's Journey Over the Last Century', as the park is to be named, will be completed by 1999 and, in the style of modern edu-tainment displays, it will feature a century of Chinese patriotism arranged in a theme park in the shape of a scaled-down version of China. See Quan Xin, '"Zhongguo shiji zhi lu: guoqing bainian aiguozhuyi jiaoyu

A period of relative political stability and intellectual stagnation has combined with economic frenzy to create the possibility for a rough-and-ready confluence of interests under the umbrella of patriotism. While many prominent dissidents are still banned from returning to the mainland and others are periodically persecuted in China — in particular when their activities among workers threaten the *status quo* — there are those who can travel freely and have become involved in various business ventures. One could speculate that it is only a matter of time before some aberrant exiles will be welcomed back into the fold as 'patriotic Overseas Chinese' (*aiguo huaqiao*).

In the broader context of Chinese society, since 1989 there have been numerous indications of a growing disenchantment with the West and its allies. People have been sorely aware that the post-'89 transformation in Eastern Europe and the Soviet Union has not been as rapid or as positive as first expected. As in many other parts of the world, there is a general belief that the West, its values and systems, have not made that much difference to post-Communist countries. For those who supported the 1989 student movement, there is the added realization that if China had then successfully undergone a major political upheaval, the nation could well have been faced with the disorder that now dogs Russia's rulers.

Coupled with this is the underlying sentiment that the world (that is, the West) owes China something. Past humiliations are often used as an excuse to demand better treatment from the West. This has been repeatedly revealed in official Chinese responses to the question of human rights abuses, in particular in the White Paper of 1991.[15] The popular Mao cult that flourished in the early 1990s had a perceptible anti-foreign edge to it. Mao ruled a China that was effectively closed off from the West, and he instilled in the nation a sense of pride and self-worth that it has lost as the result of Deng's open-door and reform policies. While Deng is admired for what he has done for the economy, Mao is revered, among other things, for keeping the superpowers, the United States and the Soviet Union, at bay.[16]

The demand for better treatment from the international community was particularly obvious during China's Olympic bid in 1993 when the mainland media called on the rest of the world to 'give China a chance' (*gei Zhongguo*

---

gongcheng" jingqi tuichu' ['China's Journey Over the Last One Hundred Years' Will Soon be Launched], *Beijing qingnian bao*, 16 October 1994.

15 See *Zhongguode renquan zhuangkuang (baipishu) xuexi cailiao* [Materials for Studying *The Human Rights Situation in China (White Paper)*] (Hongqi chubanshe, Beijing, 1991), p.3. See also the long article on human rights abuses in *Guangming ribao* [Guangming Daily], 11 September 1994.

16 The new Mao cult (c. 1988-93) was an extremely complex phenomenon and the anti-Western dimension of it was, of course, only a small aspect of it. See Geremie Barmé, *Shades of Mao: The Posthumous Cult of the Great Leader* (M. E. Sharpe, Armonk, 1996).

yige jihui). The internal propaganda campaign emphasized the primacy of a unique Chinese national spirit and the ability of the people to 'move mountains and drain the oceans' in their quest to create a perfect homeland (*jiayuan*), a paradise on earth.[17] The eventual failure of the Chinese bid was deemed to have been orchestrated by Western bullies, and the Olympic Committee's decision to give the 2000 Olympics to Sydney was seen as an affront to Chinese national sentiment (not to mention a lost business opportunity).[18]

While nationalist sentiment is repackaged and flourishes, the clamp-down on oppositionist opinion in the media after 1989 has meant that few divergent voices have an outlet in any wide-based public forum. Mass opinion is thus formed either by the salacious tabloid press and electronic media or by classified publications and news sources that reinforce accepted dogma and politico-cultural stereotypes. Although intellectuals have regrouped and produced a number of significant publications since 1992, the diversification of the Chinese media and the wholesale commercialisation of the non-propaganda media have meant that their impact is marginal at best. Without public intellectuals or public debate, few of the more extreme opinions that do appear — for example, those of Yuan Hongbing in his 1990 *Winds on the Plain* (discussed below) or Wang Shan in his 1994 book *China Through the Third Eye*[19] — get challenged except by pro-Party propagandists.

At the same time, as the older comrades and their dated politics fade from the scene, a major generational and ideological shift is becoming irreversible. Until now, narrow sectarian fundamentalists — people like the veteran propagandists Hu Qiaomu (recently deceased), Deng Liqun and Xu Weicheng, as well as elderly political figures like Wang Zhen (recently deceased) — favoured some form of ideological constraint on the unbridled passions of national aspiration and economic power. But the Maoist worldview that gave China some form of vision and sense of self-worth has been dismantled and

---

17   For a typical example of this kind of propaganda, see 'Zhongguorende jingshen neng yishan daohai' [The Spirit of the Chinese People Can Move Mountains and Drain the Oceans], *Beijing qingnian bao*, 2 August 1991. The language of such writing is highly reminiscent of Maoist propaganda (in regard to the Red Flag Canal, Dazhai, Daqing, the Tangshan Earthquake and so on) that spoke constantly of the ability of the Chinese labouring people to overcome all obstacles and remake the world. After 1989, this type of language was employed in promoting the Asian Games in 1990, fighting the 1991 floods in South China and pursuing the Olympic bid in 1993.

18   See Nayan Chanda and Lincoln Kaye, 'Circling Hawks', *Far Eastern Economic Review*, 7 October 1993, pp.12-13.

19   Wang Shan, *Disan zhi yanjing kan Zhongguo* (Shanxi renmin chubanshe, Taiyuan, 1994). Attributed to an fictitious 'German' writer, the book was actually written by Wang Shan, its putative translator.

lacks committed advocates.[20] What remains is a crude pre-World War I positivism that has been revised since the late 1970s and further enhanced by the international media's myth-making and hype regarding the economic and cultural rise of 'East Asia'. There is a faith in science, material wealth, capitalism and national strength. It is a faith tempered neither by the moderating influences of traditional culture nor, for all the talk about China's burgeoning middle class, by any modern bourgeois angst. Nationalistic and ultra-nationalistic sentiments are now found across the political spectrum, and we can speculate that many of the individuals and groups who hold such views have a following in the broader society. This essay will attempt to reflect the range of expression that such sentiments take.

Oriental, Orientalism

It's a state of mind/ It's peace of mind/ If you don't mind/ Orientalism/
It's east and west/ Forget the rest/ So can you guess?/ Orientalism[21]

Much of the more serious cultural/nationalist debate that has unfolded in the mainland Chinese media since the early 1990s has appeared in the pages of a number of journals that are based mostly in Beijing. These include *Dushu* [Reading], the oldest 'liberal' monthly, which has weathered the extraordinary ideological upheavals of the reform period; the two main organs of Chinese-style 'national studies' (*guoxue*),[22] *Zhongguo wenhua* [Chinese Culture] and *Xueren* [Scholar];[23] *Dongfang* [Oriental], the joint effort of a coalition of cultural conservatives and 'liberals'; and *Zhanlüe yu guanli* [Strategy and Management], a publication edited by younger conservatives, the latter two journals both first appearing in 1993.

While articles and dialogues published in the more easily labelled 'liberal' journals like *Dushu* and *Dongfang* generally skirt the issues of one-party rule and authoritarianism/totalitarianism, or only discuss them in the oblique esoteric code common to the media in a repressive environment,

---

20 See, for example, Willy Wo-Lap Lam, *China after Deng Xiaoping: The Power Struggle in Beijing since Tiananmen* (John Wiley & Sons, Singapore, 1995), pp.185-91.

21 These lyrics come from the Singaporean rocker Dick Lee's pop-rap song 'Orientalism'. My thanks to Gloria Davies for bringing Lee's work to my attention.

22 For the comments of a number of noted scholars on the revival of 'national studies' in recent years, its relevance to the question of cultural nationalism and Western thought, see 'Guoxue, chuantong wenhua yu shehuizhuyi shicang jingji' [National Studies, Traditional Culture and the Socialist Market Economy], *Renmin ribao*, 6 and 27 December 1994.

23 For a review of these magazines, see Cheng Nong, 'Fuchu haimian' [Floating to the Surface], *Dushu*, no.2 (1994), pp.47-52. Numerous other publications both in China and elsewhere, like the Hong Kong-based *Ershiyi shiji* [21st Century] which circulates in China, also play a significant role in mainland intellectual debates.

Zhanlüe yu guanli is more direct in its approach. The general tenor of the many articles in its pages on the subject of nationalism[24] is that the single-party state you have is better than the free-wheeling chaos you do not. Its editors and many of its writers are troubled by the lack of morals, spiritual vacuity and cultural lawlessness in China today.

In the first issue of *Zhanlüe yu guanli*, Wang Xiaodong, one of the journal's editors, rebuffed Samuel P. Huntington's notion that future world conflicts would be primarily cultural in nature, dividing the world into the West, Islam and Confucian cultural blocs.[25] Wang denies that China can meaningfully be classified as a Confucian nation/civilization and asserts that there is no desire on the part of the Chinese to Confucianize the rest of the world. He notes that Western values and civilization are generally welcomed by the Chinese, apart from instances where their transmission involves economic or other forms of imperialism. Any future conflicts will depend on economic interests. Ideological, cultural and other clashes, he claims, are and will remain little more than a guise for clashes of national interest.[26] He argues that China will come into conflict with other powers because of its present economic strength and potential, which will make it seem a threat to the United States. He quotes Prime Minister Mahathir of Malaysia, commenting that following the collapse of the Soviet Union and the emergence of one superpower, small countries have no choice but either to be obedient to that power or to resist it.[27]

Wang notes that over the past decade Chinese intellectuals have generally sought foreign nostrums as a solution to China's dilemmas. According to these intellectuals, the greatest obstacle to China's progress is a vaguely defined collection of 'national traditions' (*minzu chuantong*). But Wang questions: what happens if the Chinese come to perceive that there are active exterior obstacles to this 'garnering from the outside' (*waiqu*)? Such obstacles might be expressed in terms of trade, migration or some other form. His argument uses references gleaned from the novelist Bao Mi's apocalyptic view of

---

24   The Chinese terms for 'nationalism' most often used in these discussions are *minzuzhuyi* and, more rarely, *mincuizhuyi*. *Mincuizhuyi* has, however, a more narrow definition and strong elements of cultural determinism. One writer for *Zhanlüe yu guanli* notes the *mincuizhuyi* elements of Maoism and their appeal to people in the present age of economic dislocation. See Hu Weixi, 'Zhongguo jinxiandaide shehui zhuanxing yu mincuizhuyi' [Social Transformation in Modern China and Nationalism], *Zhanlüe yu guanli*, no.5 (1994), pp.26-7.

25   See Shi Zhong (Wang Xiaodong), 'Weilaide chongtu' [Future Conflicts], *Zhanlüe yu guanli*, no.1 (1993), pp.46-50. Huntington's original article was 'The Clash of Civilizations', *Foreign Affairs*, vol.72, no.3 (Summer 1993), pp.22-49. For Shi Zhong's article in English, see *Strategy and Management* (English edition of *Zhanlüe yu guanli*), no.1 (1995), pp.66-73.

26   Shi Zhong, 'Weilaide chongtu', p.47.

27   Ibid., p.49.

China's future as presented in the popular futuristic *samizdat* novel *Huanghuo* [Yellow Peril],[28] which is concerned with a war that results both from a struggle for resources in South China and international conflicts.[29]

Others, like Xiao Gongqin, the Shanghai-based historian who came to prominence in the late 1980s as a supporter of 'new authoritarianism', are more restrained. From the early 1990s onward, Xiao has issued warnings about the dangers of weak central government control. Xiao has pointed out that local mafias, corrupt police and economic cartels will soon have the country in a stranglehold and Beijing will be increasingly incapable of imposing its will. Xiao sees no solution in Western nostrums or in any political alternatives to firm Party rule. He has written on the role nationalism can play during the present period of 'ideological transformation' in China.[30]

Wang Hui, another critic of Huntington, commented in the same journal that the culturalism of Huntington's argument and the critical tendencies of Orientalism, introduced into China in the early 1990s, have been conflated by Chinese intellectuals and have added fuel to the debates on nationalism.[31] One of the most important points raised by writers like Wang Hui is that Western theories presently being introduced to China, including much post-modernist theorizing, although challenging and relatively subversive in the context of the West, can be used to advance or consolidate cultural conservatism in the present Chinese environment[32] or, as the Shanghai academic and cultural critic

---

[28] Bao Mi, *Huanghuo* [Yellow Peril] (Fengyun shidai chuban youxian gongsi, Taibei, 1991). In particular, Wang uses Li Ming's 'Zongkan Zhongguode weiji' [An Overview of China's Crisis], ibid., vol.III, pp.279-313.

[29] The novel was written on the mainland and often circulated on computer diskette, and a version was published in Taiwan amidst considerable fanfare. The author's concerns and reflections were supposed to be a direct response to the events of 1989. The book is certainly in the style of the 'crisis writings' common on the mainland from the late 1980s. Bao Mi told a Beijing-based reporter for *Time Magazine* that the book was 'a philosophical tract against consumerism, not an attack on the communist regime'. Jaime A. FlorCruz, 'Secrets of a Hot Novel', *Time Magazine*, 30 March 1992.

[30] Xiao Gongqin, 'Minzuzhuyi yu Zhongguo zhuanxing shiqide yishi xingtai' [Nationalism and Ideology in China during the Period of Transformation], *Zhanlüe yu guanli*, no.4 (1994), pp.21-5. Similar sentiments have been expressed by a number of Chinese analysts and 'wannabe' government advisers. See, for example, Wang Shaoguang and Hu Angang's 1993 report on the state of the Chinese economy and central government power, discussed by Shuang Yi in 'Xuezhe xiance, quanzhe juece' [Academics Offer Policy Advice, the Powers-That-Be Make the Decisions], *Zhongguo shibao zhoukan* [China Times Weekly], no.94 (17-23 October 1993), pp.16-18.

[31] Wang Hui and Zhang Tianwei in conversation, 'Wenhui pipan lilun yu dangdai Zhongguo minzuzhuyi wenti' [Cultural Criticism Theory and Contemporary Chinese Nationalism], *Zhanlüe yu guanli*, no.4 (1994), p.19. Wang's work also appears in *Dushu*.

[32] Ibid., p.19. In his comments, Wang uses the dichotomy between political and cultural nationalism in a way that is highly reminiscent of John Hutchinson's work on the subject. See Hutchinson, *The Dynamics of Cultural Nationalism* (Allen & Unwin,

Xu Jilin has said, be yet another 'subterfuge in the cultural cold war' (*wenhua lengzhande dunci*) with the West.[33] In early 1995, the London-based academic Zhao Yiheng published a lengthy critique of how what he calls Western 'post-studies' (*houxue*) had aided the development of a new conservatism among mainland intellectuals.[34] There is an ever-expanding literature on a range of 'post-' subjects in China (post-structuralism, post-modernism, post-colonialism, and so on) and, as a number of critics like Zhao have noted, such theoretical strategies are more often than not used to validate the place of mass commercial culture in the society and negate the independent and critical role of the informed intellectual.[35] This plethora of Sino-post-modernisms, it could be argued, serves members of the intelligentsia as a means for abdicating their role as critics, a role that has often proved uncomfortable and even dangerous in the past. At the same time, theoretical approaches like post-colonialism are used to affirm the value of local and nativist cultural elements (*bentuhua*, as it is termed in Chinese, or 'sinicization') and even, one could speculate, a cultural and political *status quo* — and to reject 'Western' thought (socio-cultural as well as political) as colonizing, imperialist and altogether unsuited to Chinese realities. By redefining intellectual debate in terms of 'Chineseness', these mainland disciples of post-modernism[36] lend conservative and nationalistic discourse a cloak of up-to-date respectability.

London, 1987), p.12ff. Wang makes similar points about the political and nationalist nature of commercial culture and post-modernist debate in his essay 'Jiushi niandai Zhongguo dalude wenhua yanjiu yu wenhua piping' [Cultural Research and Criticism in 1990s' Mainland China], *Dianying yishu* [The Art of Cinema], no.1 (1995), summarized in *Dushu*, no.5 (1995), pp.151-2.

33   Xu Jilin, '"Houzhimin wenhua piping" mianmianguan' [Staring Down 'Post-Colonial Cultural Criticism'], *Dongfang*, no.4 (1994), p.23.

34   Zhao Yiheng, '"Houxue" yu Zhongguo xin baoshouzhuyi' ['Post-studies' and China's New Conservatism], *Ershiyi shiji*, no.2 (1995), pp.4-15. See also Xu Ben's '"Disan shijie piping" zai dangjin Zhongguode chujing' [The Predicament of 'Third World Criticism' in China Today] in the same issue, pp.16-27. For a critique of these articles — and rejection of their approach — by Zhang Yiwu, associate professor in Chinese literature at Beijing University and a leading figure in this debate, see Zhang, 'Chanshi "Zhongguo" de jiaolü' [The Anxiety of Interpreting 'China'], *Ershiyi shiji*, no.4 (1995), pp.128-35.

35   Some critics also claim in private that the hue and cry over theory in China is part of a complex battle for intellectual and ideological supremacy (*zhengduo huayuquan*) launched by up-and-coming younger academics.

36   They are, in particular, the Beijing-based literary critics Chen Xiaoming and Zhang Yiwu, although their fellows are legion. For some of Chen and Zhang's views, see, for example, the record of round-table discussion 'Jingshen tuibaizhede kuangwu' [The Wild Dance of the Spiritually Decadent], *Zhongshan*, no.6 (1993), pp.142-62, and 'Dongfangzhuyi yu zhouzhimin wenhua' [Orientalism and Post-Colonial Culture], *Zhongshan*, no.1 (1994), pp.126-48.

Given the cultural confusion in China today, it is little wonder then that the works of Edward W. Said[37] have been so well received. From mid-1993 onward there has been talk of Said's work on Orientalism and the imperialist West's distortion of Middle Eastern and Asian Others. A group of intellectuals writing in the January 1994 issue of the 'liberal' journal *Dushu* averred that the deployment of Orientalism is something pursued only by marginalized Western and minority intellectuals who are trying to validate their own flimsy cultural positions. Sun Jin, a scholar of theology, expressed what seems to be a fairly widely-held view: when China becomes a truly strong nation, niggardly theoretical and intellectual questions like Orientalism, Post-modernist discourse, and talk of a global Centre and Periphery will be easily dealt with. Then, and only then, it is argued, can China enter into an equal dialogue with the world.

But for many, an equal 'dialogue' with the outside world is seen as virtually impossible. A number of noted Chinese writers from Lu Xun onward have commented on exchanges with the outside as reflecting either a slavish mentality or an attitude of pompous, unquestioning superiority.

Self-Hate and Self-Approbation

> The religion of the Chinese today is cheating, deceit, blackmail and theft, eating, drinking, whoring, gambling and smoking . . . We think any honest, humble gentleman a fool and regard any good person who works hard and demands little in return as an idiot. Crooks are our sages; thieves and swindlers our supermen . . . there are no greater cynics than the Chinese people.[38]

Many Chinese pride themselves on being the harshest and most perceptive critics of themselves. There is a powerful, if hard-to-define, tradition of self-loathing in China. Its roots can be found in the late Ming Dynasty of the 16th-17th centuries when some literati used the language of Buddhism and Confucian thought to engage in self-reflection.[39] From the mid-19th century this impulse of self-criticism surfaced again. For over a century there has been a vigorous trend in both popular and intellectual circles to

---

[37]   In particular, the writings by Said that have gained attention in China are *Orientalism*, 1978, and *Culture and Imperialism*, 1993.

[38]   He Xin, 'Gudu yu tiaozhan — wode fendou yu sikao' [Solitude and Challenge — My Struggle and Reflections], *Zixue zazhi* [Autodidact Magazine], no.10 (1988), p.39, quoted in Barmé and Jaivin, *New Ghosts, Old Dreams*, pp.213 and 254. For a more recent and full-blown catalogue of the ills of the national spirit, see Jia Lusheng, *Wode bing* [My Sickness] (Guoji wenhua chuban gongsi, Beijing, 1992).

[39]   See, for example, Wu Pei-yi, *The Confucian's Progress: Autobiographical Writings in Traditional China* (Princeton University Press, Princeton, 1990); and Wm. Theodore de Bary, 'Individualism and Humanitarianism in Late Ming Thought', in de Bary et al. (eds), *Self and Society in Ming Thought* (Columbia University Press, New York, 1970), pp.145-247.

denounce the Chinese and China. In 1897, Tan Sitong, a young political reformist who was later martyred for his activities, saw the fate of China in Buddhist terms:

> A calamitous destiny is now unfolding in China. It has been brought about by the evils committed by generations of tyrannical rulers, and also by the karmic deeds of the people during incalculable cycles of transmigration. When I look at China, I know that a great disaster is at hand.[40]

These sentiments are reflected in the writings and comments of many Chinese writers this century (the names Lu Xun, Li Zongwu, Li Ao, Bo Yang, Lung-kee Sun, Long Yingtai and Liu Xiaobo come readily to mind),[41] and it is common to hear such remarks whenever politics, the economy, culture or the future of the nation are privately discussed today.

For many people, there is a sense that China has somehow fallen from grace, that the glories of the longest continuing civilization (summed up in the popular mind by the phrase 'five thousand years of history') are buried in the past and can in no way help China cope with its position in the modern world. The legacy of this history is felt to have been exposed as impotent when the Qing court was confronted with the military and economic might of other nations. The complexities and wealth of the written language and its culture have been felt by such critics to be a barrier to communication with the rest of the world. The political and social legacy of some two millenia is often characterized by the words 'feudal' or 'Confucian', deemed a deadening weight, forming a 'deep structure' that stymies change, repressive and ultimately conducive to neither social nor political harmony.

According to this view, every element of Chinese reality only adds to the crisis that is endemic to Chinese civilization, and one so profound that widespread economic development does not necessarily alleviate it. The list of problems is long and harrowing.

---

[40]   Tan Sitong, 'Renxue' [On Humanity], *Tan Sitong quanji* [The Complete Works of Tan Sitong] (Sanlian shudian, Beijing, 1954), p.73, quoted in Barmé and Jaivin, *New Ghosts, Old Dreams*, p.117.

[41]   Li Zongwu's work was first reprinted on the mainland in 1989, and Li Ao's essays began to appear the same year. Bo Yang's controversial *The Ugly Chinaman* and Lung-kee Sun's *The 'Deep Structure' of Chinese Culture* were published in China in 1986. Long Yingtai's essays, which are highly critical of Taiwan and 'Chineseness', have also been available for some years. Ironically, the mainland critic Liu Xiaobo is banned on the mainland, although he regularly published social and political critiques following his release from jail in 1991. Of these writers, Bo Yang is probably the most vociferous critic of the Chinese national character. Some of his satirical essays (*zawen*) of the 1960s were first published on the mainland in 1993. In those writings he remarked, among other things, that what appears to be Chinese nationalism is little more than a disguised refusal to accept superior institutions and practices that are generally identified as being 'Western'.

The population is catastrophically large. The political system (cosmetic Marxist-Leninist socialism with the characteristics of a police state) hinders the development of a mature society that can live rationally with the wealth that the economic reforms are creating. Environmental problems are of such a magnitude that they may well condemn future generations to illness and poverty. An arbitrary legal system relies on government whim and personal connections coupled with an erratic police mechanism that combines elements of Maoist draconianism with both traditional and modern methods of coercion. The media lacks independence and serves either Party fiat or fritters away its energies on consumeristic and cultural trivia; journalists devoted to the higher calling of pursuing truth and justice in their work are persecuted and hounded into silence. The carpetbagger, get-rich-quick mentality of both private entrepreneurs and large numbers of state cadres are self-centred, short-sighted and unprincipled. This murky soup of a society is overseen by a Party leadership ridden with nepotism and one that rules according to the precepts of clan elders (a 'Chinese mafia', as some Chinese have dubbed it). It directs the life of the nation through a bureaucracy of such size and labyrinthine structure that it is little better than an administrative 'black hole'. The educational tradition sanctifies learning by rote, and the educational ills have been aggravated by a utilitarian approach to knowledge. In the society at large there is a widespread lack of sympathy for the disadvantaged and poor, coupled with malicious jealousy of the successful; an interest in the new that is satisfied by buying up foreign technology and gadgets; a fascination with strong rulers and a pseudo emperor cult without a system of succession that can ensure political stability. This self-critique is topped off with laments concerning the Chinese populace's complacency about the depth and seriousness of the crises facing the country.[42]

This modern tradition of self-loathing is widespread and powerful. Born of a deep-felt anxiety over material backwardness, military weakness and political inadequacy, those engaged in this self-loathing recognize the role of the colonial powers in China's crisis but tend to look for the origins of the nation's troubles internally and in historical terms. Under Mao moral/political

---

[42]   This far-from-exhaustive list of ills is taken for the most part from the many publications dwelling on national crises that have appeared on mainland China since the late 1980s. See, for example, Lu Yi et al., *Qiuji: yige shijixingde xuanze* [Belonging to the World: A Choice for the Future] (Baijia chubanshe, Shanghai, 1989); Li Ming (ed.), *Zhongguode weiji yu sikao* [China's Crisis and Reflections on It], restricted circulation (Tianjin renmin chubanshe, Tianjin, 1989); He Bochuan, *Shan'aoshangde Zhongguo: wenti, kunjing, tongkude xuanze* [In the Hills of China: A Choice Between Problems, Dilemmas and Agony], revised edition (Sanlian shudian, Hong Kong, 1990); Su Ya and Jia Lusheng, *Shei lai chengbao?* [Who'll Take this Contract?] (Huacheng chubanshe, Guangzhou, 1990); Shi Zhongwen, *Zhongguo ren: zouchu sihutong* [The Chinese: Escaping a Dead-end] (Zhongguo fazhan chubanshe, Beijing, 1991); and, more recently, Qiao Lijun, Chen Tianze et al., *Zhongguo buneng luan* [China Cannot Afford Chaos] (Zhonggong zhongyang dangxiao chubanshe, Beijing, 1994).

supremacy had been seen as an answer to China's dilemma and the key to ensuring that the Chinese were not 'expelled from the human race' (*kaichu qiuji*);[43] with Deng's reforms, material strength coupled with the innate and abiding moral power of the Chinese world is believed by many to be the only way to overcome the nation's various inadequacies. However, there are intellectuals who feel that without systemic change and political reform, not to mention national moral reconstruction, no amount of wealth and power will make China a 'modern' or responsible country. During the late 1980s, articles and books dealing with a powerful sense of impending national crisis, by authors ostensibly troubled by the mood of nihilism born of a rejection of the Party-state, repeatedly claimed that unless something was done the Chinese may finally be 'expelled from the human race'.

Self-loathing satisfies a need to explain China's woeful modern history while at the same time reaffirming a prevalent sense of national uniqueness. Shame, weakness and aggrieved sentiments of national humiliation are devices that are regularly used by propagandists and politicians to inculcate patriotic ire. It is not surprising then that not all the views on the differences between China and the Western Other are macho and self-assertive. Wang Shuo, the Beijing novelist and master of irony, chortles about the superiority of the Chinese tradition of self-destruction. A writer who has delighted in excoriating Chinese foibles, from 1988 Wang made national nihilism into something of a hip youth cult, satirically validating as a national achievement China's all-pervasive corruption. Wang has claimed that the Chinese know how to abuse themselves better than anyone else. In a book-length interview published in 1992, he remarked in a tone of smug abnegation:

> Generally speaking, foreigners are pretty naive . . . They're materially extremely wealthy, but impoverished in the realm of spiritual culture. They've just cottoned on to smoking dope, and that's an artificial form of stimulation! We Chinese know how to get our kicks out of self-annihilation.[44]

According to this view, which entails a kind of celebratory cultural determinism, China has not been able to inherit and utilize the past creatively yet remains different from every other nation in the world in that it has greater problems, a more complex burden of tradition and a more vile populace. In this there is also a strong streak of *Schadenfreude*. Hannah Arendt summed up this attitude in regard to a nation traumatized by recent totalitarianism,

---

43   This expression was commonly used in the late 1980s. Mao had used it on 30 August 1956 in his speech at the preparatory conference for the Party's Eighth Congress. He said that if China did not overtake America economically after implementing the supposedly superior socialist system for 50-60 years then it deserved to be 'expelled from the human race'.

44   Wang Yiming, *Wo shi Wang Shuo* [I'm Wang Shuo] (Guoji wenhua chuban gongsi, Beijing, 1992).

analysing the German situation in 1950, and it adumbrates an attitude readily found among the urban elite of China:

> . . . *Schadenfreude*, malicious joy in ruination. It is as though the Germans, denied the power to rule the world, had fallen in love with impotence as such, and now find a positive pleasure in contemplating international tensions and the unavoidable mistakes that occur in the business of governing, regardless of the possible consequences for themselves.[45]

Many of the aspects of self-loathing were reflected in *Heshang* [River Elegy], the highly-controversial six-part documentary series that was screened in 1988.[46] 'River Elegy' gives a sweeping overview of the nation's history, symbols and contemporary ills. Later denounced by the authorities, the series' reflections on China infuriated conservatives and nationalists throughout the Chinese commonwealth. The debate concerning 'River Elegy' provided the first public occasion when ideological opponents on the mainland and in Taiwan shared a common response out of a sense of wounded national pride. One of the key elements of the series was that it equated older civilizations (China, Egypt, Africa, and so on) with decadence, non-competitive economies and backwardness. This rhetorical device was aimed, on one level at least, at provoking the viewer into a patriotic response and feelings of outrage that the 'Chinese tradition' along with past Party policies have combined to reduce China to its present (1988) status.[47]

In short, one of the recurrent themes of 'River Elegy' was the sense of frustration and hopelessness that its intellectual-journalist writers felt about the failure of China to have become a powerful, modern trading nation. The series' critique of the traditional polity and its ideology, along with its oblique references to the present regime, can be construed as being an indictment of both the past and present systems' inability to turn China into a modern international power.[48]

---

45   Hannah Arendt, 'The Aftermath of Nazi Rule: Report from Germany' (1950), in Arendt, *Essays in Understanding, 1930-1954* (Harcourt Brace & Company, New York, 1994), p.250.

46   For the full text of the series, see Su Xiaokang and Wang Luxiang, *Heshang* [River Elegy] (Xiandai chubanshe, Beijing, 1988); and Su Xiaokang and Wang Luxiang, *Deathsong of the River: A Reader's Guide to the Chinese TV Series Heshang* (Cornell University, Ithaca, 1991). For sections relevant to this discussion, see, for example, *Heshang*, pp.16-22.

47   See W. L. Chong, 'Su Xiaokang On His Film "River Elegy"', *China Information*, vol.4, no.3 (Winter 1989-90), p.46.

48   A point forcefully made by Dong Leshan in 'Dongfangzhuyi dahechang?', pp.99-100, 101. The debate surrounding 'River Elegy' was partially revived in 1995 when Tang Yijie, a leading Beijing University academic, commented publicly that the series was valuable in representing a 1980s current of thought that was critical of 'Chinese tradition'. Academics like Tang, it was reported, are concerned that the revival of

While a number of the writers behind the series, including Su Xiaokang and Jin Guantao, have moved in different directions since leaving China in 1989, it is interesting to note that Xia Jun, the China Central TV director of the series, having weathered the storms of the post-Tiananmen purge in Beijing, teamed up with the reportage writer Mai Tianshu to produce two acclaimed peasant-based tele-documentaries. 'The Peasants' (*Nongmin*) and 'The East' (*Dongfang*)[49] are multi-episode documentaries made in northwest China and produced in 1992 and 1993 respectively. Filmed in southern Shanxi, one ·of the most ancient agrarian cultural centres of China (the 'Hedong' — 'east of the Yellow River' — area in southwest Shanxi), the makers of 'The East' limn a Chinese rural world marked by its cultural integrity; a pre-modern Chinese civilization not disrupted or atomized by social upheavals, political uncertainty or chaotic modernization. Commentators on the series have remarked that after seeing 'The East' it is evident that it is the 'peripheral world' which should now succour the spiritually depleted 'centre' of mainstream culture. Mai Tianshu, who wrote the series' narration, calls for a rejection of theories introduced from the West (he hints but does not specify that Marxism-Leninism is included in this blanket condemnation of foreign thought).[50] One commentator notes that the significance of a work like 'The East' is that it underlines

> the most significant stage in the spiritual evolution of Chinese intellectuals in the closing years of this century: they have abandoned the fleeting perspective of pseudo-Western tourists looking down on their own land and instead now look thoughtfully to 'Mother Earth'; they have gone through the baptism of enthusiastically accepting all fads of Western thought and returned to their native soil, the land that has nurtured our Chinese culture; they have left behind romanticism and passion in favour of practicality and rationalism; they have turned from cultural criticism to cultural construction and conservatism.[51]

The world that 'The East' reveals, however, is hardly a utopian pastoral idyll suffused with cultural value and abiding lessons for urban dwellers. Behind its veneer of folksy voyeurism, the series affirms some of the most

---

interest in traditonal studies (*guoxue*) may be manipulated by Party conservatives to negate modern Chinese, in particular reformist, culture. See Zhongyangshe (Taipei), 'Xuezhe kending "Heshang" fanxing jiazhi, xuejie chuxian pipan fanxing shengyin' [An Academic Approves of the Value of Self-Reflection in 'River Elegy'; Voices Raised in Academic Circles Critical of Self-Reflection], *Shijie ribao* [World Journal] (North American Edition), 13 June 1995.

49   The full title is 'Dongfang — yige weide wenmingde shengwuxue jiepou' [The East — The Anatomy of a Great Civilization]. The series consisted of six 50-minute episodes.

50   Mai Tianshu, 'Faxian Dongfang' [Discovering the East], *Beijing qingnian bao*, 24 April 1994.

51   Zou Yanfeng, '"Dongfang" de qishi' [The Inspiration of 'The East'], *Beijing qingnian bao*, 24 April 1994.

backward-looking, pre-modern aspects of the Chinese rural world, including male domination, semi-feudal social hierarchies and educational inequalities. Both series present a loving portrayal of peasant culture and traditional values that reflects some of the most conservative dimensions of the 'national essence'. Of course, such native-soil conservatism is hardly unique to these television documentaries. China's 'new wave' directors like Zhang Yimou,[52] Chen Kaige, Tian Zhuangzhuang and Li Shaohong have been creating works that contain undeniable elements of rural nostalgia (and voyeurism) for years. Their own complex brand of cinematic chauvinism (one that is informed both by the tradition of self-hate and national narcissism) fits in neatly with a film industry that was born of nationalist aspirations in the 1920s and 1930s.[53]

Elements of self-hate and moral disgust, as well as the more commonly reported aspects of protest and rebellion, were crucial to the student-led demonstrations of 1989. For large numbers of intellectuals and students, the movement seemed to provide an opportunity for the educated elite to move back onto the centre-stage of Chinese history after decades of being persecuted and sidelined by the Party. For their part, many Beijing citizens supported the protests in the belief that the peaceful demonstrations showed that the Chinese had a moral sense, were willing to stand up for questions of principle and, with a concerted effort, could overcome the negative legacies of both the imperial and socialist past. As the students so rightly claimed, the movement had a powerful patriotic and redemptive message, one which played a key role in mobilizing mass support.[54] With the failure of that movement and the continued stability (and transformation) of Party rule, it is not surprising that an entrenched pattern of political activism in 20th-century China has reappeared once more, one in which political activism and extremism once frustrated are transformed into egregious nationalism.[55]

---

[52] For a critique of Zhang's work in this regard and its relevance to the debate on the 'loss of the humanist spirit' in China that began in late 1993 (see below), see Xu Lin and Zhang Hong's comments in Wang Xiaoming et al., 'Kuangyeshangde feixu — wenxue he wenren jingshende weiji' [Ruins in the Wilderness — The Crisis of Literature and the Humanist Spirit], *Shanghai wenxue* [Shanghai Literature], no.6 (1993), pp.65-6.

[53] See Ma Junxiang, 'Minzuzhuyi suo suzaode xiandai Zhongguo dianying' [Chinese Cinema: A Creation of Nationalism], in Liu Qingfeng (ed.), *Minzuzhuyi yu Zhongguo xiandaihua* [Nationalism and China's Modernization] (Zhongwen daxue chubanshe, Hong Kong, 1994), pp.521-32.

[54] See Jeffrey N. Wasserstrom and Elizabeth J. Perry (eds), *Popular Protest and Political Culture in Modern China*, 2nd ed. (Westview Press, Boulder, 1994); and Geremie Barmé, 'Confession, Redemption, and Death: Liu Xiaobo and the Protest Movement of 1989', in George Hicks (ed.), *The Broken Mirror: China after Tiananmen* (Longman, Essex, 1990), pp.70-80.

[55] For a Chinese view of this historical pattern this century, see Yang Xiong, 'Cong jijinzhuyi dao minzuzhuyi — shilun Zhongguo qingnian yundongde fazhan dongji jiqi wuqu' [From Extremism to Nationalism — A Tentative Discussion of the Causes and

The massacre of 4 June 1989 led for a time to an affirmation of the key elements of national self-hate: the innocent young slaughtered by an unresponsive and entrenched gerontocracy which was ruling over a nation that is corrupt, chaotic and, above all, not 'modern'. The chance for a national redemption had been lost and with it the moral force and legitimacy of the rulers.

Prior to the upheavals of 1989, there was a vocal pro-Western lobby in China. While some of their number went into exile after 4 June, many who were previously politically engaged and remained on the mainland have tried to take personal advantage of China's impressive economic performance, reasoning that money-making is not only a viable *modus vivendi* but also a revolutionary act that may presage true reform. In late 1993, a number of intellectuals in Shanghai launched a discussion on the 'loss of the humanist spirit' (*renwen jingshede shiluo*) in China.[56] They lamented the fact that the commercialisation and de-politicization of culture had marginalized serious artistic issues and, as we have noted above, that post-modernism was being sinicized by mainland intellectuals and writers who used it as a theoretical validation of their political disengagement, cowardice and moral neutrality in regard to the state.[57]

The widespread interest in the 1980s among the reading public in faddish Western theories like psychoanalysis, existentialism, structuralism and deconstruction had now dwindled. It was argued that intellectuals had suffered a new displacement in terms of social position and prestige from 1989 and that in the 1990s those who did not become involved in 'abstract debates' (*qingtan* or 'idle talk') about theory were busy themselves either hawking their talents in the market place or attempting to exercise a more overt political influence as 'strategists' for present or future powerholders.[58] A mini-debate on this

---

Misperception of Chinese Youth Movements], *Qingnian yanjiu* [Youth Studies], no.7 (1991), pp.7-13.

56   See Wang Xiaoming et al., 'Kuangyeshangde feixu, pp.63-71. This particular discussion took place in February 1993 but was not published until later in the year. This was by no means the first time such sentiments had been expressed by contemporary Chinese critics. Both Zhu Dake and Liu Xiaobo, for example, were noted for their criticisms of the vacuity of the reformist literature of the 1980s. See Geremie Barmé, 'The Chinese Velvet Prison: Culture in the "New Age", 1976-89', *Issues & Studies*, vol.25, no.8 (August 1989), p.58, n.13 and p.61.

57   Mindful of various political and social taboos these views are generally expressed in an elliptical fashion. See, for example, Xiao Tongqing, 'Xunqiu jiazhi mubiao yu lishi jinchengde qihe' [In Search of a Correspondence Between Meaningful Goals and Historical Progress], *Dongfang*, no.1 (1995), summarized in *Dushu*, no.5 (1995), p.154.

58   See Li Tiangang's comments in Gao Ruiquan et al., 'Renwen jingshen xunzong' [Searching for Traces of the Humanistic Spirit], *Dushu*, no.4 (1994), p.75. For more details of this major discussion — one of the most important of its type since 1989, see also Zhang Rulun et al., 'Renwen jingshen xunsilu zhi yi' [Thoughts on the Humanistic Spirit], *Dushu*, no.3 (1994), pp.3-13; Xu Jilin et al., 'Daotong, xuetong yu zhengtong'

question of 'humanism', social commitment and moral perfectionism was sparked by Zhang Chengzhi, the Beijing-based Muslim novelist and proto-nationalist, when the leading Shanghai daily *Wenhui bao* published a vociferous attack by Zhang on the greed, vanity and lack of patriotic backbone among Chinese intellectuals and writers.[59]

From the early 1990s onward, following the nation's increased economic growth, there has been a new twist in this tradition of self-loathing. People observe that China continues to advance economically without embarking on a drastic reform of the political or social system, and the debate about the 'humanist spirit', mentioned above, was part of a cautious attempt by some thoughtful intellectuals to air these fears in public. There are many who believe that the acquisition and maintenance of wealth will gradually transform the 'national character', or at least obviate the need for any major shift in the public perception of the national character.[60] Consumerism as the ultimate revolutionary action is seen by many as playing a redemptive role in national life, for it enables people to remake themselves not through some abstract national project but through the self-centred power of possession.

Whereas there was a strong spirit of self-reflection in the 1980s, economic success in the 1990s coupled with restrictions on intellectual debate and political repression have encouraged a sense of bravado. The national spirit that is being reformulated in the 1990s is not one based on mature reflection or open discussion but rather on a cocky, even vengeful, and perhaps a purblind self-assurance.

The faith in Chinese exclusivity is reflected even in that particularly Westernized art form: Chinese rock'n'roll. Cui Jian, the godfather of the Chinese rock scene, has claimed that northern, Beijing-based rock is completely different from Hong Kong and Taiwan imports. He averred in an interview published in late 1993 that northern Chinese can produce a robust, positive and socially progressive type of music that is quite different from the

---

[The Tradition of the Way, Tradition of Scholarship and Rectitude], *Dushu*, no. 5 (1994), pp.46-55; Wu Xuan et al., 'Women xuyao zenyangde renwen jingshen' [What Kind of Humanistic Spirit Do We Need?], *Dushu*, no.6 (1994), pp.66-74; and Wang Yichuan's response in *Zhonghua dushubao* [The China Reader's Newspaper], 3 August 1994, summarized in *Dushu*, no.10 (1994), pp.154-5.

59   See Zhang Chengzhi, 'Shiren, ni wei shenme bu fennu?!' [Poets, Why Aren't You Outraged?!], *Wenhui bao*, 7 August 1994. Xu Jilin rebutted Zhang in the same issue of the paper and the debate continued for some weeks. See the feature 'Renwen jingshen yu wenren caoshou' [The Humanist Spirit and the Integrity of the Literati], *Wenhui bao*, 7 August 1994, 21 August 1994, 4 September 1994, and 18 September 1994.

60   In terms of the 'humanist spirit' discussion, the bureaucrat-writer Wang Meng sums up this view most succinctly while questioning its validity. See Wang Meng's remarks, 'Renwen jingshen wenti ougan' [Random Thoughts on the Question of the Humanist Spirit], *Dongfang*, no.5 (1994), summarized in *Dushu*, no.12 (1994), p.146, where he says that ironically the very proponents of cultural integrity and independence still expect to be given handouts by the state.

negative and decadent rock of the West.[61] Other song-writers like Hou Muren, and Kong Yongqian, the designer of the controversial 'cultural T-shirts' (*wenhuashan*) of 1991, have pursued their work not because they want to overthrow the *status quo* as such, but rather to enrich the cultural sphere of China and make their nation more competitive with the rest of the world (including other areas of the Chinese commonwealth: Hong Kong and Taiwan). The authorities may view their cultural products as divisive and dangerous, but in the larger realm of China they are actually patriots. Others, going further, are emerging as super-patriots.

Yuan Hongbing: Pissing in the Wind

> This race that dwells on the continent of East Asia once shone with a brilliance bestowed by the sun. Now it has its back to the icy wall of history, driven there by the forces of Fate. We must prove whether we are an inferior race or not, for now Fate is pissing in our very faces.[62]

Today, radical views do not necessarily issue from pro-Maoist ideologues or conservatives. One firebrand is Yuan Hongbing, a lawyer formerly at Beijing University and labour organizer, whose involvement with a 'Peace Charter' reportedly modelled on the Czechoslovak 'Charter 77'[63] and detention in February 1994 put him in the front ranks of China's small public dissident movement,[64] although his philosophy is more akin to New Age Nietzscheanism than liberalism.[65]

---

[61]   See Xue Ji (ed.), *Yaogun xunmeng — Zhongguo yaogunyue shilu* [In Search of the Rock'n'Roll Dream — The True Story of Chinese Rock] (Zhongguo dianying chubanshe, Beijing, 1993), pp.2-3. Chinese rock'n'rollers, while superficially 'Westernized', are often in private rabidly anti-foreign. See also Andrew F. Jones, 'The Politics of Popular Music in Post-Tiananmen China', in Wasserstrom and Perry, *Popular Protest and Political Culture*, pp.158-61.

[62]   Yuan Hongbing, *Huangyuan feng* [Winds on the Plain] (Xiandai chubanshe, Beijing, 1990), p.127. The remainder of the chapter, entitled 'Restless Soul', continues very much in this vein.

[63]   This Chinese 'Peace Charter', published in transaltion as an appendix to 'China: New Arrests Linked to Worker Rights', *Human Rights Watch/Asia*, vol.6, no.2 (11 March 1994), is highly revealing. The authors use Party-style rhetoric to appeal to a wide audience (and perhaps even the authorities), and the egregious nationalistic sentiments and elitism of the document are in marked contrast to the contents of Charter 77. Yuan's co-author, Zhou Guoqiang, who was detained in early 1994, has always impressed this author in private as being a strongly patriotic rather than democratic figure.

[64]   See 'China's Most Distrusted', *Newsweek*, 21 March 1994, p.8; Ying Fu, 'Yuan Hongbing kangyi zhengzhi qishi' [Yuan Hongbing Protests Against Political Discrimination], *Zhongguo shibao zhoukan*, no.101 (5-11 December 1993), p.17; and Merle Goldman, *Sowing the Seeds of Democracy in China: Political Reform in the Deng Xiaoping Era* (Harvard University Press, Cambridge, Mass., 1994). Official persecution

Yuan was one of the organizers of the controversial publication *Lishide chaoliu* [The Tide of History] in 1992, noted for its anti-conservative, reformist tone.[66] Yet an earlier volume authored by Yuan entitled *Winds on the Plain*, which appeared in 1990, is perhaps more revealing of his mindset and that of some of his coevals.[67] Seen by some readers as a philosophical tract of considerable individuality, in the repressive intellectual atmosphere of post-Tiananmen China it soon gained a considerable following among university students.[68]

In the book Yuan propounds what he calls 'new heroicism' (*xin yingxiong zhuyi*), a cause that is primarily concerned with the 'fate of the race' and the strongman as national hero and saviour.[69] Like Nietzsche (a philosopher whose high standing among Chinese intellectuals has a long history), he talks of the need for madness and irrationality.[70] Yuan condemns all individual attempts to achieve freedom as a betrayal of the race, whether it be to engage in politics or to flee China in search of a new life. He condemns those who seek from the West a solution to China's problems. Indulging in what could be called 'Sino-fascism',[71] he proposes that the answer to the political, social and cultural 'ugliness' of the Chinese is purification through fire and blood: total warfare 'even if this creation means that our blue skies darken with the colour of blood that will not fade for a thousand years'.

---

has led the non-mainland media to classify Yuan as a 'liberal' or 'democratic activist'. There is little in his writing to support this.

65   Matei Mihalca, 'China's New Heroes Signal New Nationalism', *Asian Wall Street Journal*, 20 December 1994.

66   *Lishide chaoliu — xuexi Deng Xiaoping nanxun zhongyao jianghua fudao cailiao* [The Tide of History — Study Materials for Important Speeches Made by Deng Xiaoping During His Tour of the South] (Zhongguo renmin daxue chubanshe, Beijing, 1992). Yuan wrote one of the two introductory essays to the book. See Yuan Hongbing, 'Rang lishi buzai beiqi' [Don't Let History Cry in Anguish Any More], ibid., pp.13-28. He was reportedly cashiered from Beijing University for his involvement with this publication and attempted to sue the University Party Committee for expelling him. See 'China: New Arrests Linked to Worker Rights', p.2.

67   Yuan Hongbing, *Huangyuan feng* (see note 62).

68   Luo Wen, 'Bashezhe, xiong lang, yemanren — *Huangyuan feng* shi zenyang yiben shu?' [Trekker, Vicious Wolf, Barbarian — Just What Type of Book Is *Winds on the Plain*?], *Zhongguo tushu pinglun* [China Book Review], no.3 (1991), p.8. See also Chen Ping, 'Choulou yu ziside linghun — ping *Huangyuan feng* de "meide zhuti"' [An Ugly and Selfish Soul — On the 'Subject of Beauty' in *Winds on the Plain*], *Zhongguo tushu pinglun*, no.3 (1991), pp.11-12.

69   Yuan Hongbing, *Huangyuan feng*, p.216.

70   Ibid., p.250.

71   For example, Yuan writes: 'On the battlefield of racial competition the l.. t moving clarion call is the concept of racial superiority . . . Only the fresh blood of others can prove the strength of one race'. Ibid., p.193.

In Yuan's vision, the first step toward national renewal is a 'totalitarian style' (*jiquande xingshi*). 'Only with totalitarianism will it be possible to fuse the weak, ignorant and selfish individuals of the race into a powerful whole'. The race needs strong, idealistic, dignified and free men to achieve this end. In his own formulation of the neo-authoritarian/conservatism debate that has developed in China since the late 1980s,[72] Yuan says that his *soi-disant* 'freedom fighter' must be crowned by a 'democracy' that he uses to break the nexus between totalitarian rule and authoritarianism. This hero must put the welfare of the race above all other concerns, including those of the family.[73] Indeed, race is an easy way of coping with the complex legacies of cultural superiority, political exclusivity and self-loathing that have been discussed. By emphasizing race, the question of humanity is happily circumvented, as are all of the knotty problems of political, social and personal morality and ethics that are germaine to it.[74]

Winds on the Plain shares much in common with other views that are inward-looking and reject the outside world apart from the economic benefits that can be reaped from a relationship with it. As Yuan remarks when putting the case against the West: 'Scientific rationalism has said all it can within the context of Western civilization'.[75]

While couched in excessively purple prose, few of the views Yuan expresses in this book — one that was banned by the authorities for its 'bourgeois liberalism'![76] — are particularly new, or Chinese. Nor are Yuan's views on male primacy[77] and racial strength unrelated to earlier trends among

---

[72]   The debate concerning neo-authoritarianism versus mass democracy developed in 1988 and has continued under various guises to the present day. See, for example, Barry Sautman, 'Sirens of the Strongman: Neo-Authoritarianism in Recent Chinese Political Theory', *The China Quarterly*, no.129 (March 1992), pp.72-102.

[73]   This is a summary of the parting words of the author. See Yuan Hongbing, *Huangyuan feng*, pp.267-73.

[74]   As Hannah Arendt puts it, people 'have recoiled more and more from the idea of humanity and become more susceptible to the doctrine of race, which denies the very possibility of a common humanity. They instinctively felt that the idea of humanity, whether it appears in a religious or humanistic form, implies the obligation of a general responsibility which they do not wish to assume. For the idea of humanity, when purged of all sentimentality, has the very serious consequence that in one form or another men must assume responsibility for all crimes committed by men and that all nations share the onus of evil committed by all others. Shame at being a human being is the purely individual and still non-political expression of this insight'. See Hannah Arendt, 'Organized Guilt and Universal Responsibility', in Arendt, *Essays in Understanding, 1930-1954*, p.130.

[75]   Yuan Hongbing, *Huangyuan feng*, p.210.

[76]   See *Zhongguo tushu pinglun*, no.3 (1991), pp.8, 11-12 (which is an official publishing journal.

[77]   See, for example, Yuan Hongbing, *Huangyuan feng*, pp.87-96

the priapic proponents of the avant-garde in the early 1980s. The well-known 'misty' poet Yang Lian's 'Nuoerlang' cycle of poems, although set in Tibet, gave voice to Han male dominance, and something of Yang's tone is reflected in the recent writings of another poet, Zhou Lunyou. Known as a dissenting writer since his advocacy of Not-Not (*feifei*) poetry in the mid-1980s, the Sichuan poet Zhou Lunyou was jailed following 1989 and after his release published an attack on post-Tiananmen cultural trends.[78] Lambasting the raffishness championed by Beijing writers like Wang Shuo, Zhou calls for 'red purity' (*hongse chucui*) in a tone of self-righteousness not that dissimilar to the tenor of Yuan Hongbing's work. Zhou came out in favour of a robust, 'muscular' poetry, pitting himself against all that was weak, effete and clannish in the Beijing and regional arts scene.[79]

A Beijing Bastard in New York[80]

'By the way, fuck you!'[81]

In 1993, the intellectual portrayals of the national spirit were overshadowed by a tele-drama that brought into focus many of the questions discussed in this essay. This was 'A Beijing Man in New York', referred to in the opening paragraphs of this essay.

This tele-series involved the archetypical trip by a hero to foreign parts, where he overcomes adversity, obtains fortune and sires offspring by ravishing beauties, leaving behind a legacy of riches and empire.[82] Wang Qiming, the

---

78   Zhou Lunyou, 'Hongse xiezuode jingyi shenru gutou yu zhidu' [The Significance of Red Writing has Entered our Bones and the System], *Kaifang zazhi* [Open Magazine], no.8 (1993), pp.101-102.

79   Zhou states that 'red writing' champions books that 'are written with blood', the blood of the heart'. Ibid., p.102. The relationship between the Beijing cultural avant-garde and its practitioners in the provinces is a complex one. Many provincials aspire to the recognition, both local and international, that has been enjoyed by Beijing-based cultural and intellectual figures. Many have relocated themselves in the Chinese capital in search of fame and fortune (witness, for example, the careers of various film-makers, writers and artists). Others regard Beijing as being decadent and 'effeminate'. Writers like Zhou in the southwest or Li Jie, the Shanghai literary critic, have been scornful of the faux masculinity of the Beijing-style. It is significant that Wang Shuo, a part Manchu whose work has mined a vein first uncovered by the Republican-period Manchu writer, Lao She, is the object of scorn. Some Han patriots have blamed the world-weary Manchu canker for many of China's ills in the past.

80   'Beijing Bastards' (*Beijing zazhong*) was the title of the director Zhang Yuan's unofficial 1993 film about Beijing youth culture.

81   In 'A Beijing Man in New York', this was the Chinese hero's remark, in English, to his white American business competitor and rival in love.

82   See Eric J. Leed, *The Mind of the Traveler: From Gilgamesh to Global Tourism* (Basic Books, New York, 1991), p.114.

protagonist of the series, gives birth not to a lineage as do the heroes of other travel-and-conquest epics but to wealth, the legitimate product of his labours in New York and the means whereby the perceived cultural malaise and social impotence of China, as embodied by Wang,[83] a dishevelled Beijing artiste, are mollified. For Wang, money = wealth = potency = self-validation = continuity. The series enthralled audiences. Its tone also fortuitously fulfilled some of the needs of post-1989 propaganda — as well as satisfying popular curiosity and prurience — in that it depicted the horrors of Western capitalism at the same time as affirming the positive dimensions (rags-to-riches) of the market economy which China is pursuing with such energy.

Official and semi-official reviews of the series generally concentrated on aspects of Sino-American differences, emphasizing that the work 'focused on conflicts between Chinese and Western culture, psychology, and concepts of values' and that it would 'help Chinese TV viewers better understand American society and help those who entertain a rosy American dream to become more realistic'.[84] China's physical poverty, wrote one commentator in *Dushu*, will give birth to many people like Wang Qiming, but the spiritual vacuity of New York will force more people to search for spiritual values.[85] But one critic who writes for both the mainland and Hong Kong press commented that the unifying theme of the series can be summed up in one line: 'Screw you America' (*Meiguo, wo cao ni daye*).[86] And audiences — bureaucrats, masses and intellectuals — with a few vocal exceptions were at one in their praise of the show.

Wang Qiming, the protagonist of the series, is forced to give up his wholesome Chinese values to be successful in America.[87] Yet his success shows how those native values have informed his actions and help him

---

[83]   Wang is played by Jiang Wen, China's most popular male lead and a popular director. Following his work on the series in New York, Jiang Wen expressed a number of strong anti-Western sentiments and stated, among other things, that while the Chinese are increasingly being freed from their prejudices about the outside world, foreigners (namely Americans) are still deeply biased against China. See Jiang Wen and Luo Xueying, 'Jiang Wen yanlide shijie' [The World as Jiang Wen Sees It], *Wenhui dianying shibao* [Wenhui Film Times], 21 September 1992.

[84]   Yu Wentao, 'TV Series Tells about Beijingers in New York', *China Daily*, 13 October 1993.

[85]   Wu Hong, 'Beijingren, Niuyueren' (Beijing Men and New York Men), *Dushu*, no.1 (1994), p.84.

[86]   Zha Xiduo, 'Youse yanjinglide xiyangjing', p.17. Zha Xiduo is the penname of Jianying Zha, whose book *China Pop: How Soap Operas, Tabloids, and Bestsellers Are Transforming a Culture* (The New Press, New York, 1995) generally gives a more benign view of the significance of mainland popular culture.

[87]   See Bao Lai, 'Jingshen guizude lunluo — tan dianshiju "Beijingren zai Niuyue"' [The Decadence of the Spiritual Gentry — Comments on the TV Series 'A Beijing Man in New York], *Kaifang zazhi*, no.1 (1994), p.95.

maintain a certain superiority and humanity quite absent from the foreigners characters in the story. And, in reality, Wang retains elements of what is quintessentially Chinese — expressed in both negative and positive elements of his personality — despite the ravages of American commercial life. Xu Jilin, a Shanghai critic, summed up a large segment of intellectual opinion when he wrote that Wang was in fact the television embodiment of Wang Shuo's 'ruffians' or 'smart-arses' (pizi).[88] Xu also opined that the intentional misrepresentation of the United States validates a view of reformist China that is increasingly common among the Chinese themselves: the world created by a competitive market economy, the model of which is to be found in the United States, is one in which there are no ground rules, no morality or rectitude, a place where the strong devour the weak.

Conclusion: There's No Time Like the Future

As the children of the Cultural Revolution and the reform era come into power and money, they are finding a new sense of self-importance and worth. They are resentful of the real and imagined slights that they and their nation have suffered in the past, and their desire for strength and revenge is increasingly reflected in contemporary Chinese culture. Unofficial culture has reached or is reaching an uncomfortable accommodation with the economic if not always the political realities of contemporary China. As its practitioners negotiate a relationship with both the state in all of its complex manifestations and capital (often, but not always, the same thing), national pride and achievement act as a glue that further bonds the relationship. The patriotic consensus, aptly manipulated by diverse Party organs, acts as a crucial element in the coherence of the otherwise increasingly fragmented Chinese world.

For decades Chinese education and propaganda have emphasized the role of History in the fate of the Chinese nation-state. While many Chinese disciples of post-modernism and post-colonialism are busy talking themselves out of a role as social and intellectual critics of the traditional and Communist heritages to which they are the heirs, the ideology of progress, national wealth and power continue to inform public opinion. History and its supposedly inexorable workings determine for China a triumphant march toward a strong and modern future in which all of the progressivist dreams of the past century — and the promise of Chinese civilization — shall supposedly be realized.

---

[88]   Xu Jilin, 'Wudu zhi houde jiazhi anshi — zai shuo "Beijingren zai Niuyue"' [Values Hinted at by a Misreading — Further Comments on 'A Beijing Man in New York'], *Wenhui bao*, 13 November 1993. Xu's first criticism of the *pizi* Wang Qiming was 'Ancang xuanjide haiwai "youshi"' [The Hidden Agenda of an Overseas 'Wanderer'], *Wenxue bao (shikan)* [Literature Press, trial issue] (Shanghai), no.3 (1993). For more on *pizi, liumang,* and their place in contemporary Chinese culture, see Geremie Barmé, 'Wang Shuo and *liumang* ("Hooligan") Culture', *The Australian Journal of Chinese Affairs*, no.28 (July 1992), p.34ff.

While Marxism-Leninism and Mao Thought have been abandoned in all but name, the role of History in China's future remains steadfast.

In the late 1950s, China's utopian hopes were to surpass Britain and America within decades. In the Cultural Revolution, China became the centre of world revolution and publicly deemed itself the most 'progressive' force on the international scene.[89] Now, it is the 'Asia-Pacific century' that beckons and beguiles.[90] The new mythology of East Asian material strength and spiritual worth touted equally by regional propagandists and the Western media feeds into the century-old Chinese dreams of national revival and supremacy. Whatever the economic and political realities of that future may be, it is important to be aware that the cultural attitudes and awareness that form the basis for the attitudes of Chinese across political spectrum have been shaped by defunct Party propaganda and express deeply-frustrated and compelling nationalistic aspirations. This is evident in the official Chinese media today, as well as in the mass media, and non-official intellectual and cultural circles. It is likely to be evident too in the future, regardless of the political direction the country happens to take.

---

[89]   Liu Qingfeng calls this 'neo-Sinocentrism' (*xin huaxia zhongxinzhuyi*). See her 'Wenhua gemingzhongde huaxia zhongxinzhuyi' [Sinocentrism in the Cultural Revolution], in *Minzuzhuyi yu Zhongguo xiandaihua*, pp.359-66.

[90]   Beckoning, too, is the age of what one mainland writer, presumably inspired by Tu Wei-ming's work on 'cultural China', has called 'Pacific Confucianism' (*Taipingyang ruxue*). See Wu Huailian, 'Taipingyang shidai yu Zhonghuazhuyi' [The Pacific Age and China-ism], *Qingnian tansuo* [Youth Inquiry], no.4 (1994), pp.9-11.

Index